Safety Symbols

These symbols appear in laboratory activities. They warn of possible dangers in the laboratory and remind you to work carefully.

Safety Goggles Wear safety goggles to protect your eyes in any activity involving chemicals, flames or heating, or glassware.

Lab Apron Wear a laboratory apron to protect your skin and clothing from damage.

Breakage Handle breakable materials, such as glassware, with care. Do not touch broken glassware.

Heat-Resistant Gloves Use an oven mitt or other hand protection when handling hot materials such as hot plates or hot glassware.

Plastic Gloves Wear disposable plastic gloves when working with harmful chemicals and organisms. Keep your hands away from your face, and dispose of the gloves according to your teacher's instructions.

Heating Use a clamp or tongs to pick up hot glassware. Do not touch hot objects with your bare hands.

Flames Before you work with flames, tie back loose hair and clothing. Follow instructions from your teacher about lighting and extinguishing flames.

No Flames When using flammable materials, make sure there are no flames, sparks, or other exposed heat sources present.

Corrosive Chemical Avoid getting acid or other corrosive chemicals on your skin or clothing or in your eyes. Do not inhale the vapors. Wash your hands after the activity.

Poison Do not let any poisonous chemical come into contact with your skin, and do not inhale its vapors. Wash your hands when you are finished with the activity.

Fumes Work in a ventilated area when harmful vapors may be involved. Avoid inhaling vapors directly. Only test an odor when directed to do so by your teacher, and use a wafting motion to direct the vapor toward your nose.

Sharp Object Scissors, scalpels, knives, needles, pins, and tacks can cut your skin. Always direct a sharp edge or point away from yourself and others.

Animal Safety Treat live or preserved animals or animal parts with care to avoid harming the animals or yourself. Wash your hands when you are finished with the activity.

Plant Safety Handle plants only as directed by your teacher. If you are allergic to certain plants, tell your teacher; do not do an activity involving those plants. Avoid touching harmful plants such as poison ivy. Wash your hands when you are finished with the activity.

Electric Shock To avoid electric shock, never use electrical equipment around water, or when the equipment is wet or your hands are wet. Be sure cords are untangled and cannot trip anyone. Unplug equipment not in use.

Physical Safety When an experiment involves physical activity, avoid injuring yourself or others. Alert your teacher if there is any reason you should not participate.

Disposal Dispose of chemicals and other laboratory materials safely. Follow the instructions from your teacher.

Hand Washing Wash your hands thoroughly when finished with the activity. Use soap and warm water. Rinse well.

General Safety Awareness When this symbol appears, follow the instructions provided. When you are asked to develop your own procedure in a lab, have your teacher approve your plan before you go further.

PEARSON

Boston, Massachusetts
Glenview, Illinois
Shoreview, Minnesota
Upper Saddle River, New Jersey

Environmental Science

Book-Specific Resources
Student Edition
StudentExpress™ CD-ROM
Interactive Textbook Online
Teacher's Edition
All-in-One Teaching Resources
Color Transparencies
Guided Reading and Study Workbook
Student Edition in MP3 Audio
Discovery Channel School® Video
Consumable and Nonconsumable Materials Kits

Program Print Resources
Integrated Science Laboratory Manual
Computer Microscope Lab Manual
Inquiry Skills Activity Books
Progress Monitoring Assessments
Test Preparation Workbook
Test-Taking Tips With Transparencies
Teacher's ELL Handbook
Reading Strategies for Science Content

Differentiated Instruction Resources
Adapted Reading and Study Workbook
Adapted Tests
Differentiated Instruction Guide for Labs and Activities

Program Technology Resources
TeacherExpress™ CD-ROM
Interactive Textbooks Online
PresentationExpress™ CD-ROM
ExamView® Test Generator CD-ROM
Lab zone™ Easy Planner CD-ROM
Probeware Lab Manual With CD-ROM
Computer Microscope and Lab Manual
Materials Ordering CD-ROM
Discovery Channel School® DVD Library
Lab Activity Video Library—DVD and VHS
Web Site at PearsonSchool.com

Spanish Print Resources
Spanish Student Edition
Spanish Guided Reading and Study Workbook
Spanish Teaching Guide With Tests

Acknowledgments appear on p. 230, which constitutes an extension of this copyright page.

Cover
Mosses drape the trees of this temperate rain forest in Washington State (top). Hundreds of butterfly species live in the tropical rain forests of Ecuador (bottom).

13-digit ISBN 978-0-13-365104-1
10-digit ISBN 0-13-365104-5
2 3 4 5 6 7 8 9 10 11 10 09 08

Program Authors

Michael J. Padilla, Ph.D.
Associate Dean and Director
Eugene T. Moore School of Education
Clemson University
Clemson, South Carolina

Michael Padilla is a leader in middle school science education. He has served as an author and elected officer for the National Science Teachers Association and as a writer of the National Science Education Standards. As lead author of Science Explorer, Mike has inspired the team in developing a program that meets the needs of middle grades students, promotes science inquiry, and is aligned with the National Science Education Standards.

Ioannis Miaoulis, Ph.D.
President
Museum of Science
Boston, Massachusetts

Originally trained as a mechanical engineer, Ioannis Miaoulis is in the forefront of the national movement to increase technological literacy. As dean of the Tufts University School of Engineering, Dr. Miaoulis spearheaded the introduction of engineering into the Massachusetts curriculum. Currently he is working with school systems across the country to engage students in engineering activities and to foster discussions on the impact of science and technology on society.

Martha Cyr, Ph.D.
Director of K–12 Outreach
Worcester Polytechnic Institute
Worcester, Massachusetts

Martha Cyr is a noted expert in engineering outreach. She has over nine years of experience with programs and activities that emphasize the use of engineering principles, through hands-on projects, to excite and motivate students and teachers of mathematics and science in grades K–12. Her goal is to stimulate a continued interest in science and mathematics through engineering.

Book Authors

Marylin Lisowski, Ph.D.
Professor of Science and Environmental Education
Eastern Illinois University
Charleston, Illinois

Linda Cronin Jones, Ph.D.
Associate Professor of Science and Environmental Education
University of Florida
Gainesville, Florida

Contributing Writer

Thomas R. Wellnitz
Science Instructor
The Paideia School
Atlanta, Georgia

Consultants

Reading Consultant

Nancy Romance, Ph.D.
Professor of Science Education
Florida Atlantic University
Fort Lauderdale, Florida

Mathematics Consultant

William Tate, Ph.D.
Professor of Education and Applied Statistics and Computation
Washington University
St. Louis, Missouri

Reviewers

Tufts University Content Reviewers

Faculty from Tufts University in Medford, Massachusetts, developed *Science Explorer* chapter projects and reviewed the student books.

Astier M. Almedom, Ph.D.
Department of Biology

Wayne Chudyk, Ph.D.
Department of Civil and Environmental Engineering

John L. Durant, Ph.D.
Department of Civil and Environmental Engineering

George S. Ellmore, Ph.D.
Department of Biology

David Kaplan, Ph.D.
Department of Biomedical Engineering

Samuel Kounaves, Ph.D.
Department of Chemistry

David H. Lee, Ph.D.
Department of Chemistry

Douglas Matson, Ph.D.
Department of Mechanical Engineering

Karen Panetta, Ph.D.
Department of Electrical Engineering and Computer Science

Jan A. Pechenik, Ph.D.
Department of Biology

John C. Ridge, Ph.D.
Department of Geology

William Waller, Ph.D.
Department of Astronomy

Content Reviewers

Paul Beale, Ph.D.
Department of Physics
University of Colorado
Boulder, Colorado

Jeff Bodart, Ph.D.
Chipola Junior College
Marianna, Florida

Michael Castellani, Ph.D.
Department of Chemistry
Marshall University
Huntington, West Virginia

Eugene Chiang, Ph.D.
Department of Astronomy
University of California – Berkeley
Berkeley, California

Charles C. Curtis, Ph.D.
Department of Physics
University of Arizona
Tucson, Arizona

Daniel Kirk-Davidoff, Ph.D.
Department of Meteorology
University of Maryland
College Park, Maryland

Diane T. Doser, Ph.D.
Department of Geological Sciences
University of Texas at El Paso
El Paso, Texas

R. E. Duhrkopf, Ph.D.
Department of Biology
Baylor University
Waco, Texas

Michael Hacker
Co-director, Center for Technological Literacy
Hofstra University
Hempstead, New York

Michael W. Hamburger, Ph.D.
Department of Geological Sciences
Indiana University
Bloomington, Indiana

Alice K. Hankla, Ph.D.
The Galloway School
Atlanta, Georgia

Donald C. Jackson, Ph.D.
Department of Molecular Pharmacology, Physiology, & Biotechnology
Brown University
Providence, Rhode Island

Jeremiah N. Jarrett, Ph.D.
Department of Biological Sciences
Central Connecticut State University
New Britain, Connecticut

David Lederman, Ph.D.
Department of Physics
West Virginia University
Morgantown, West Virginia

Becky Mansfield, Ph.D.
Department of Geography
Ohio State University
Columbus, Ohio

Elizabeth M. Martin, M.S.
Department of Chemistry and Biochemistry
College of Charleston
Charleston, South Carolina

Joe McCullough, Ph.D.
Department of Natural and Applied Sciences
Cabrillo College
Aptos, California

Robert J. Mellors, Ph.D.
Department of Geological Sciences
San Diego State University
San Diego, California

Joseph M. Moran, Ph.D.
American Meteorological Society
Washington, D.C.

David J. Morrissey, Ph.D.
Department of Chemistry
Michigan State University
East Lansing, Michigan

Philip A. Reed, Ph.D.
Department of Occupational & Technical Studies
Old Dominion University
Norfolk, Virginia

Scott M. Rochette, Ph.D.
Department of the Earth Sciences
State University of New York, College at Brockport
Brockport, New York

Laurence D. Rosenhein, Ph.D.
Department of Chemistry
Indiana State University
Terre Haute, Indiana

Ronald Sass, Ph.D.
Department of Biology and Chemistry
Rice University
Houston, Texas

George Schatz, Ph.D.
Department of Chemistry
Northwestern University
Evanston, Illinois

Sara Seager, Ph.D.
Carnegie Institution of Washington
Washington, D.C.

Robert M. Thornton, Ph.D.
Section of Plant Biology
University of California
Davis, California

John R. Villarreal, Ph.D.
College of Science and Engineering
The University of Texas – Pan American
Edinburg, Texas

Kenneth Welty, Ph.D.
School of Education
University of Wisconsin–Stout
Menomonie, Wisconsin

Edward J. Zalisko, Ph.D.
Department of Biology
Blackburn College
Carlinville, Illinois

Teacher Reviewers

David R. Blakely
Arlington High School
Arlington, Massachusetts

Jane E. Callery
Two Rivers Magnet Middle School
East Hartford, Connecticut

Melissa Lynn Cook
Oakland Mills High School
Columbia, Maryland

James Fattic
Southside Middle School
Anderson, Indiana

Dan Gabel
Hoover Middle School
Rockville, Maryland

Wayne Goates
Eisenhower Middle School
Goddard, Kansas

Katherine Bobay Graser
Mint Hill Middle School
Charlotte, North Carolina

Darcy Hampton
Deal Junior High School
Washington, D.C.

Karen Kelly
Pierce Middle School
Waterford, Michigan

David Kelso
Manchester High School Central
Manchester, New Hampshire

Benigno Lopez, Jr.
Sleepy Hill Middle School
Lakeland, Florida

Angie L. Matamoros, Ph.D.
ALM Consulting, Inc.
Weston, Florida

Tim McCollum
Charleston Middle School
Charleston, Illinois

Bruce A. Mellin
Brooks School
North Andover, Massachusetts

Ella Jay Parfitt
Southeast Middle School
Baltimore, Maryland

Evelyn A. Pizzarello
Louis M. Klein Middle School
Harrison, New York

Kathleen M. Poe
Fletcher Middle School
Jacksonville, Florida

Shirley Rose
Lewis and Clark Middle School
Tulsa, Oklahoma

Linda Sandersen
Greenfield Middle School
Greenfield, Wisconsin

Mary E. Solan
Southwest Middle School
Charlotte, North Carolina

Mary Stewart
University of Tulsa
Tulsa, Oklahoma

Paul Swenson
Billings West High School
Billings, Montana

Thomas Vaughn
Arlington High School
Arlington, Massachusetts

Susan C. Zibell
Central Elementary
Simsbury, Connecticut

Safety Reviewers

W. H. Breazeale, Ph.D.
Department of Chemistry
College of Charleston
Charleston, South Carolina

Ruth Hathaway, Ph.D.
Hathaway Consulting
Cape Girardeau, Missouri

Douglas Mandt, M.S.
Science Education Consultant
Edgewood, Washington

Activity Field Testers

Nicki Bibbo
Witchcraft Heights School
Salem, Massachusetts

Rose-Marie Botting
Broward County Schools
Fort Lauderdale, Florida

Colleen Campos
Laredo Middle School
Aurora, Colorado

Elizabeth Chait
W. L. Chenery Middle School
Belmont, Massachusetts

Holly Estes
Hale Middle School
Stow, Massachusetts

Laura Hapgood
Plymouth Community Intermediate School
Plymouth, Massachusetts

Mary F. Lavin
Plymouth Community Intermediate School
Plymouth, Massachusetts

James MacNeil, Ph.D.
Cambridge, Massachusetts

Lauren Magruder
St. Michael's Country Day School
Newport, Rhode Island

Jeanne Maurand
Austin Preparatory School
Reading, Massachusetts

Joanne Jackson-Pelletier
Winman Junior High School
Warwick, Rhode Island

Warren Phillips
Plymouth Public Schools
Plymouth, Massachusetts

Carol Pirtle
Hale Middle School
Stow, Massachusetts

Kathleen M. Poe
Fletcher Middle School
Jacksonville, Florida

Cynthia B. Pope
Norfolk Public Schools
Norfolk, Virginia

Anne Scammell
Geneva Middle School
Geneva, New York

Karen Riley Sievers
Callanan Middle School
Des Moines, Iowa

David M. Smith
Eyer Middle School
Allentown, Pennsylvania

Gene Vitale
Parkland School
McHenry, Illinois

Contents

Environmental Science

Reference Section

VIDEO

Enhance understanding through dynamic video.

Preview Get motivated with this introduction to the chapter content.

Field Trip Explore a real-world story related to the chapter content.

Assessment Review content and take an assessment.

Get connected to exciting Web resources in every lesson.

SCI LINKS NSTA Find Web links on topics relating to every section.

Active Art Interact with selected visuals from every chapter online.

Planet Diary® Explore news and natural phenomena through weekly reports.

Science News® Keep up to date with the latest science discoveries.

Experience the complete textbook online and on CD-ROM.

Activities Practice skills and learn content.

Videos Explore content and learn important lab skills.

Audio Support Hear key terms spoken and defined.

Self-Assessment Use instant feedback to help you track your progress.

Activities

Lab zone™ Chapter Project — Opportunities for long-term inquiry

Lab zone Discover Activity — Exploration and inquiry before reading

Lab zone Try This Activity — Reinforcement of key concepts

Lab zone Skills Activity — Practice of specific science inquiry skills

Labs — In-depth practice of inquiry skills and science concepts

At-Home **Activity** — Quick, engaging activities for home and family

• Tech & Design • — Design, build, test, and communicate

Math — Point-of-use math practice

active art — Illustrations come alive online

Careers in **Science**

Treetop Scientist

It is shortly after daybreak when biologist Margaret Lowman begins her climb. She moves quickly up the ladder attached to a giant tree in the rain forest of Belize in Central America. Five meters, ten meters, fifteen—within minutes, she is ten stories up. As she clambers onto a wooden platform, she stops to admire the forest. Brilliantly colored macaws fly overhead while spider monkeys swing through the branches above her.

"It is a fantastic feeling," Meg says. "Almost every organism in the world sees the forest canopy from the inside or from above. But humans are an exception. Most of the time we can do no better than look up at it from below."

The rain forest canopy is the dense covering formed by the leafy tops of tall trees. It can be 20 to 40 meters above the ground. Working as a field biologist, Meg studies the insects that feed on the plants in the canopy.

Meg Lowman climbs high into the rain forest canopy in Belize. ▶

Talking With Dr. Margaret Lowman

A macaw bursts into flight in the canopy.

How did you get interested in science?

I probably got started at about age 3 by making forts in bushes. My friends and I made nature trails. We made zoos with earthworms, and I collected everything from birds and insects to twigs. By the fifth grade I had accumulated quite a wildflower collection. I carefully pressed and identified the wildflowers on cards by habitat, color, size, and so on. That collection won me second place in the New York state science fair. I felt proud to be among all those boys with their electronic and chemistry experiments.

Why did you choose to study forests?

In college, I started out as a geology major. But I found myself looking at the living things while everyone else was looking at rocks. Fortunately, the college that I attended had a research forest that interested me. When it came time to do the research for my doctorate, I had thought I would study butterflies. But they can be quite difficult to track, so I chose to focus on something much less mobile—trees.

Meg Lowman, on a canopy sled, collects insect specimens in Cameroon.

Career Path

Margaret Lowman grew up in upstate New York and attended Williams College in Massachusetts. She received a Ph.D. in botany from the University of Sydney in Australia. Formerly the director of the Marie Selby Botanical Gardens in Sarasota, Florida, she is now a professor at the New College of Florida. The mother of two boys, she juggles career and family.

A balloon tows a canopy sled that can rest in the upper rain forest canopy.

What are the challenges of studying the canopy?

When the canopy is far above the ground, it is not easy to study. I started out in Australia using a rope to climb into the canopy. Then another scientist and I came up with a different approach. On the back of a napkin, we drew a plan to build a bridge between trees.

The idea of a bridge between trees evolved into what I call my little "highways in the sky." I've built them in several places. They are collections of platforms and bridges that are strung together through the treetops. The platforms allow a group of people to stop and examine the canopy in detail, while the bridges allow people to keep moving.

Besides these walkways, we've used hot-air balloons and large cranes to get us up into the canopy. But these technologies are expensive.

What did you want to learn about rain forests?

There are two questions in particular that I have been asking throughout my career. First, how many leaves on a tree do insects consume? And, second, how does insect damage affect the health of the trees?

How much do insects consume?

One dramatic discovery was in the rain forest of Australia. Every spring something was eating up to 50 percent of the young leaves of the Antarctic beech trees and then mysteriously disappearing. I watched the trees for two years before I was able to capture the beetle larvae that were responsible for the damage. There was a reason I had missed the larvae for so long: After the larvae feed on the leaves, they fall off the trees into the leaves and soil on the ground below.

Once I raised the larvae to adult beetles, I found that I had uncovered a previously unknown species—*Nothofagus novacastria.* I called it the gul beetle.

How do the insects affect the health of the forests?

The most surprising thing I learned is that trees can put up with a lot more insect damage than we ever dreamed. Before scientists were able to access the canopy, they had to make estimates based on what they could learn from working on the ground. Those studies found that insects damaged about 5 to 7 percent of a tree's leaves in any given year. But once we got up into the canopy, we realized that there are a lot more insects and a lot more leaves damaged—nearly four or five times what we had originally thought.

Meg discovered beetle larvae that feed on young leaves of the Antarctic beech. The scientific name of the beetle is *Nothofagus novacastria.*

Meg carefully collects and records data on plant and animal species.

How do forests grow back?

Along with my work as a leaf detective, I got interested in yet another question: What forces affect the regrowth of a rain forest? Once the trees and other plants are killed in an area of the forest, whether by natural forces such as lightning-triggered fires or by people cutting trees, what does it take to return the forest to its natural state?

We've learned that once the canopy is seriously damaged, it will take far longer for it to grow back than we imagined. For over 30 years, we have been monitoring the regrowth of the canopy in Australia. It is surprising how slowly it grows back. We have seen four-inch-high seedlings that are 50 years old. In the tropics we're not looking at a hundred years, we're looking at a thousand years to grow again.

What are some memorable moments in the canopy?

Some memories are of little things, such as watching a yellow-bellied sapsucker eating a gypsy moth. It was very messy, like a child eating a caramel apple with his hands. Other memories are the moments of discovery—like finally finding that gul beetle larvae munching on the Antarctic beech leaves.

Writing in Science

Career Link Meg says that one of her greatest challenges as a field biologist is to find ways of getting into the canopy. In a paragraph, describe several methods that Meg uses to solve the problem. Then add a method of your own for reaching the canopy.

For: More on this career
Visit: PHSchool.com
Web Code: ceb-5000

Chapter 1

Populations and Communities

The BIG Idea

Populations and Ecosystems

How do the living and nonliving parts of an ecosystem interact?

Chapter Preview

1 Living Things and the Environment

Discover What's in the Scene?

Try This With or Without Salt?

Skills Lab A World in a Bottle

2 Studying Populations

Discover What's the Population of Beans in a Jar?

Skills Activity Calculating

Math Skills Inequalities

Active Art Graphing Changes in a Population

Try This Elbow Room

Skills Lab Counting Turtles

Science and Society Animal Overpopulation

3 Interactions Among Living Things

Discover Can You Hide a Butterfly?

Analyzing Data Predator-Prey Interactions

Skills Activity Classifying

At-Home Activity Feeding Frenzy

4 Changes in Communities

Discover What Happened Here?

At-Home Activity Community Changes

A population of Grant's zebras roams on the Masai Mara Reserve in Kenya. ▶

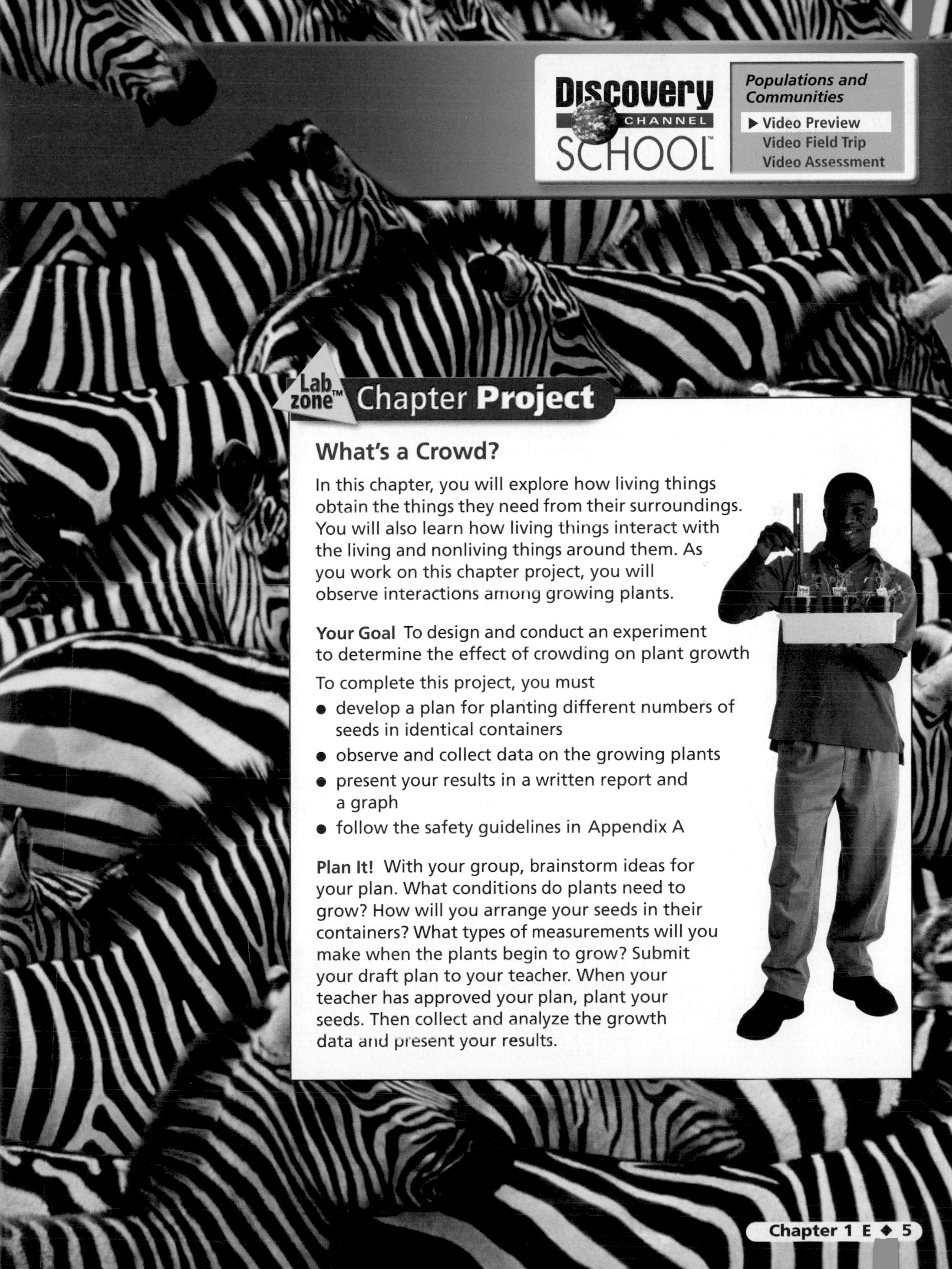

Lab zone™ Chapter **Project**

What's a Crowd?

In this chapter, you will explore how living things obtain the things they need from their surroundings. You will also learn how living things interact with the living and nonliving things around them. As you work on this chapter project, you will observe interactions among growing plants.

Your Goal To design and conduct an experiment to determine the effect of crowding on plant growth

To complete this project, you must

- develop a plan for planting different numbers of seeds in identical containers
- observe and collect data on the growing plants
- present your results in a written report and a graph
- follow the safety guidelines in Appendix A

Plan It! With your group, brainstorm ideas for your plan. What conditions do plants need to grow? How will you arrange your seeds in their containers? What types of measurements will you make when the plants begin to grow? Submit your draft plan to your teacher. When your teacher has approved your plan, plant your seeds. Then collect and analyze the growth data and present your results.

Section 1

Living Things and the Environment

Reading Preview

Key Concepts

- What needs are met by an organism's environment?
- What are the two parts of an organism's habitat with which it interacts?
- What are the levels of organization within an ecosystem?

Key Terms

- organism • habitat
- biotic factor • abiotic factor
- photosynthesis • species
- population • community
- ecosystem • ecology

Target Reading Skill

Identifying Main Ideas As you read the Habitats section, write the main idea—the biggest or most important idea—in a graphic organizer like the one below. Then write three supporting details that give examples of the main idea.

Main Idea

An organism obtains food . . .		
Detail	Detail	Detail

Lab zone Discover Activity

What's in the Scene?

1. Choose a magazine picture of a nature scene. Paste the picture onto a sheet of paper, leaving space all around the picture.
2. Locate everything in the picture that is alive. Use a colored pencil to draw a line from each living thing. If you know its name, write it on the line.
3. Using a different colored pencil, label each nonliving thing.

Think It Over

Inferring How do the living things in the picture depend on the nonliving things? Using a third color, draw lines connecting the living things to the nonliving things they need.

As the sun rises on a warm summer morning, the Nebraska town is already bustling with activity. Some residents are hard at work building homes for their families. They are working underground, where it is dark and cool. Other inhabitants are collecting seeds for breakfast. Some of the town's younger residents are at play, chasing each other through the grass.

Suddenly, an adult spots a threatening shadow—an enemy has appeared in the sky! The adult cries out several times, warning the others. Within moments, the town's residents disappear into their underground homes. The town is silent and still, except for a single hawk circling overhead.

Have you guessed what kind of town this is? It is a prairie dog town on the Nebraska plains. As these prairie dogs dug their burrows, searched for food, and hid from the hawk, they interacted with their environment, or surroundings.

Black-Tailed Prairie Dog ▶

FIGURE 1
An Organism in Its Habitat
Like all organisms, this red-tailed hawk obtains food, water, and shelter from its habitat. Prairie dogs are a major source of food for the red-tailed hawk.

Habitats

A prairie dog is one type of **organism,** or living thing. Different types of organisms must live in different types of environments. **An organism obtains food, water, shelter, and other things it needs to live, grow, and reproduce from its environment.** An environment that provides the things the organism needs to live, grow, and reproduce is called its **habitat.**

One area may contain many habitats. For example, in a forest, mushrooms grow in the damp soil, salamanders live on the forest floor, and woodpeckers build nests in tree trunks.

Organisms live in different habitats because they have different requirements for survival. A prairie dog obtains the food and shelter it needs from its habitat. It could not survive in a tropical rain forest or on the rocky ocean shore. Likewise, the prairie would not meet the needs of a spider monkey or hermit crab.

Why do different organisms live in different habitats?

Biotic Factors

To meet its needs, a prairie dog must interact with more than just the other prairie dogs around it. **An organism interacts with both the living and nonliving parts of its habitat.** The living parts of a habitat are called **biotic factors** (by AHT ik). Biotic factors in the prairie dogs' habitat include the grass and plants that provide seeds and berries. The hawks, ferrets, badgers, and eagles that hunt the prairie dogs are also biotic factors. In addition, worms, fungi, and bacteria are biotic factors that live in the soil underneath the prairie grass.

Name a biotic factor in your environment.

FIGURE 2
Abiotic Factors
The nonliving things in an organism's habitat are abiotic factors. **Applying Concepts** *Name three abiotic factors you interact with each day.*

▲ This orangutan is enjoying a drink of water.

▲ Sunlight enables this plant to make its own food.

▲ This banjo frog burrows in the soil to stay cool.

Abiotic Factors

Abiotic factors (ay by AHT ik) are the nonliving parts of an organism's habitat. They include water, sunlight, oxygen, temperature, and soil.

Water All living things require water to carry out their life processes. Water also makes up a large part of the bodies of most organisms. Your body, for example, is about 65 percent water. Plants and algae need water, along with sunlight and carbon dioxide, to make their own food in a process called **photosynthesis** (foh toh SIN thuh sis). Other living things depend on plants and algae for food.

Sunlight Because sunlight is needed for photosynthesis, it is an important abiotic factor for most living things. In places that do not receive sunlight, such as dark caves, plants and algae cannot grow. Because there are no plants or algae to provide food, few other organisms can live in such places.

Oxygen Most living things require oxygen to carry out their life processes. Oxygen is so important to the functioning of the human body that you can live only a few minutes without it. Organisms that live on land obtain oxygen from air, which is about 20 percent oxygen. Fish and other water organisms obtain oxygen that is dissolved in the water around them.

Temperature The temperatures that are typical of an area determine the types of organisms that can live there. For example, if you took a trip to a warm tropical island, you might see colorful orchid flowers and tiny lizards. These organisms could not survive on the frozen plains of Siberia.

Some animals alter their environments so they can survive very hot or very cold temperatures. Prairie dogs, for example, dig underground dens to find shelter from the hot summer sun and cold winter winds.

Soil Soil is a mixture of rock fragments, nutrients, air, water, and the decaying remains of living things. Soil in different areas consists of varying amounts of these materials. The type of soil in an area influences the kinds of plants that can grow there. Many animals, such as the prairie dogs, use the soil itself as a home. Billions of microscopic organisms such as bacteria also live in the soil.

How do abiotic factors differ from biotic factors?

FIGURE 3
A Population
All these garter snakes make up a population.

Levels of Organization

Of course, organisms do not live all alone in their habitat. Instead, organisms live together in populations and communities, and with abiotic factors in their ecosystems.

Populations In 1900, travelers saw a prairie dog town in Texas that covered an area twice the size of the city of Dallas. The town contained more than 400 million prairie dogs! These prairie dogs were all members of one species, or single kind, of organism. A **species** (SPEE sheez) is a group of organisms that are physically similar and can mate with each other and produce offspring that can also mate and reproduce.

All the members of one species in a particular area are referred to as a **population.** The 400 million prairie dogs in the Texas town are one example of a population. All the pigeons in New York City make up a population, as do all the bees that live in a hive. In contrast, all the trees in a forest do not make up a population, because they do not all belong to the same species. There may be pines, maples, birches, and many other tree species in the forest.

Communities A particular area usually contains more than one species of organism. The prairie, for instance, includes prairie dogs, hawks, grasses, badgers, and snakes, along with many other organisms. All the different populations that live together in an area make up a **community.**

To be considered a community, the different populations must live close enough together to interact. One way the populations in a community may interact is by using the same resources, such as food and shelter. For example, the tunnels dug by prairie dogs also serve as homes for burrowing owls and black-footed ferrets. The prairie dogs share the grass with other animals. Meanwhile, prairie dogs themselves serve as food for many species.

Lab zone Try This **Activity**

With or Without Salt?

In this activity you will explore salt as an abiotic factor.

1. Label four 600-mL beakers A, B, C, and D. Fill each with 500 mL of room-temperature spring water.
2. Set beaker A aside. Add 2.5 grams of noniodized salt to beaker B, 7.5 grams of salt to beaker C, and 15 grams of salt to beaker D. Stir each beaker.
3. Add $\frac{1}{8}$ spoonful of brine shrimp eggs to each beaker.
4. Cover each beaker with a square of paper. Keep them away from direct light or heat. Wash your hands.
5. Observe the beakers daily for three days.

Drawing Conclusions In which beakers did the eggs hatch? What can you conclude about the amount of salt in the shrimps' natural habitat?

For: Links on biotic and abiotic factors
Visit: www.SciLinks.org
Web Code: scn-0511

Ecosystems The community of organisms that live in a particular area, along with their nonliving surroundings, make up an **ecosystem.** A prairie is just one of the many different ecosystems found on Earth. Other ecosystems in which living things make their homes include mountain streams, deep oceans, and evergreen forests.

Figure 4 shows the levels of organization in a prairie ecosystem. **The smallest level of organization is a single organism, which belongs to a population that includes other members of its species. The population belongs to a community of different species. The community and abiotic factors together form an ecosystem.**

Because the populations in an ecosystem interact with one another, any change affects all the different populations that live there. The study of how living things interact with each other and with their environment is called **ecology.** Ecologists are scientists who study ecology. As part of their work, ecologists study how organisms react to changes in their environment. An ecologist, for example, may look at how a fire affects a prairie ecosystem.

What is ecology?

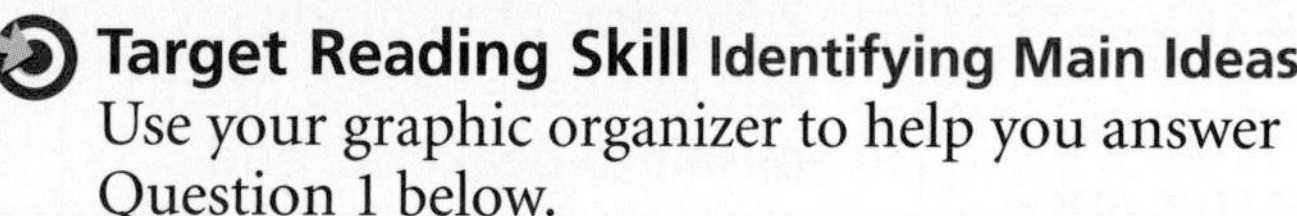

Target Reading Skill Identifying Main Ideas Use your graphic organizer to help you answer Question 1 below.

Reviewing Key Concepts

1. a. **Listing** What basic needs are provided by an organism's habitat?
   b. **Predicting** What might happen to an organism if its habitat could not meet one of its needs?
2. a. **Defining** Define the terms *biotic factors* and *abiotic factors.*
   b. **Interpreting Illustrations** List all the biotic and abiotic factors in Figure 4.
   c. **Making Generalizations** Explain why water and sunlight are two abiotic factors that are important to most organisms.
3. a. **Sequencing** List these terms in order from the smallest level to the largest: *population, organism, ecosystem, community.*
   b. **Classifying** Would all the different kinds of organisms in a forest be considered a population or a community? Explain.
   c. **Relating Cause and Effect** How might a change in one population affect other populations in a community?

Writing in Science

Descriptive Paragraph What habitat do you live in? Write a one-paragraph description of your habitat. Describe how you obtain the food, water, and shelter you need from your habitat. How does this habitat meet your needs in ways that another would not?

FIGURE 4
Ecological Organization

The smallest level of organization is the organism. The largest is the entire ecosystem.

Organism: Prairie dog

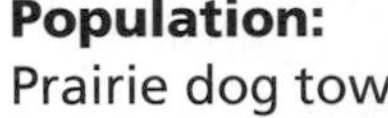

Population: Prairie dog town

Community: All the living things that interact on the prairie

Ecosystem: All the living and nonliving things that interact on the prairie

Lab zone **Skills Lab**

A World in a Bottle

Problem

How do organisms survive in a closed ecosystem?

Skills Focus

making models, observing

Materials

- gravel • soil • moss plants • plastic spoon
- charcoal • spray bottle • large rubber band
- 2 vascular plants • plastic wrap
- pre-cut, clear plastic bottle

Procedure   

1. In this lab, you will place plants in moist soil in a bottle that then will be sealed. This setup is called a terrarium. Predict whether the plants can survive in this habitat.
2. Spread about 2.5 cm of gravel on the bottom of a pre-cut bottle. Then sprinkle a spoonful or two of charcoal over the gravel.
3. Use the spoon to layer about 8 cm of soil over the gravel and charcoal. After you add the soil, tap it down to pack it.
4. Scoop out two holes in the soil. Remove the vascular plants from their pots. Gently place their roots in the holes. Then pack the loose soil firmly around the plants' stems.
5. Fill the spray bottle with water. Spray the soil until you see water collecting in the gravel.
6. Cover the soil with the moss plants, including the areas around the stems of the vascular plants. Lightly spray the mosses with water.
7. Tightly cover your terrarium with plastic wrap. Secure the cover with a rubber band. Place the terrarium in bright, indirect light.
8. Observe your terrarium daily for two weeks. Record your observations in your notebook. If its sides fog, move the terrarium to an area with a different amount of light. You may need to move it a few times. Note any changes you make in your terrarium's location.

Analyze and Conclude

1. **Making Models** List all of the biotic factors and abiotic factors that are part of your ecosystem model.
2. **Observing** Were any biotic or abiotic factors able to enter the terrarium? If so, which ones?
3. **Predicting** Suppose a plant-eating insect were added to the terrarium. Predict whether it would be able to survive. Explain your prediction.
4. **Communicating** Write a paragraph that explains how your terrarium models an ecosystem on Earth. How does your model differ from that ecosystem?

Design an Experiment

Plan an experiment that would model a freshwater ecosystem. How would this model be different from the land ecosystem? *Obtain your teacher's approval before carrying out your plan.*

Section 2

Integrating Mathematics

Studying Populations

Reading Preview

Key Concepts

- How do ecologists determine the size of a population?
- What causes populations to change in size?
- What factors limit population growth?

Key Terms

- estimate
- birth rate
- death rate
- immigration
- emigration
- population density
- limiting factor
- carrying capacity

Target Reading Skill

Asking Questions Before you read, preview the red headings. In a graphic organizer like the one below, ask a question for each heading. As you read, write the answers to your questions.

Studying Populations

Question	Answer
How do you determine population size?	Some methods of determining population size are . . .

Lab zone Discover Activity

What's the Population of Beans in a Jar?

1. Fill a plastic jar with dried beans. This is your model population.
2. Your goal is to determine the bean population size, but you will not have time to count every bean. You may use any of the following to help you: a ruler, a small beaker, another large jar. Set a timer for two minutes when you are ready to begin.
3. After two minutes, record your answer. Then count the beans. How close was your answer?

Think It Over

Forming Operational Definitions In this activity, you came up with an estimate of the size of the bean population. Write a definition of the term *estimate* based on what you did.

How would you like to be an ecologist today? Your assignment is to study the albatross population on an island. One question you might ask is how the size of the albatross population has changed over time. Is the number of albatrosses on the island more than, less than, or the same as it was 50 years ago? To answer this question, you must first determine the current size of the albatross population.

FIGURE 5
Studying Populations
These young albatrosses are part of a larger albatross population in the Falkland Islands.

Determining Population Size

Some methods of determining the size of a population are direct and indirect observations, sampling, and mark-and-recapture studies.

Direct Observation The most obvious way to determine the size of a population is to count all of its members. For example, you could try to count all the crabs in a tide pool.

Indirect Observation Sometimes it may be easier to observe signs of organisms rather than the organisms themselves. Look at the mud nests built by cliff swallows in Figure 6. Each nest has one entrance hole. By counting the entrance holes, you can determine the number of swallow nests in this area. Suppose that the average number of swallows per nest is four: two parents and two offspring. If there are 120 nests, you can multiply 120 by 4 to determine that there are 480 swallows.

Sampling In many cases, it is not even possible to count signs of every member of a population. The population may be very large or spread over a wide area. In such cases, ecologists usually make an estimate. An **estimate** is an approximation of a number, based on reasonable assumptions.

FIGURE 6
Determining Population Size
Scientists use a variety of methods to determine the size of a population.

Indirect Observation
One way to determine this cliff swallow population is to count their cone-shaped nests.

Direct Observation
Counting these crabs one by one is an example of direct observation.

One way to estimate the size of a population is to count the number of organisms in a small area (a sample), and then multiply to find the number in a larger area. To get the most accurate estimate, your sample area should be typical of the larger area. Suppose you count 8 birch trees in 100 square meters of a forest. If the entire forest were 100 times that size, you would multiply your count by 100 to estimate the total population, or 800 birch trees.

Mark-and-Recapture Studies Another estimating method is called "mark and recapture." Here's an example showing how mark and recapture works. First, turtles in a bay are caught in a way that does not harm them. Ecologists count the turtles and mark each turtle's shell with a dot of paint before releasing it. Two weeks later, the researchers return and capture turtles again. They count how many turtles have marks, showing that they have been recaptured, and how many are unmarked. Using a mathematical formula, the ecologists can estimate the total population of turtles in the bay. You can try this technique for yourself in the Skills Lab at the end of this section.

When might an ecologist use indirect observation to estimate a population?

Lab zone **Skills Activity**

Calculating

An oyster bed is 100 meters long and 50 meters wide. In a 1-square-meter area you count 20 oysters. Estimate the population of oysters in the bed. (*Hint:* Drawing a diagram may help you set up your calculation.)

Sampling
To estimate the birch tree population in a forest, count the birches in a small area. Then multiply to find the number in the larger area.

Mark and Recapture
This researcher is releasing a marked turtle as part of a mark-and-recapture study.

Changes in Population Size

By returning to a location often and using one of the methods described on the previous pages, ecologists can monitor the size of a population over time. **Populations can change in size when new members join the population or when members leave the population.**

Births and Deaths The main way in which new individuals join a population is by being born into it. The **birth rate** of a population is the number of births in a population in a certain amount of time. For example, suppose that a population of 100 cottontail rabbits produces 600 young in a year. The birth rate in this population would be 600 young per year.

The main way that individuals leave a population is by dying. The **death rate** is the number of deaths in a population in a certain amount of time. If 400 rabbits die in a year in the population, the death rate would be 400 rabbits per year.

The Population Statement When the birth rate in a population is greater than the death rate, the population will generally increase. This can be written as a mathematical statement using the "is greater than" sign:

If birth rate > death rate, population size increases.

However, if the death rate in a population is greater than the birth rate, the population size will generally decrease. This can also be written as a mathematical statement:

If death rate > birth rate, population size decreases.

Immigration and Emigration The size of a population also can change when individuals move into or out of the population, just as the population of your town changes when families move into town or move away. **Immigration** (im ih GRAY shun) means moving into a population. **Emigration** (em ih GRAY shun) means leaving a population. For instance, if food is scarce, some members of an antelope herd may wander off in search of better grassland. If they become permanently separated from the original herd, they will no longer be part of that population.

Graphing Changes in Population Changes in a population's size can be displayed on a line graph. Figure 7 shows a graph of the changes in a rabbit population. The vertical axis shows the numbers of rabbits in the population, while the horizontal axis shows time. The graph shows the size of the population over a ten-year period.

Math Skills

Inequalities

The population statement is an example of an inequality. An inequality is a mathematical statement that compares two expressions. Two signs that represent inequalities are

< (is less than)

> (is greater than)

For example, an inequality comparing the fraction to the decimal 0.75 would be written

$$\frac{1}{2} < 0.75$$

Practice Problems Write an inequality comparing each pair of expressions below.

1. 5 ■ −6
2. 0.4 ■ $\frac{3}{5}$
3. −2 − (−8) ■ 7 − 1.5

FIGURE 7
This line graph shows how the size of a rabbit population changed over a ten-year period. **Interpreting Graphs** *In what year did the rabbit population reach its highest point? What was the size of the population in that year?*

Go Online *active art*

For: Changes in Population activity
Visit: PHSchool.com
Web Code: cep-5012

▼ Young cottontail rabbits in a nest

From Year 0 to Year 4, more rabbits joined the population than left it, so the population increased.

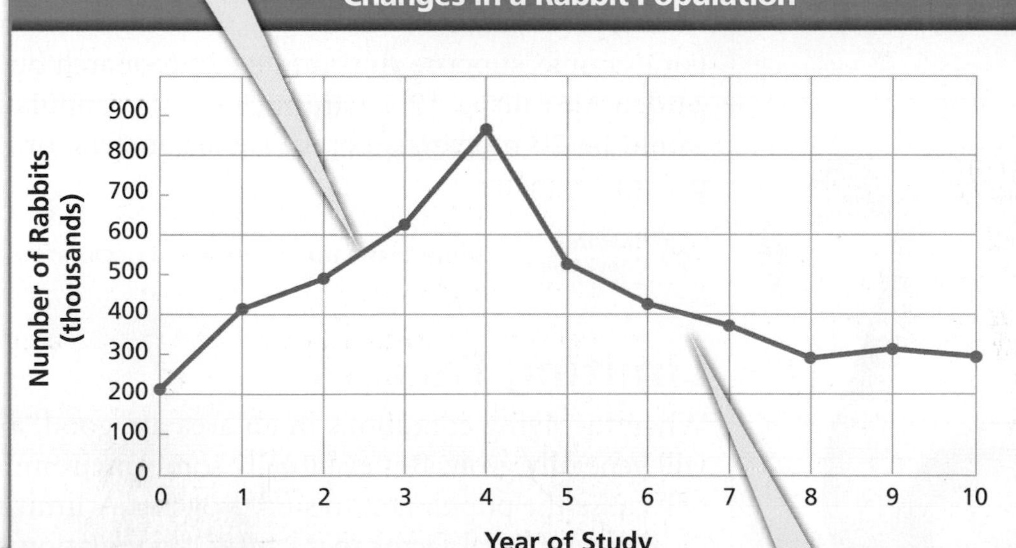

From Year 4 to Year 8, more rabbits left the population than joined it, so the population decreased.

◀ Cottontail rabbit caught by a fox

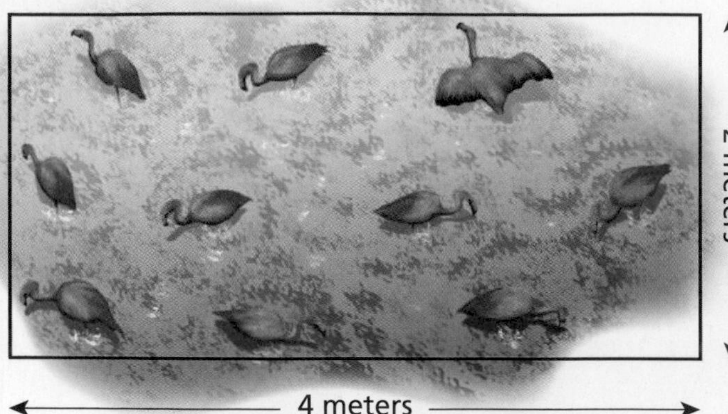

FIGURE 8
Population Density
In the pond on the top left, there are ten flamingos in 8 square meters. The population density is 1.25 flamingos per square meter.
Calculating *What is the population density of the flamingos in the pond on the top right?*

Population Density Sometimes an ecologist may need to know more than just the total size of a population. In many situations, it is helpful to know the **population density**—the number of individuals in an area of a specific size. Population density can be written as an equation:

$$\text{Population density} = \frac{\text{Number of individuals}}{\text{Unit area}}$$

For example, suppose you counted 20 monarch butterflies in a garden measuring 10 square meters. The population density would be 20 monarchs per 10 square meters, or 2 monarchs per square meter.

What is meant by the term *population density*?

Limiting Factors

When the living conditions in an area are good, a population will generally grow. But eventually some environmental factor will cause the population to stop growing. A **limiting factor** is an environmental factor that causes a population to decrease. **Some limiting factors for populations are food and water, space, and weather conditions.**

Food and Water Organisms require food and water to survive. Since food and water are often in limited supply, they are often limiting factors. Suppose a giraffe must eat 10 kilograms of leaves each day to survive. The trees in an area can provide 100 kilograms of leaves a day while remaining healthy. Five giraffes could live easily in this area, since they would only require a total of 50 kilograms of food. But 15 giraffes could not all survive—there would not be enough food. No matter how much shelter, water, and other resources there were, the population would not grow much larger than 10 giraffes.

◀ **Greater flamingo**

The largest population that an area can support is called its **carrying capacity.** The carrying capacity of this giraffe habitat would be 10 giraffes. A population usually stays near its carrying capacity because of the limiting factors in its habitat.

FIGURE 9
Food as a Limiting Factor
These jackals are fighting over the limited food available to them.

Space Space is another limiting factor for populations. Gannets are seabirds that are usually seen flying over the ocean. They come to land only to nest on rocky shores. But the nesting shores get very crowded. If a pair does not find room to nest, they will not be able to add any offspring to the gannet population. So nesting space on the shore is a limiting factor for gannets. If there were more nesting space, more gannets would be able to nest, and the population would increase.

Space is also a limiting factor for plants. The amount of space in which a plant grows determines whether the plant can obtain the sunlight, water, and soil nutrients it needs. For example, many pine seedlings sprout each year in a forest. But as the seedlings grow, the roots of those that are too close together run out of space. Branches from other trees may block the sunlight the seedlings need. Some of the seedlings then die, limiting the size of the pine population.

FIGURE 10
Space as a Limiting Factor
Could any more sunflower plants grow in this field? If not, the field has reached its carrying capacity for sunflowers.

Lab zone Try This **Activity**

Elbow Room

1. Using masking tape, mark off several one-meter squares on the floor of your classroom.
2. Your teacher will set up groups of 2, 4, and 6 students. Each group's task is to put together a small jigsaw puzzle in one of the squares. All the group members must keep their feet within the square.
3. Time how long it takes your group to finish the puzzle.

Making Models How long did it take each group to complete the task? How does this activity show that space can be a limiting factor? What is the carrying capacity of puzzle-solvers in a square meter?

FIGURE 11
Weather as a Limiting Factor
A snowstorm can limit the size of an orange crop.
Applying Concepts *What other weather conditions can limit population growth?*

Weather Weather conditions such as temperature and the amount of rainfall can also limit population growth. A cold snap in late spring can kill the young of many species of organisms, including birds and mammals. A hurricane or flood can wash away nests and burrows. Such unusual events can have long-lasting effects on population size.

What is one weather condition that can limit the growth of a population?

Section 2 Assessment

Target Reading Skill Asking Questions Use the answers to the questions you wrote about the headings to help you answer the questions below.

Reviewing Key Concepts

1. a. **Listing** What are four methods of determining population size?
   b. **Applying Concepts** Which method would you use to determine the number of mushrooms growing on the floor of a large forest? Explain.
2. a. **Identifying** Name two ways organisms join a population and two ways organisms leave a population.
   b. **Calculating** Suppose a population of 100 mice has produced 600 young. If 200 mice have died, how many mice are in the population now? (Assume for this question that no mice have moved into or out of the population for other reasons.)
   c. **Drawing Conclusions** Suppose that you discovered that there were actually 750 mice in the population. How could you account for the difference?
3. a. **Reviewing** Name three limiting factors for populations.
   b. **Describing** Choose one of the limiting factors and describe how it limits population growth.
   c. **Inferring** How might the limiting factor you chose affect the pigeon population in your town?

Math Practice

4. **Inequalities** Complete the following inequality showing the relationship between carrying capacity and population size. Then explain why the inequality is true.

   If population size ■ carrying capacity, then population size will decrease.

Lab zone **Skills Lab**

Counting Turtles

Problem

How can the mark-and-recapture method help ecologists monitor the size of a population?

Skills Focus

calculating, graphing, predicting

Materials

- model paper turtle population
- calculator
- graph paper

Procedure

1. The data table shows the results from the first three years of a population study to determine the number of snapping turtles in a pond. Copy the table into your notebook.

Data Table				
Year	Number Marked	Total Number Captured	Number Recaptured (With Marks)	Estimated Total Population
1	32	28	15	
2	25	21	11	
3	23	19	11	
4	15			

2. Your teacher will give you a box representing the pond. Fifteen of the turtles have been marked, as shown in the data table for Year 4.
3. Capture a member of the population by randomly selecting one turtle. Set it aside.
4. Repeat Step 3 nine times. Record the total number of turtles you captured.
5. Examine each turtle to see whether it has a mark. Count the number of recaptured (marked) turtles. Record this number in your data table.

Analyze and Conclude

1. **Calculating** Use the equation below to estimate the turtle population for each year. The first year is done for you as a sample. If your answer is a decimal, round it to the nearest whole number. Record the population for each year in the last column of the data table.

$$\text{Total population} = \frac{\text{Number marked} \times \text{Total number captured}}{\text{Number recaptured (with marks)}}$$

Sample (Year 1):

$$\frac{32 \times 28}{15} = 59.7 \text{ or } 60 \text{ turtles}$$

2. **Graphing** Graph the estimated total populations for the four years. Mark years on the horizontal axis. Mark population size on the vertical axis.
3. **Interpreting Data** Describe how the turtle population has changed over the four years of the study. Suggest three possible causes for the changes.
4. **Predicting** Use your graph to predict what the turtle population will be in Year 5. Explain your prediction.
5. **Communicating** Write a paragraph that explains why the mark-and-recapture method is a useful tool for ecologists. When is this technique most useful for estimating a population's size?

More to Explore

Suppose that only six turtles had been recaptured in Year 2. How would this change your graph?

Animal Overpopulation: How Can People Help?

White-Tailed Deer
To obtain food, deer are moving into people's yards.

Populations of white-tailed deer are growing rapidly in many parts of the United States. As populations soar, food becomes a limiting factor. Many deer die of starvation. Others grow up small and unhealthy. In search of food, hungry deer move closer to where humans live. There they eat farm crops, garden vegetables, shrubs, and even trees. In addition, increased numbers of deer near roads can cause automobile accidents.

People admire the grace and swiftness of deer. Most people don't want these animals to suffer from starvation or illness. Should people take action to limit growing deer populations?

Wildlife Technician
This wildlife researcher in Virginia studies white-tailed deer populations. Here he prepares to tag a young deer.

The Issues

Should People Take Direct Action?

Many people argue that hunting is the best way to reduce animal populations. Wildlife managers look at the supply of resources in an area and determine its carrying capacity. Then hunters are issued licenses to help reduce the number of deer. Hunting is usually not allowed in cities or suburbs, however.

Some people favor nonhunting approaches to control deer populations. One plan is to trap the deer and relocate them. But this method is expensive and requires finding another location that can accept the deer without upsetting the balance of its own ecosystem.

Scientists are also working to develop chemicals to reduce the birth rate in deer populations. But this plan is effective for only one year at a time.

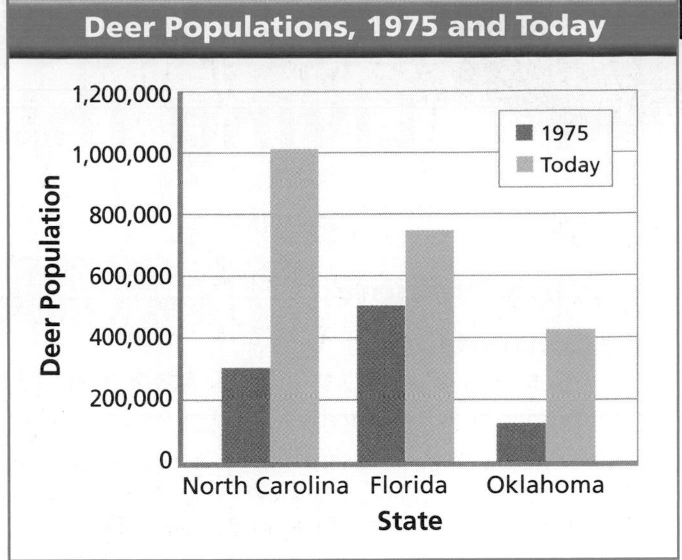

White-Tailed Deer Populations
This graph shows how the deer populations have grown in North Carolina, Florida, and Oklahoma.

Should People Take Indirect Action?

Some suggest bringing in natural predators of deer, such as wolves, mountain lions, and bears, to areas with too many deer. But these animals could also attack cattle, dogs, cats, and even humans. Other communities have built tall fences around areas to keep out the deer. However, this solution is impractical for farmers or ranchers.

Should People Do Nothing?

Some people oppose any kind of action. They support leaving the deer alone and allowing nature to take its course. Animal populations in an area naturally cycle up and down over time. Doing nothing means that some deer will die of starvation or disease. But eventually, the population will be reduced to a size within the carrying capacity of the environment.

You Decide

1. **Identify the Problem**
   In your own words, explain the problem created by the overpopulation of white-tailed deer.
2. **Analyze the Options**
   List the ways that people can deal with the overpopulation of white-tailed deer. State the positive and negative points of each method.
3. **Find a Solution**
   Suppose you are an ecologist in an area that has twice as many deer as it can support. Propose a way for the community to deal with the problem.

For: More on white-tailed deer overpopulation
Visit: PHSchool.com
Web Code: ceh-5010

Section

3 Interactions Among Living Things

Reading Preview

Key Concepts

- How do an organism's adaptations help it to survive?
- What are the major ways in which organisms in an ecosystem interact?
- What are the three types of symbiotic relationships?

Key Terms

- natural selection
- adaptations • niche
- competition • predation
- predator • prey • symbiosis
- mutualism • commensalism
- parasitism • parasite • host

Target Reading Skill

Using Prior Knowledge Before you read, look at the section headings and visuals to see what this section is about. Then write what you know about how living things interact in a graphic organizer like the one below. As you read, continue to write in what you learn.

What You Know
1. Organisms interact in different ways. 2.

What You Learned
1. 2.

Lab zone Discover Activity

Can You Hide a Butterfly?

1. Trace a butterfly on a piece of paper, using the outline shown here.
2. Look around the classroom and pick a spot where you will place your butterfly. You must place your butterfly out in the open. Color your butterfly so it will blend in with the spot you choose.
3. Tape your butterfly down. Someone will now have one minute to find the butterflies. Will your butterfly be found?

Think It Over

Predicting Over time, do you think the population size of butterflies that blend in with their surroundings would increase or decrease?

Can you imagine living in a cactus like the one in Figure 12? Ouch! You probably wouldn't want to live in a house covered with sharp spines. But many species live in, on, and around saguaro cactuses.

As day breaks, a twittering sound comes from a nest tucked in one of the saguaro's arms. Two young red-tailed hawks are preparing to fly for the first time. Farther down the stem, a tiny elf owl peeks out of its nest in a small hole. This owl is so small it could fit in your palm! A rattlesnake slithers around the base of the saguaro, looking for lunch. Spying a shrew, the snake strikes it with its needle-like fangs. The shrew dies instantly.

Activity around the saguaro continues after sunset. Long-nosed bats come out to feed on the nectar from the saguaro's blossoms. The bats stick their faces into the flowers to feed, dusting their long snouts with white pollen. As they move from plant to plant, they carry the pollen to other saguaros. This enables the cactuses to reproduce.

Adapting to the Environment

Each organism in the saguaro community has unique characteristics. These characteristics affect the individual's ability to survive in its environment.

Natural Selection A characteristic that makes an individual better suited to its environment may eventually become common in that species through a process called **natural selection.** Natural selection works like this: Individuals whose unique characteristics are best suited for their environment tend to survive and produce offspring. Offspring that inherit these characteristics also live to reproduce. In this way, natural selection results in **adaptations,** the behaviors and physical characteristics that allow organisms to live successfully in their environments.

Individuals with characteristics that are poorly suited to the environment are less likely to survive and reproduce. Over time, poorly suited characteristics may disappear from the species.

Niche **Every organism has a variety of adaptations that are suited to its specific living conditions.** The organisms in the saguaro community have adaptations that result in specific roles. The role of an organism in its habitat, or how it makes its living, is called its **niche.** A niche includes the type of food the organism eats, how it obtains this food, and which other organisms use the organism as food. A niche also includes when and how the organism reproduces and the physical conditions it requires to survive.

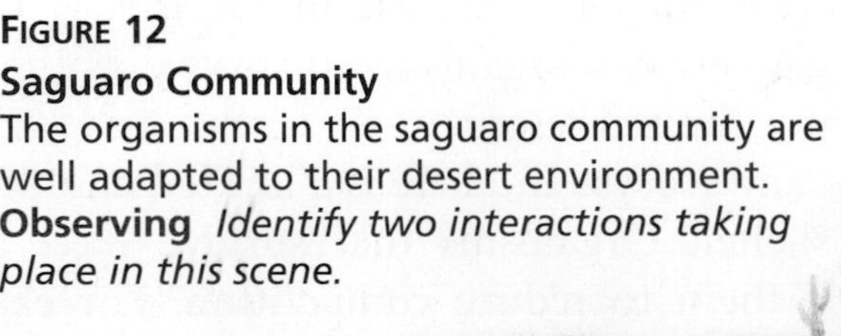

FIGURE 12
Saguaro Community
The organisms in the saguaro community are well adapted to their desert environment.
Observing *Identify two interactions taking place in this scene.*

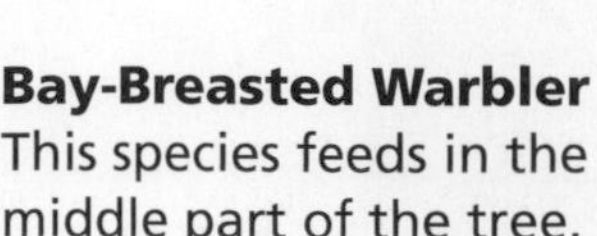

Cape May Warbler
This species feeds at the tips of branches near the top of the tree.

Bay-Breasted Warbler
This species feeds in the middle part of the tree.

Yellow-Rumped Warbler
This species feeds in the lower part of the tree and at the bases of the middle branches.

FIGURE 13
Niche and Competition
Each of these warblers occupies a different niche in its spruce tree habitat. By feeding in different areas of the tree, the birds avoid competing for food.
Comparing and Contrasting *How do the niches of these three warblers differ?*

Competition

During a typical day in the saguaro community, a range of interactions takes place among organisms. **There are three major types of interactions among organisms: competition, predation, and symbiosis.**

Different species can share the same habitat and food requirements. For example, the roadrunner and the elf owl both live on the saguaro and eat insects. However, these two species do not occupy exactly the same niche. The roadrunner is active during the day, while the owl is active mostly at night. If two species occupy the same niche, one of the species will eventually die off. The reason for this is **competition,** the struggle between organisms to survive as they attempt to use the same limited resource.

In any ecosystem, there is a limited amount of food, water, and shelter. Organisms that survive have adaptations that enable them to reduce competition. For example, the three species of warblers in Figure 13 live in the same spruce forest habitat. They all eat insects that live in the spruce trees. How do these birds avoid competing for the limited insect supply? Each warbler "specializes" in feeding in a certain part of a spruce tree. This is how the three species coexist.

Why can't two species occupy the same niche?

For: More on population interactions
Visit: PHSchool.com
Web Code: ced-5013

Predation

A tiger shark lurks below the surface of the clear blue water, looking for shadows of albatross chicks floating above. The shark spots a chick and silently swims closer. Suddenly, the shark bursts through the water and seizes the albatross with one snap of its powerful jaw. This interaction between two organisms has an unfortunate ending for the albatross.

An interaction in which one organism kills another for food is called **predation.** The organism that does the killing, in this case the tiger shark, is the **predator.** The organism that is killed, in this case the albatross, is the **prey.**

The Effect of Predation on Population Size Predation can have a major effect on the size of a population. Recall from Section 2 that when the death rate exceeds the birth rate in a population, the size of that population usually decreases. So if there are many predators, the result is often a decrease in the size of the population of their prey. But a decrease in the number of prey results in less food for their predators. Without adequate food, the predator population starts to decline. So, generally, populations of predators and their prey rise and fall in related cycles.

FIGURE 14
Predation
This green tree python and mouse are involved in a predator-prey interaction.

Math Analyzing Data

Predator-Prey Interactions

On Isle Royale, an island in Lake Superior, the populations of wolves (the predator) and moose (the prey) rise and fall in cycles. Use the graph to answer the questions.

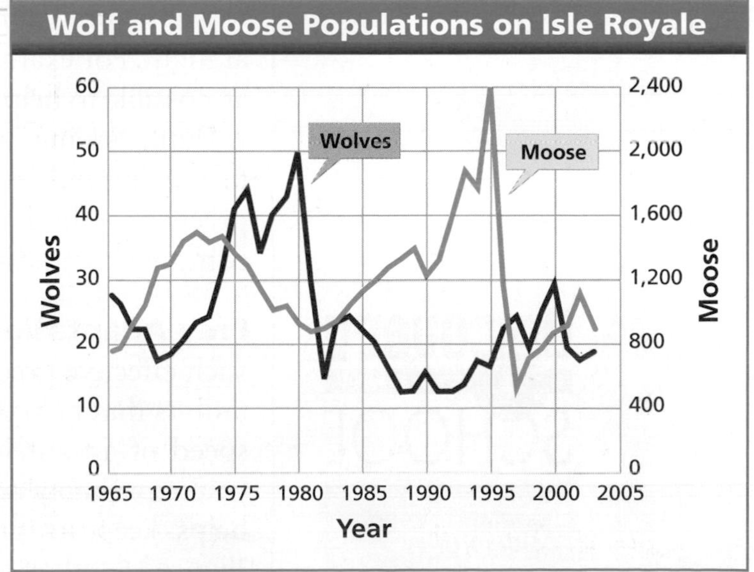

1. **Reading Graphs** What variable is plotted on the *x*-axis? What two variables are plotted on the *y*-axis?
2. **Interpreting Data** How did the moose population change between 1965 and 1972? What happened to the wolf population from 1973 through 1976?
3. **Inferring** How might the change in the moose population have led to the change in the wolf population?
4. **Drawing Conclusions** What is one likely cause of the dip in the moose population between 1974 and 1981?
5. **Predicting** How might a disease in the wolf population one year affect the moose population the next year?

FIGURE 15
Predator Adaptations
This greater horseshoe bat has adaptations that allow it to find prey in the dark. The bat produces pulses of sound and locates prey by interpreting the echoes.
Inferring *What other adaptations might contribute to the bat's success as a predator?*

Predator Adaptations Predators have adaptations that help them catch and kill their prey. For example, a cheetah can run very fast for a short time, enabling it to catch its prey. A jellyfish's tentacles contain a poisonous substance that paralyzes tiny water animals. Some plants, too, have adaptations for catching prey. The sundew is covered with sticky bulbs on stalks—when a fly lands on the plant, it remains snared in the sticky goo while the plant digests it.

Some predators have adaptations that enable them to hunt at night. For example, the big eyes of an owl let in as much light as possible to help it see in the dark. Insect-eating bats can hunt without seeing at all. Instead, they locate their prey by producing pulses of sound and listening for the echoes. This precise method enables a bat to catch a flying moth in complete darkness.

Prey Adaptations How do organisms avoid being killed by such effective predators? Organisms have many kinds of adaptations that help them avoid becoming prey. The alertness and speed of an antelope help protect it from its predators. And you're probably not surprised that the smelly spray of a skunk helps keep its predators at a distance. As you can see in Figure 16, other organisms also have some very effective ways to avoid becoming a predator's next meal.

What are two predator adaptations?

FIGURE 16

Defense Strategies

Organisms display a wide array of adaptations that help them avoid becoming prey.

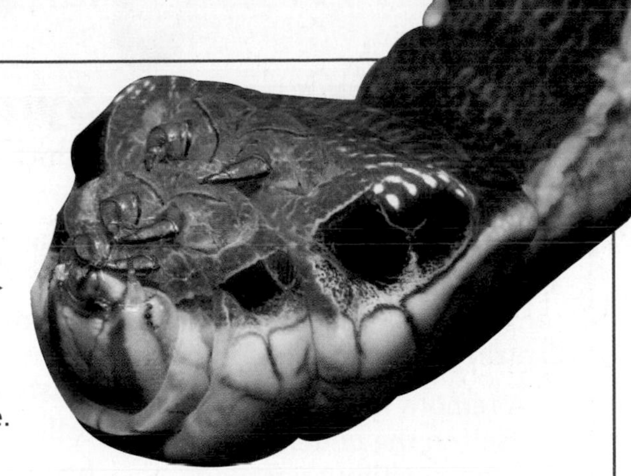

Mimicry ▶
If you're afraid of snakes, you'd probably be terrified to see this organism staring at you. But this caterpillar only looks like a snake. Its convincing resemblance to a viper tricks would-be predators into staying away.

Protective Covering ▼
Have you ever seen a pine cone with a face? This organism is actually a pangolin, a small African mammal. When threatened, the pangolin protects itself by rolling up into a scaly ball.

False Coloring ▲
If you saw this moth in a dark forest, you might think you were looking into the eyes of a large mammal. The large false eyespots on the moth's wings scare potential predators away.

Camouflage ▲
Is it a leaf? Actually, it's a walking leaf insect. But if you were a predator, you might be fooled into looking elsewhere for a meal.

▼ Warning Coloring
A grasshopper this brightly colored can't hide. So what defense does it have against predators? Like many brightly colored animals, this grasshopper is poisonous. Its bright blue and yellow colors warn predators not to eat it.

Lab zone Skills Activity

Classifying

Classify each interaction as an example of mutualism, commensalism, or parasitism. Explain your answers.

- A remora fish attaches itself to the underside of a shark without harming the shark, and eats left-over bits of food from the shark's meals.
- A vampire bat drinks the blood of horses.
- Bacteria living in cows' stomachs help them break down the cellulose in grass.

Symbiosis

Many of the interactions in the saguaro community you read about are examples of symbiosis. **Symbiosis** (sim bee OH sis) is a close relationship between two species that benefits at least one of the species. **The three types of symbiotic relationships are mutualism, commensalism, and parasitism.**

Mutualism A relationship in which both species benefit is called **mutualism** (MYOO choo uh liz um). The relationship between the saguaro and the long-eared bats is an example of mutualism. The bats benefit because the cactus flowers provide them with food. The saguaro benefits as its pollen is carried to another plant on the bat's nose.

In some cases of mutualism, two species are so dependent on each other that neither could live without the other. This is true for some species of acacia trees and stinging ants in Central and South America. The stinging ants nest only in the acacia tree, whose thorns discourage the ants' predators. The tree also provides the ants' only food. The ants, in turn, attack other animals that approach the tree and clear competing plants away from the base of the tree. To survive, each species needs the other.

Commensalism A relationship in which one species benefits and the other species is neither helped nor harmed is called **commensalism** (kuh MEN suh liz um). The red-tailed hawks' interaction with the saguaro is an example of commensalism. The hawks benefit by having a place to build their nest, while the cactus is not affected by the hawks.

Commensalism is not very common in nature because two species are usually either helped or harmed a little by any interaction. For example, by creating a small hole for its nest in the cactus stem, the elf owl slightly damages the cactus.

FIGURE 17
Mutualism
Three yellow-billed oxpeckers get a cruise and a snack aboard an obliging hippopotamus. The oxpeckers eat ticks living on the hippo's skin. Since both the birds and the hippo benefit from this interaction, it is an example of mutualism.

Parasitism **Parasitism** (PA ruh sit iz um) involves one organism living on or inside another organism and harming it. The organism that benefits is called a **parasite,** and the organism it lives on or in is called a **host.** The parasite is usually smaller than the host. In a parasitic relationship, the parasite benefits from the interaction while the host is harmed.

Some common parasites are fleas, ticks, and leeches. These parasites have adaptations that enable them to attach to their host and feed on its blood. Other parasites live inside the host's body, such as tapeworms that live inside the digestive systems of dogs, wolves, and some other mammals.

Unlike a predator, a parasite does not usually kill the organism it feeds on. If the host dies, the parasite loses its source of food. An interesting example of this rule is shown by a species of mite that lives in the ears of moths. The mites almost always live in just one of the moth's ears. If they live in both ears, the moth's hearing is so badly affected that it is likely to be quickly caught and eaten by its predator, a bat.

Why doesn't a parasite usually kill its host?

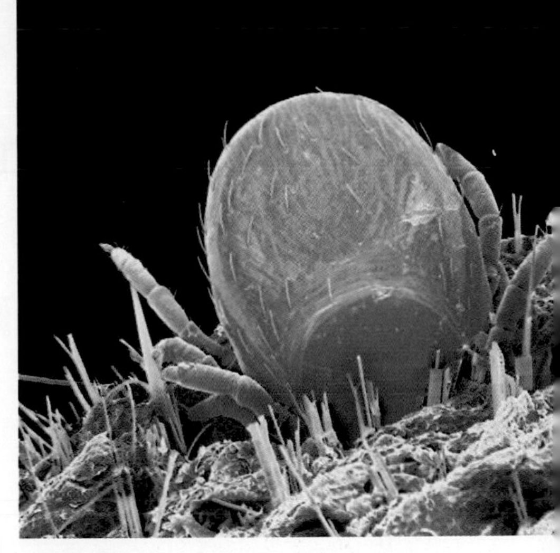

FIGURE 18
Parasitism
Ticks feed on the blood of certain animals. **Classifying** *Which organism in this interaction is the parasite? Which organism is the host?*

Section 3 Assessment

Target Reading Skill **Using Prior Knowledge** Review your graphic organizer and revise it based on what you just learned in the section.

Reviewing Key Concepts

1. a. **Defining** What are adaptations?
   b. **Explaining** How are a snake's sharp fangs an adaptation that helps it survive in the saguaro community?
   c. **Developing Hypotheses** Explain how natural selection in snakes might have led to adaptations such as sharp fangs.
2. a. **Reviewing** What are three main ways in which organisms interact?
   b. **Classifying** Give one example of each type of interaction.
3. a. **Listing** List the three types of symbiotic relationships.
   b. **Comparing and Contrasting** For each type of symbiotic relationship, explain how the two organisms are affected.
   c. **Applying Concepts** Some of your classroom plants are dying. Others that you planted at the same time and cared for in the same way are growing well. When you look closely at the dying plants, you see tiny mites on them. Which symbiotic relationship is likely occurring between the plants and mites? Explain.

Lab zone At-Home Activity

Feeding Frenzy You and your family can observe interactions among organisms at a bird feeder. Fill a clean, dry, 2-liter bottle with birdseed. With paper clips, attach a plastic plate to the neck of the bottle. Then hang your feeder outside where you can see it easily. Observe the feeder at different times of the day. Keep a log of all the organisms you see near it and how they interact.

Section 4

Changes in Communities

Reading Preview

Key Concept

- How do primary and secondary succession differ?

Key Terms

- succession
- primary succession
- pioneer species
- secondary succession

Target Reading Skill

Comparing and Contrasting As you read, compare and contrast primary and secondary succession by completing a table like the one below.

Factors in Succession	Primary Succession	Secondary Succession
Possible cause	Volcanic eruption	
Type of area		
Existing ecosystem?		

Lab zone Discover Activity

What Happened Here?

1. The two photographs at the bottom of this page show the same area in Yellowstone National Park in Wyoming. The photograph on the left was taken soon after a major fire. The photograph on the right was taken a few years later. Observe the photographs carefully.
2. Make a list of all the differences you notice between the two scenes.

Think It Over

Posing Questions How would you describe what happened during the time between the two photographs? What questions do you have about this process?

In 1988, huge fires raged through the forests of Yellowstone National Park. The fires were so hot that they jumped from tree to tree without burning along the ground. Huge trees burst into flame from the intense heat. It took months for the fires to burn themselves out. All that remained were thousands of blackened tree trunks sticking out of the ground like charred toothpicks.

Could a forest community recover from such disastrous fires? It might seem unlikely. But within just a few months, signs of life had returned. First, tiny green shoots of new grass poked through the sooty ground. Then, small tree seedlings began to grow. The forest was coming back! After 15 years, young forests were flourishing in many areas.

Fires, floods, volcanoes, hurricanes, and other natural disasters can change communities very quickly. But even without disasters, communities change. The series of predictable changes that occur in a community over time is called **succession.**

Changes in a Yellowstone community ▼

1 Volcanic Eruption
Shortly after a volcanic eruption, there is no soil, only ash and rock.

2 Pioneer Species
The first species to grow are pioneer species such as mosses and lichens.

3 Soil Creation
As pioneer species grow and die, soil forms. Some plants grow in this new soil.

4 Fertile Soil and Maturing Plants
As more plants die, they decompose and make the soil more fertile. New plants grow and existing plants mature in the fertile soil.

FIGURE 19
Primary Succession
Primary succession occurs in an area where no soil and no organisms exist.
Applying Concepts *What determines the particular species that appear during succession?*

Primary Succession

Primary succession is the series of changes that occur in an area where no soil or organisms exist. Such an area might be a new island formed by the eruption of an undersea volcano or an area of rock uncovered by a melting sheet of ice.

Figure 19 shows the series of changes an area might undergo after a violent volcanic eruption. The first species to populate the area are called **pioneer species.** They are often carried to the area by wind or water. Typical pioneer species are mosses or lichens, which are fungi and algae growing in a symbiotic relationship. As pioneer species grow, they help break up the rocks. When the organisms die, they provide nutrients that enrich the thin layer of soil that is forming on the rocks.

Over time, plant seeds land in the new soil and begin to grow. The specific plants that grow depend on the climate of the area. For example, in a cool, northern area, early seedlings might include alder and cottonwood trees. Eventually, succession may lead to a community of organisms that does not change unless the ecosystem is disturbed. Reaching this mature community can take centuries.

What are some pioneer species?

1 Abandoned Field
Grasses and wildflowers have taken over this abandoned field.

2 Tree Growth Begins
After a few years, pine seedlings and other plants replace some of the grasses and wildflowers.

FIGURE 20
Secondary Succession
Secondary succession occurs following a disturbance to an ecosystem, such as clearing a forest for farmland.

Secondary Succession

The changes following the Yellowstone fire were an example of secondary succession. **Secondary succession** is the series of changes that occur in an area where the ecosystem has been disturbed, but where soil and organisms still exist. Natural disturbances that have this effect include fires, hurricanes, and tornadoes. Human activities, such as farming, logging, or mining, may also disturb an ecosystem. **Unlike primary succession, secondary succession occurs in a place where an ecosystem currently exists.**

Secondary succession usually occurs more rapidly than primary succession. Consider, for example, an abandoned field in the southeastern United States. You can follow the process of succession in such a field in Figure 20. After a century, a hardwood forest is developing. This forest community may remain for a long time.

What are two natural events that can disturb an ecosystem?

For: Links on succession
Visit: www.SciLinks.org
Web Code: scn-0514

3 A Forest Develops
As tree growth continues, the trees begin to crowd out the grasses and wildflowers.

4 Mature Community
Eventually, a mixed forest of pine, oak, and hickory dominates the landscape.

Section 4 Assessment

Target Reading Skill Comparing and Contrasting Use the information in your table to help you answer Question 1 below.

Reviewing Key Concepts

1. a. **Defining** What is primary succession? What is secondary succession?
   b. **Comparing and Contrasting** How do primary succession and secondary succession differ?
   c. **Classifying** Grass poking through a crack in a sidewalk is an example of succession. Is it primary succession or secondary succession? Explain.

Lab zone At-Home Activity

Community Changes Interview a family member or neighbor who has lived in your neighborhood for a long time. Ask the person to describe how the neighborhood has changed over time. Have areas that were formerly grassy been paved or developed? Have any farms, parks, or lots returned to a wild state? Write a summary of your interview. Can you classify any of the changes as examples of succession?

Chapter 1 Study Guide

The BIG Idea **Populations and Ecosystems** Ecosystems are composed of populations that interact with their nonliving surroundings and with the community of other organisms.

1 Living Things and the Environment

Key Concepts

- An organism obtains food, water, shelter, and other things it needs to live, grow, and reproduce from its environment.
- An organism interacts with both the living and nonliving parts of its habitat.
- An organism belongs to a population that includes other members of its species. The population belongs to a community of different species. The community and abiotic factors together form an ecosystem.

Key Terms

organism	species
habitat	population
biotic factor	community
abiotic factor	ecosystem
photosynthesis	ecology

2 Studying Populations

Key Concepts

- Some methods of determining the size of a population are direct and indirect observations, sampling, and mark-and-recapture studies.
- Populations can change in size when members join or leave the population.
- Population density can be determined using the following equation:

$$\text{Population density} = \frac{\text{Number of individuals}}{\text{Unit area}}$$

- Some limiting factors for populations are food and water, space, and weather conditions.

Key Terms

estimate	emigration
birth rate	population density
death rate	limiting factor
immigration	carrying capacity

3 Interactions Among Living Things

Key Concepts

- Every organism has a variety of adaptations that are suited to its specific living conditions.
- Competition, predation, and symbiosis are interactions among organisms.
- The three types of symbiotic relationships are mutualism, commensalism, and parasitism.

Key Terms

natural selection	symbiosis
adaptations	mutualism
niche	commensalism
competition	parasitism
predation	parasite
predator	host
prey	

4 Changes in Communities

Key Concept

- Unlike primary succession, secondary succession occurs in a place where an ecosystem currently exists.

Key Terms

succession	pioneer species
primary succession	secondary succession

Review and Assessment

For: Self-Assessment
Visit: PHSchool.com
Web Code: cea-5010

Organizing Information

Identifying Main Ideas Copy the graphic organizer about determining population size onto a separate sheet of paper. Then complete it and add a title. (For more on Identifying Main Ideas, see the Skills Handbook.)

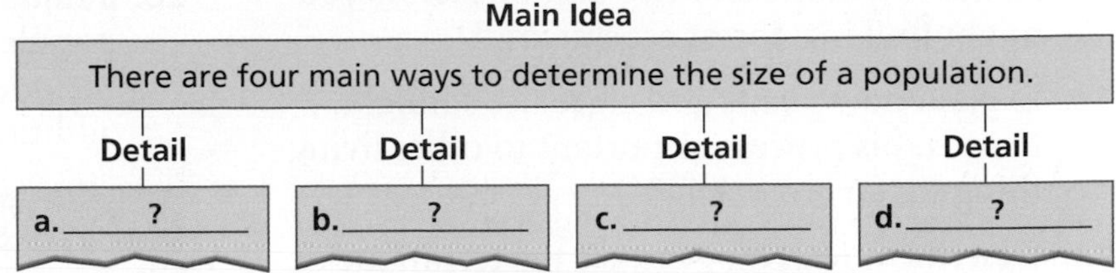

Reviewing Key Terms

Choose the letter of the best answer.

1. A prairie dog, a hawk, and a badger all are members of the same
   a. niche.
   b. community.
   c. species.
   d. population.
2. All of the following are examples of limiting factors for populations *except*
   a. space.
   b. food.
   c. time.
   d. weather.
3. In which type of interaction do both species benefit?
   a. predation
   b. mutualism
   c. commensalism
   d. parasitism
4. Which of these relationships is an example of parasitism?
   a. a bird building a nest on a tree branch
   b. a bat pollinating a saguaro cactus
   c. a flea living on a cat's blood
   d. ants protecting a tree that produces the ants' only food
5. The series of predictable changes that occur in a community over time is called
   a. natural selection.
   b. ecology.
   c. commensalism.
   d. succession.

If the statement is true, write *true*. If it is false, change the underlined word or words to make the statement true.

6. Grass is an example of a <u>biotic factor</u> in a habitat.
7. <u>Immigration</u> is the number of individuals in a specific area.
8. An organism's specific role in its habitat is called its <u>niche</u>.
9. The struggle between organisms for limited resources is called <u>mutualism</u>.
10. A parasite lives on or inside its <u>predator</u>.

Writing in Science

Descriptive Paragraph Use what you have learned about predators and prey to write about an interaction between two organisms. For each organism, describe at least one adaptation that helps it either catch prey or fend off predators.

Populations and Communities
Video Preview
Video Field Trip
▶ Video Assessment

Review and Assessment

Checking Concepts

11. Name two biotic and two abiotic factors you might find in a forest ecosystem.
12. Explain how plants and algae use sunlight. How is this process important to other living things in an ecosystem?
13. Describe how ecologists use the technique of sampling to estimate population size.
14. Give an example showing how space can be a limiting factor for a population.
15. What are two adaptations that prey organisms have developed to protect themselves? Describe how each adaptation protects the organism.

Thinking Critically

16. **Making Generalizations** Explain why ecologists usually study a specific population of organisms rather than the entire species.
17. **Problem Solving** In a summer job working for an ecologist, you have been assigned to estimate the population of grasshoppers in a field. Propose a method and explain how you would carry out your plan.
18. **Relating Cause and Effect** Competition for resources in an area is usually more intense within a single species than between two different species. Suggest an explanation for this observation. (*Hint:* Consider how niches help organisms avoid competition.)
19. **Classifying** Lichens and mosses have just begun to grow on the rocky area shown below. Which type of succession is occurring? Explain.

Math Practice

20. **Inequalities** Review the two inequalities about population size. Then revise each inequality to include immigration and emigration in addition to birth rate and death rate.

Applying Skills

Use the data in the table below to answer Questions 21–24.

Ecologists monitoring a deer population collected data during a 30-year study.

Year	0	5	10	15	20	25	30
Population (thousands)	15	30	65	100	40	25	10

21. **Graphing** Make a line graph using the data in the table. Plot years on the horizontal axis and population on the vertical axis.
22. **Interpreting Data** In which year did the deer population reach its highest point? Its lowest point?
23. **Communicating** Write a few sentences describing how the deer population changed during the study.
24. **Developing Hypotheses** In Year 16 of the study, this region experienced a very severe winter. How might this have affected the deer population?

Lab zone Chapter Project

Performance Assessment Review your report and graph to be sure that they clearly state your conclusion about the effects of crowding on plant growth. With your group, decide how you will present your results. Do a practice run-through to make sure all group members feel comfortable with their parts. After your presentation, list some improvements you could have made in your experimental plan.

Standardized Test Prep

Test-Taking Tip

Interpreting Graphs

When you are asked to interpret a line graph, look at the labels on the axes. The labels tell you what relationship is plotted—in other words, what variables are being compared. On the graph below, the axis labels show that the size of a prairie dog population is being compared over time.

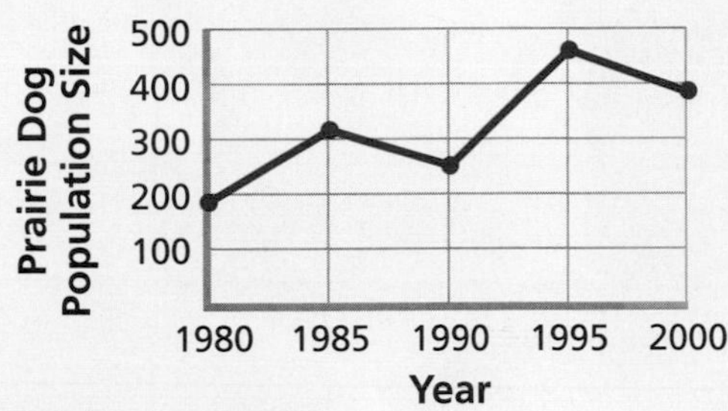

Sample Question

Based on the graph, which of the following is true?

A The prairie dog population was smaller in 1990 than in 1995.
B The prairie dog population was greater in 1990 than in 1995.
C The prairie dog population density was greater in 1990 than in 1985.
D The prairie dog population density was smaller in 1990 than in 1985.

Answer

The correct answer is **A.** You can eliminate **C** and **D** because the axis labels refer to population size rather than population density. Of the remaining choices, **A** is the only one that is correct, because the line of the graph is lower in 1990 than in 1995.

Choose the letter of the best answer.

1. According to the graph above, in what year was the prairie dog population the largest?
A 1980 **B** 1990
C 1995 **D** 2000

2. In general, which of the following is a true statement about population size?
F If birth rate < death rate, population size increases.
G If death rate < birth rate, population size decreases.
H If birth rate > death rate, population size increases.
J If death rate > birth rate, population size increases.

3. A freshwater lake has a muddy bottom, which is home to different types of algae and other organisms. Many species of fish feed on the algae. Which of the following is an *abiotic* factor in this ecosystem?
A the temperature of the water
B the color of the algae
C the number of species of fish
D the amount of food available to the fish

4. Although three different bird species all live in the same trees in an area, competition between the birds rarely occurs. The most likely explanation for this lack of competition is that these birds
F occupy different niches.
G eat the same food.
H have a limited supply of food.
J live in the same part of the trees.

5. During primary succession, a typical pioneer species is
A grass.
B lichen.
C pine trees.
D soil.

Constructed Response

6. Suppose that two species of squirrels living in the same habitat feed on the same type of nut. Describe two possible outcomes of competition between the two squirrel species.

Chapter 2 Ecosystems and Biomes

The BIG Idea

Cycles of Matter and Energy

How do matter and energy flow through ecosystems?

Chapter Preview

This macaque adds to the rich diversity of organisms in the tropical rain forest. ▶

Ecosystems and Biomes

▶ Video Preview
Video Field Trip
Video Assessment

Lab zone™ Chapter **Project**

Breaking It Down

Nothing in an ecosystem is wasted. Even when living things die, organisms such as mushrooms recycle them. This natural process of breakdown is called decomposition. When fallen leaves and other waste products decompose, a fluffy, brown mixture called compost is formed. You can observe decomposition firsthand in this chapter project by building a compost chamber.

Your Goal To design and conduct an experiment to learn more about the process of decomposition

To complete this project, you must

- build two compost chambers
- investigate the effect of one of the following variables on decomposition: moisture, oxygen, temperature, or activity of soil organisms
- analyze your data and present your results
- follow the safety guidelines in Appendix A

Plan It! Your teacher will provide you with a sample of compost material. Observe the wastes in the mixture with a hand lens. Write a hypothesis about which kinds of waste will decay and which will not. Next, decide which variable you will test and plan how you will test it. Once your teacher approves your plan, build your compost chambers and begin your experiment.

Section 1

Energy Flow in Ecosystems

Reading Preview

Key Concepts

- What energy roles do organisms play in an ecosystem?
- How does energy move through an ecosystem?
- How much energy is available at each level of an energy pyramid?

Key Terms

- producer
- consumer
- herbivore
- carnivore
- omnivore
- scavenger
- decomposer
- food chain
- food web
- energy pyramid

Target Reading Skill

Building Vocabulary A definition states the meaning of a word or phrase by telling about its most important feature or function. After you read the section, reread the paragraphs that contain definitions of Key Terms. Use all the information you have learned to write a definition of each Key Term in your own words.

Lab zone Discover **Activity**

Where Did Your Dinner Come From?

1. Across the top of a sheet of paper, list the different types of foods you ate for dinner last night.
2. Under each item, write the name of the plant, animal, or other organism that was the source of that food. Some foods have more than one source. For example, macaroni and cheese contains flour (which is made from a plant such as wheat) and cheese (which comes from an animal).

Think It Over

Classifying How many of your food sources were plants? How many were animals?

Do you play an instrument in your school band? If so, you know that each instrument has a role in a piece of music. For instance, the flute may provide the melody while the drum provides the beat.

Just like the instruments in a band, each organism has a role in the movement of energy through its ecosystem. A bluebird's role, for example, is different from that of the giant oak tree where it is perched. But all parts of the ecosystem, like all parts of a band, are necessary for the ecosystem to work.

Energy Roles

An organism's energy role is determined by how it obtains energy and how it interacts with other organisms. **Each of the organisms in an ecosystem fills the energy role of producer, consumer, or decomposer.**

Producers Energy enters most ecosystems as sunlight. Some organisms, such as plants, algae, and some bacteria, capture the energy of sunlight and store it as food energy. These organisms use the sun's energy to turn water and carbon dioxide into food molecules in a process called photosynthesis.

An organism that can make its own food is a **producer.** Producers are the source of all the food in an ecosystem. In a few ecosystems, producers obtain energy from a source other than sunlight. One such ecosystem is found in rocks deep beneath the ground. How is energy brought into this ecosystem? Certain bacteria in this ecosystem produce their own food using the energy in a gas, hydrogen sulfide, that is found in their environment.

Consumers Some members of an ecosystem cannot make their own food. An organism that obtains energy by feeding on other organisms is a **consumer.**

Consumers are classified by what they eat. Consumers that eat only plants are **herbivores.** Familiar herbivores are caterpillars and deer. Consumers that eat only animals are **carnivores.** Lions and spiders are some examples of carnivores. Consumers that eat both plants and animals are **omnivores.** Crows, bears, and most humans are omnivores.

Some carnivores are scavengers. A **scavenger** is a carnivore that feeds on the bodies of dead organisms. Scavengers include catfish and vultures.

Decomposers If an ecosystem had only producers and consumers, the raw materials of life would stay locked up in wastes and the bodies of dead organisms. Luckily, there are organisms in ecosystems that prevent this problem. **Decomposers** break down wastes and dead organisms and return the raw materials to the ecosystem.

You can think of decomposers as nature's recyclers. While obtaining energy for their own needs, decomposers return simple molecules to the environment. These molecules can be used again by other organisms. Mushrooms and bacteria are common decomposers.

What do herbivores and carnivores have in common?

Consumer—Herbivore

Producer

Consumer—Omnivore

Decomposer

FIGURE 1
Energy Roles
Each organism in an ecosystem fills a specific energy role. Producers, such as oak trees, make their own food. Consumers, such as luna moth larvae and eastern bluebirds, obtain energy by feeding on other organisms. **Classifying** *What role do decomposers play in ecosystems?*

For: Links on food chains and food webs
Visit: www.SciLinks.org
Web Code: scn-0521

Food Chains and Food Webs

As you have read, energy enters most ecosystems as sunlight and is converted into food molecules by producers. This energy is transferred to each organism that eats a producer, and then to other organisms that feed on these consumers. **The movement of energy through an ecosystem can be shown in diagrams called food chains and food webs.**

Food Chains A **food chain** is a series of events in which one organism eats another and obtains energy. You can follow one food chain in Figure 2. The first organism in a food chain is always a producer, such as the tree. The second organism feeds on the producer and is called a first-level consumer. The carpenter ant is a first-level consumer. Next, a second-level consumer eats the first-level consumer. The second-level consumer in this example is the woodpecker.

Food Webs A food chain shows only one possible path along which energy can move through an ecosystem. But just as you do not eat the same thing every day, neither do most other organisms. Most producers and consumers are part of many food chains. A more realistic way to show the flow of energy through an ecosystem is a food web. As shown in Figure 2, a **food web** consists of the many overlapping food chains in an ecosystem.

In Figure 2, you can trace the many food chains in a woodland ecosystem. Note that an organism may play more than one role in an ecosystem. For example, an omnivore such as the mouse is a first-level consumer when it eats grass. But when the mouse eats a grasshopper, it is a second-level consumer.

Just as food chains overlap and connect, food webs interconnect as well. While a gull might eat a fish at the ocean, it might also eat a mouse at a landfill. The gull, then, is part of two food webs—an ocean food web and a land food web. All the world's food webs interconnect in what can be thought of as a global food web.

What energy role is filled by the first organism in a food chain?

Lab zone Try This Activity

Weaving a Food Web

This activity shows how the organisms in a food web are interconnected.

1. Your teacher will assign you a role in the food web.
2. Hold one end of each of several pieces of yarn in your hand. Give the other ends of your yarn to the other organisms to which your organism is linked.
3. Your teacher will now eliminate an organism. All the organisms connected to the missing organism should drop the yarn that connects them.

Making Models How many organisms were affected by the removal of just one organism? What does this activity show about the importance of each organism in a food web?

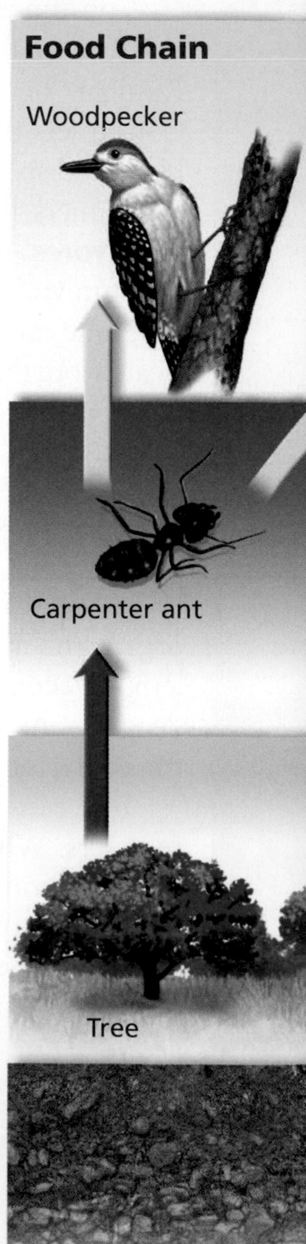

FIGURE 2
A Food Web

A food web consists of many interconnected food chains. Trace the path of energy through the producers, consumers, and decomposers. **Interpreting Diagrams** *Which organisms in the food web are acting as herbivores? Which are carnivores?*

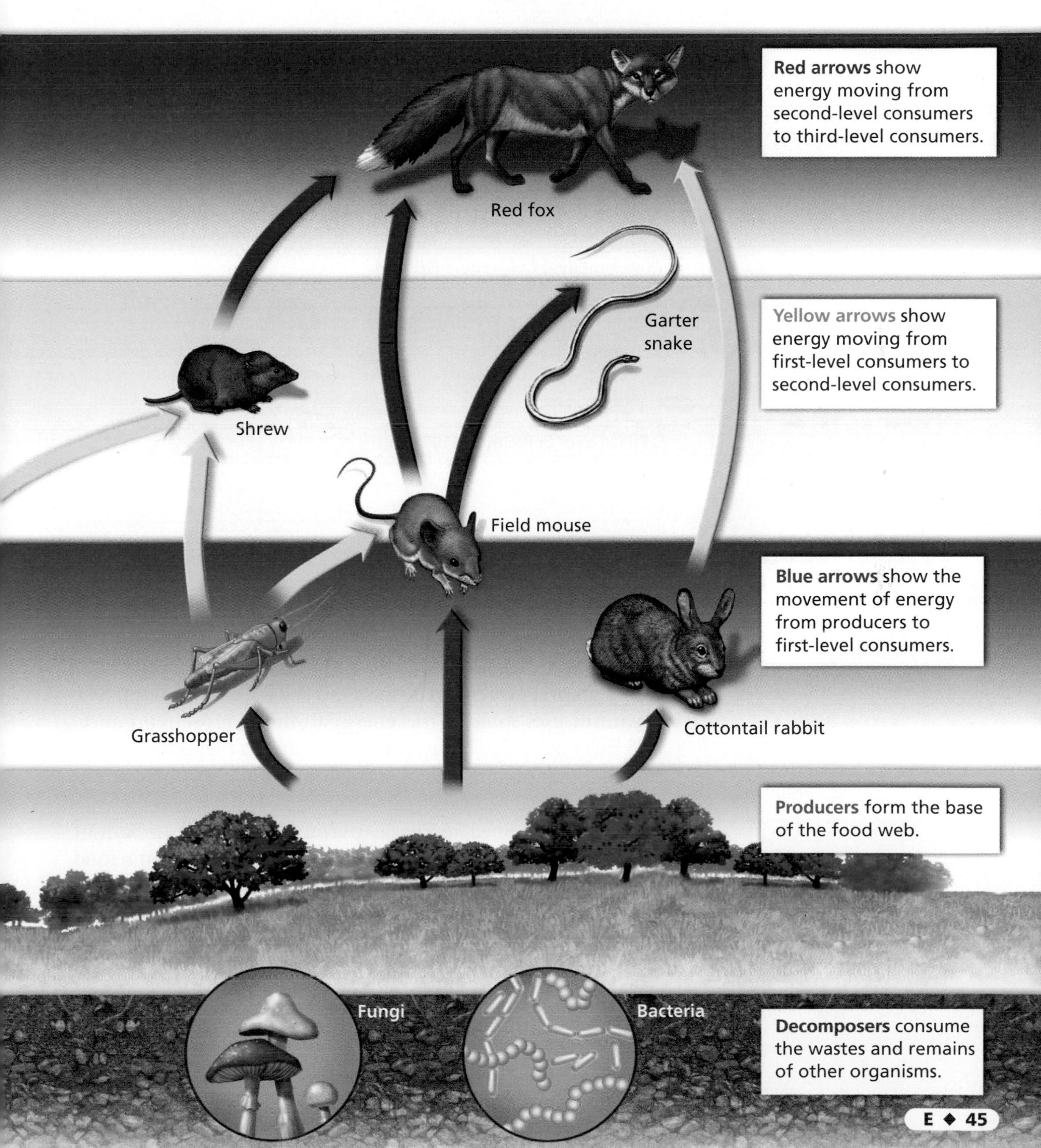

FIGURE 3
Energy Pyramid
This energy pyramid diagram shows the energy available at each level of a food web. Energy is measured in kilocalories, or kcal.
Calculating *How many times more energy is available at the producer level than at the second-level consumer level?*

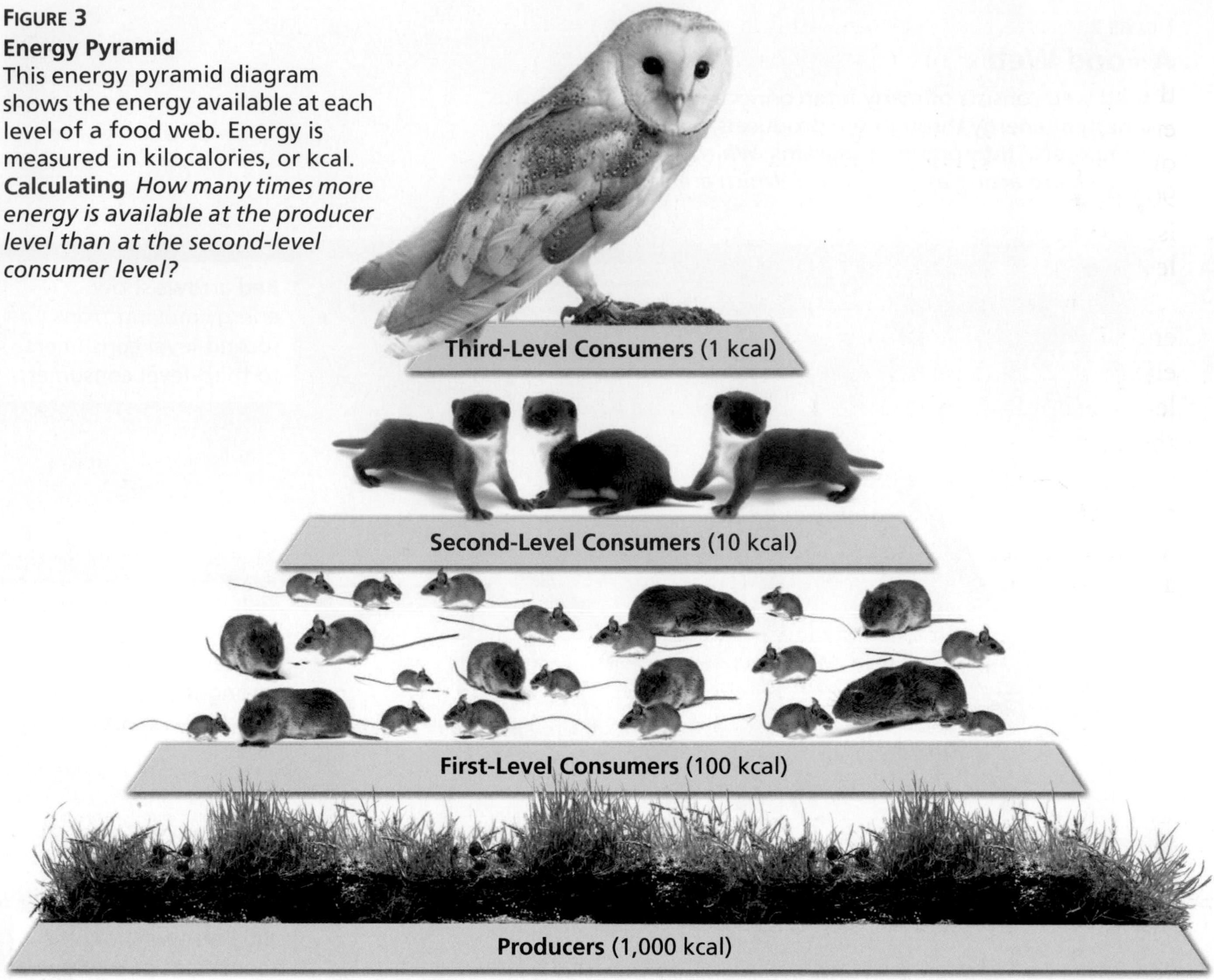

Third-Level Consumers (1 kcal)

Second-Level Consumers (10 kcal)

First-Level Consumers (100 kcal)

Producers (1,000 kcal)

Energy Pyramids

When an organism in an ecosystem eats, it obtains energy. The organism uses some of this energy to move, grow, reproduce, and carry out other life activities. This means that only some of the energy it obtains will be available to the next organism in the food web.

A diagram called an **energy pyramid** shows the amount of energy that moves from one feeding level to another in a food web. You can see an energy pyramid in Figure 3. **The most energy is available at the producer level of the pyramid. As you move up the pyramid, each level has less energy available than the level below.** An energy pyramid gets its name from the shape of the diagram—wider at the base and narrower at the top.

In general, only about 10 percent of the energy at one level of a food web is transferred to the next higher level. The other 90 percent of the energy is used for the organism's life processes or is lost to the environment as heat. Since about 90 percent of the energy is lost at each step, there is not enough energy to support many feeding levels in an ecosystem.

The organisms at higher feeding levels of an energy pyramid do not necessarily require less energy to live than do the organisms at lower levels. Since so much energy is lost at each level, the amount of energy available at the producer level limits the number of consumers that the ecosystem is able to support. As a result, there are usually few organisms at the highest level in a food web.

Reading Checkpoint **Why is the pyramid shape useful for showing the energy available at each of the levels of a food web?**

FIGURE 4
Energy Flow
This barn owl will soon use the energy contained in the rat to carry out its own life processes.

Section 1 Assessment

Target Reading Skill **Building Vocabulary** Use your definitions to help answer the questions below.

Reviewing Key Concepts

1. a. **Identifying** Name the three energy roles that organisms fill in an ecosystem.
   b. **Explaining** How do organisms in each of the three energy roles obtain energy?
   c. **Classifying** Identify the energy roles of the following organisms in a pond ecosystem: tadpole, algae, heron.
2. a. **Defining** What is a food chain? What is a food web?
   b. **Comparing and Contrasting** Why is a food web a more realistic way of portraying an ecosystem than is a food chain?
3. a. **Reviewing** What does an energy pyramid show?
   b. **Describing** How does the amount of energy available at one level of an energy pyramid compare to the amount of energy available at the next level up?
   c. **Relating Cause and Effect** Why are there usually few organisms at the top of an energy pyramid?

Lab zone At-Home Activity

Energy-Role Walk Take a short walk outdoors with a family member to look for producers, consumers, and decomposers. Create a list of the organisms and their energy roles. For each consumer, try to classify it further according to what it eats and its level. Then explain to your family member how energy flows in ecosystems.

Section 2

Integrating Chemistry

Cycles of Matter

Reading Preview

Key Concepts

- What processes are involved in the water cycle?
- How are carbon and oxygen recycled in ecosystems?
- What is the nitrogen cycle?

Key Terms

- water cycle
- evaporation
- condensation
- precipitation
- nitrogen fixation

Target Reading Skill

Sequencing A sequence is the order in which a series of events occurs. As you read, make a cycle diagram that shows the water cycle. Write each event of the water cycle in a separate oval.

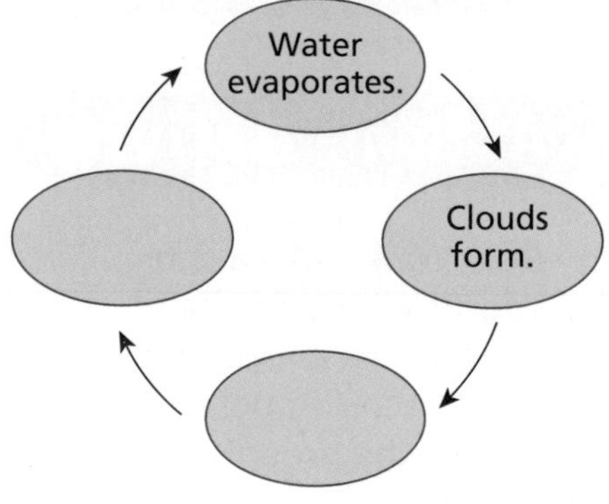

Lab zone Discover Activity

Are You Part of a Cycle?

1. Hold a small mirror a few centimeters from your mouth.
2. Exhale onto the mirror.
3. Observe the surface of the mirror.

Think It Over

Inferring What is the substance that forms on the mirror? Where did this substance come from?

A pile of crumpled cars is ready for loading into a giant compactor. The aluminum and copper pieces have already been removed so that they can be recycled, or used again. Now the steel will be reclaimed at a recycling plant. Earth has a limited supply of aluminum, copper, and the iron used in steel. Recycling old cars is one way to ensure a steady supply of these materials.

Like the supply of metal for building cars, the supply of matter in an ecosystem is limited. Matter in an ecosystem includes water, carbon, oxygen, nitrogen, and many other substances. If matter could not be recycled, ecosystems would quickly run out of the raw materials necessary for life. In this section, you will learn about some cycles of matter: the water cycle, the carbon and oxygen cycles, and the nitrogen cycle.

To understand how these substances cycle over and over through an ecosystem, you need to know a few basic terms that describe the structure of matter. Matter is made up of tiny particles called atoms. Two or more atoms that are joined and act as a unit make up a molecule. For example, a water molecule consists of two hydrogen atoms and one oxygen atom.

The Water Cycle

Water is essential for life. To ensure a steady supply, Earth's water must be recycled. The **water cycle** is the continuous process by which water moves from Earth's surface to the atmosphere and back. **The processes of evaporation, condensation, and precipitation make up the water cycle.** As you read about these processes, follow the cycle in Figure 5.

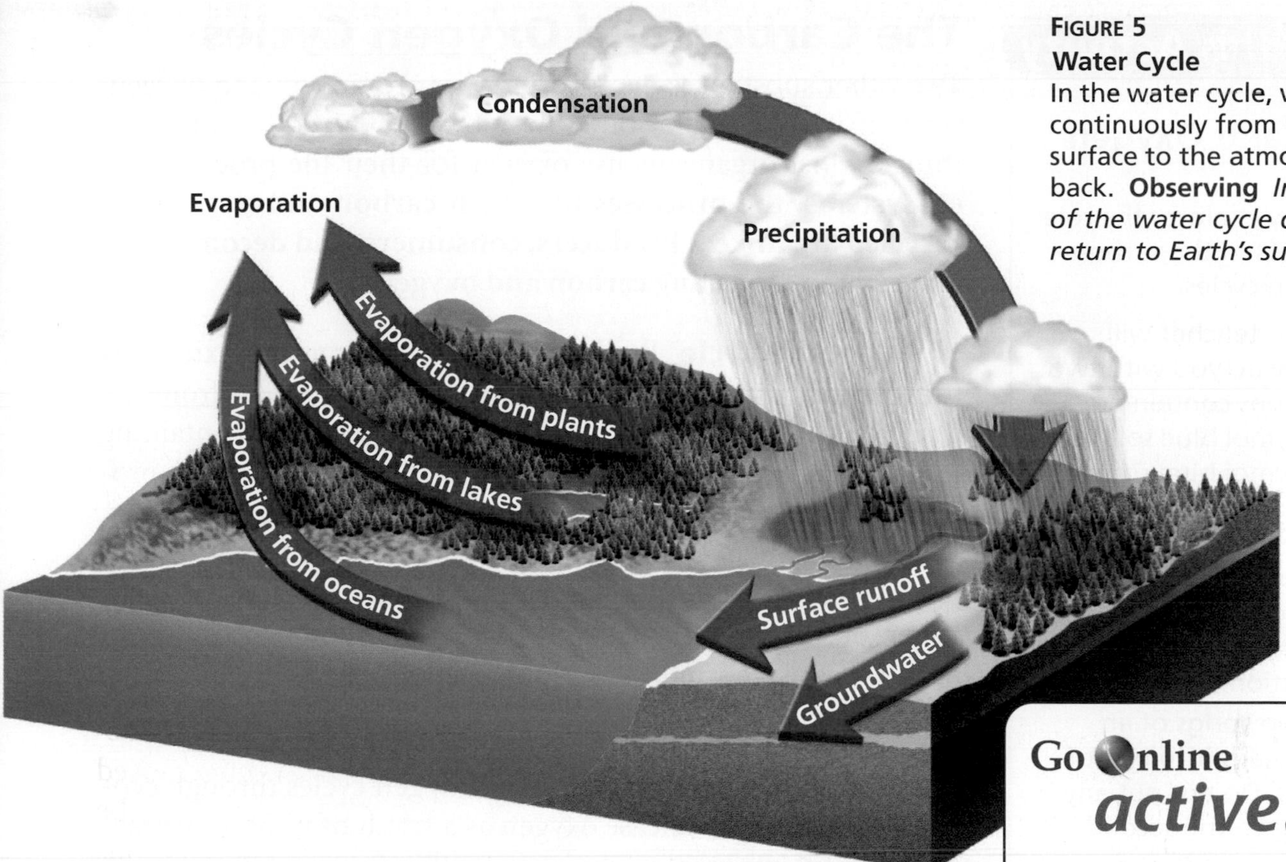

FIGURE 5
Water Cycle
In the water cycle, water moves continuously from Earth's surface to the atmosphere and back. **Observing** *In which step of the water cycle does water return to Earth's surface?*

Go Online *active art*

For: Water Cycle activity
Visit: PHSchool.com
Web Code: cfp-4024

Evaporation The process by which molecules of liquid water absorb energy and change to a gas is called **evaporation.** In the water cycle, liquid water evaporates from oceans, lakes, and other surfaces and forms water vapor, a gas, in the atmosphere. The energy for evaporation comes from the heat of the sun.

Living things also give off water. For example, plants release water vapor from their leaves. You release liquid water in your wastes and water vapor when you exhale.

Condensation As the water vapor rises higher in the atmosphere, it cools down. The cooled vapor then turns back into tiny drops of liquid water. The process by which a gas changes to a liquid is called **condensation.** The water droplets collect around particles of dust, eventually forming clouds.

Precipitation As more water vapor condenses, the drops of water in the cloud grow larger. Eventually the heavy drops fall back to Earth as **precipitation**—rain, snow, sleet, or hail. Most precipitation falls back into oceans or lakes. The precipitation that falls on land may soak into the soil and become groundwater. Or the precipitation may run off the land, eventually flowing back into a river or ocean.

What process causes water from the surface of the ocean to enter the atmosphere as water vapor?

Lab zone Skills Activity

Developing Hypotheses

You've decided to have cocoa at a friend's house on a cold, rainy day. As your friend boils some water, you notice that the inside of a window near the stove is covered with water droplets. Your friend thinks the window is leaking. Using what you know about the water cycle, can you propose another explanation for the water droplets?

Lab zone **Try This Activity**

Carbon and Oxygen Blues

This activity explores the role of producers in the carbon and oxygen cycles.

1. Your teacher will provide you with two plastic cups containing bromthymol blue solution. Bromthymol blue solution appears blue in the absence of carbon dioxide and appears yellow in the presence of carbon dioxide. Note the color of the solution.
2. Place two sprigs of an *Elodea* plant into one of the cups. Do not put any *Elodea* into the second cup. Cover both cups with plastic wrap. Wash your hands.
3. Place the cups where they will not be disturbed. Observe the two cups over the next few days. Note any color changes.

Inferring What do your observations indicate about the role of producers in the carbon and oxygen cycles?

The Carbon and Oxygen Cycles

Two other substances necessary for life are carbon and oxygen. Carbon is an essential building block in the bodies of living things. Most organisms use oxygen for their life processes. **In ecosystems, the processes by which carbon and oxygen are recycled are linked. Producers, consumers, and decomposers play roles in recycling carbon and oxygen.**

The Carbon Cycle Producers take in carbon dioxide gas from the air during photosynthesis. They use carbon from the carbon dioxide to make food molecules—carbon-containing molecules such as sugars and starches. When consumers eat producers, they take in the carbon-containing food molecules. When consumers break down these food molecules to obtain energy, they release carbon dioxide and water as waste products. When producers and consumers die, decomposers break down their remains and return carbon compounds to the soil. Some decomposers also release carbon dioxide as a waste product.

The Oxygen Cycle Like carbon, oxygen cycles through ecosystems. Producers release oxygen as a result of photosynthesis. Most organisms take in oxygen from the air or water and use it to carry out their life processes.

Human Impact Human activities also affect the levels of carbon and oxygen in the atmosphere. When humans burn oil and other fuels, carbon dioxide is released into the atmosphere. When humans clear forests for lumber, fuel, and farmland, carbon dioxide levels also rise. As you know, producers take in carbon dioxide during photosynthesis. When trees are removed from the ecosystem, there are fewer producers to absorb carbon dioxide. There is a greater effect if trees are burned down to clear a forest. If trees are burned down to clear a forest, additional carbon dioxide is released in the burning process.

Reading Checkpoint **What role do producers play in the carbon and oxygen cycles?**

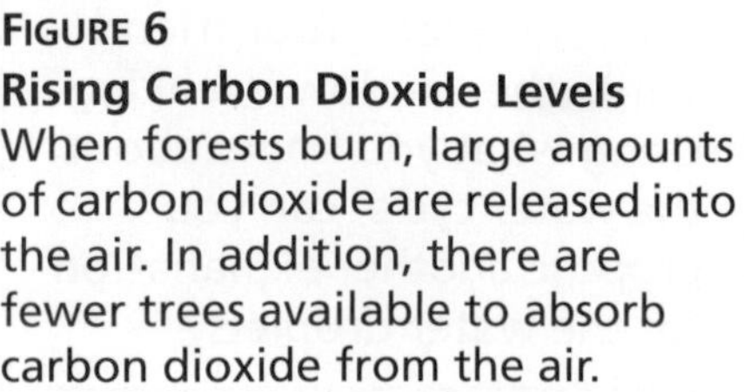

FIGURE 6
Rising Carbon Dioxide Levels
When forests burn, large amounts of carbon dioxide are released into the air. In addition, there are fewer trees available to absorb carbon dioxide from the air.

FIGURE 7

Carbon and Oxygen Cycles

This scene shows how the carbon and oxygen cycles are linked. Producers, consumers, and decomposers all play a role in recycling these two substances.

Interpreting Diagrams *How do human activities affect the carbon and oxygen cycles?*

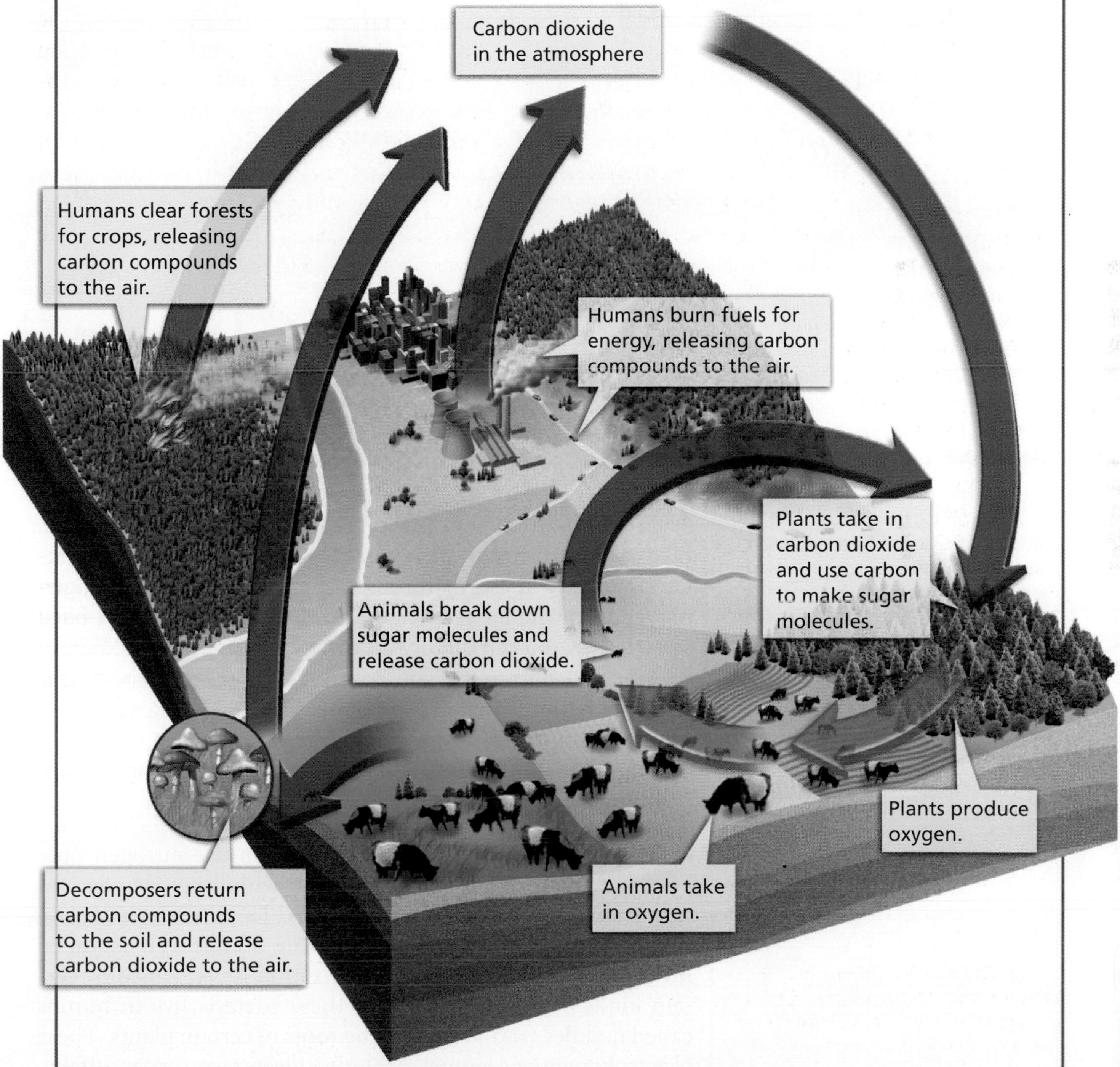

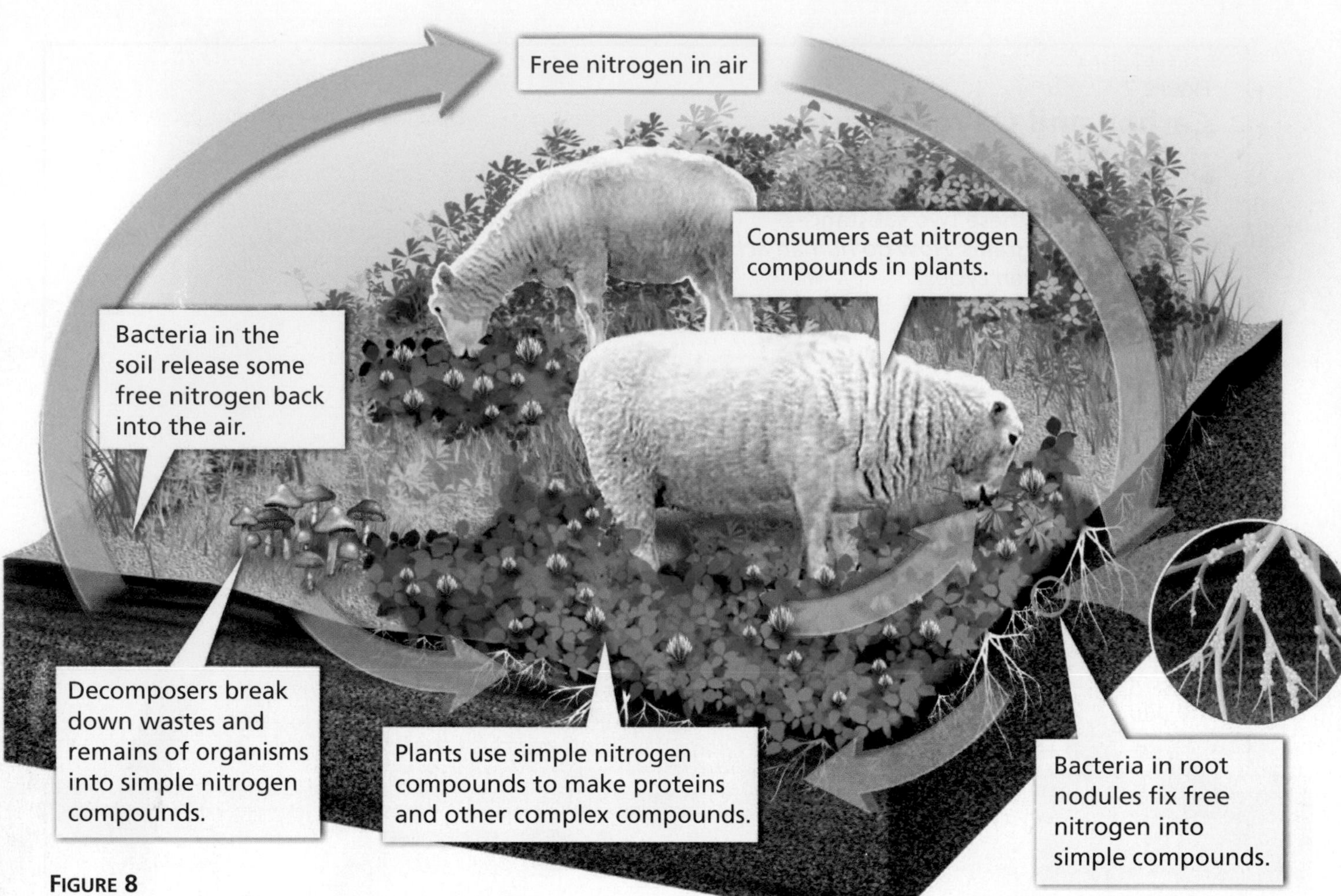

FIGURE 8
Nitrogen Cycle
In the nitrogen cycle, free nitrogen from the air is fixed into compounds. Consumers can then use these nitrogen compounds in carrying out their life processes.
Relating Cause and Effect *How does nitrogen get returned to the environment?*

The Nitrogen Cycle

Like carbon, nitrogen is a necessary building block in the matter that makes up living things. **In the nitrogen cycle, nitrogen moves from the air to the soil, into living things, and back into the air.** You can follow this process in Figure 8.

Since the air around you is about 78 percent nitrogen gas, you might think that it would be easy for living things to obtain nitrogen. However, most organisms cannot use nitrogen gas. Nitrogen gas is called "free" nitrogen because it is not combined with other kinds of atoms.

Nitrogen Fixation Most organisms can use nitrogen only once it has been "fixed," or combined with other elements to form nitrogen-containing compounds. The process of changing free nitrogen into a usable form of nitrogen is called **nitrogen fixation.** Most nitrogen fixation is performed by certain kinds of bacteria. Some of these bacteria live in bumps called nodules (NAHJ oolz) on the roots of certain plants. These plants, known as legumes, include clover, beans, peas, alfalfa, and peanuts.

The relationship between the bacteria and the legumes is an example of mutualism. Both the bacteria and the plant benefit from this relationship: The bacteria feed on the plant's sugars, and the plant is supplied with nitrogen in a usable form.

Return of Nitrogen to the Environment

Once nitrogen has been fixed, producers can use it to build proteins and other complex compounds. Decomposers, in turn, break down these complex compounds in animal wastes and the bodies of dead organisms. Decomposition returns simple nitrogen compounds to the soil. Nitrogen can cycle from the soil to producers and then to consumers many times. At some point, however, bacteria break down the nitrogen compounds completely. These bacteria then release free nitrogen back into the air. The cycle continues from there.

Where do some nitrogen-fixing bacteria live?

FIGURE 9
Growth in Nitrogen-Poor Soil
Pitcher plants can grow in nitrogen-poor soil because they have another way of obtaining nitrogen. Insects become trapped in the plant's tube-shaped leaves. The plant then digests the insects and uses their nitrogen compounds for its functions.

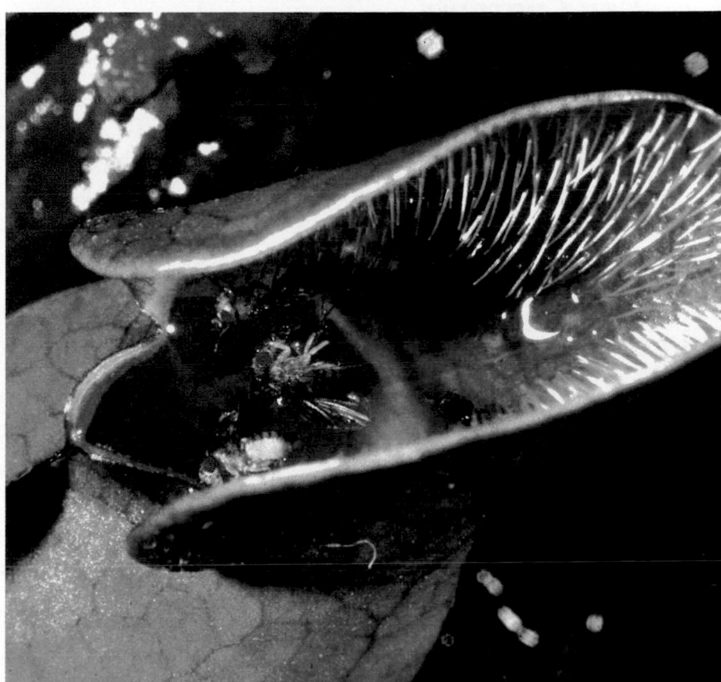

Section 2 Assessment

Target Reading Skill **Sequencing** Refer to your cycle diagram about the water cycle as you answer Question 1.

Reviewing Key Concepts

1. a. **Defining** Name and define the three major processes that occur during the water cycle.
   b. **Making Generalizations** Defend this statement: The sun is the driving force behind the water cycle.
2. a. **Reviewing** Which two substances are linked in one recycling process?
   b. **Comparing and Contrasting** What role do producers play in the carbon and oxygen cycles? What role do consumers play in these cycles?
   c. **Developing Hypotheses** How might the death of all the producers in a community affect the carbon and oxygen cycles?
3. a. **Reviewing** Why do organisms need nitrogen?
   b. **Sequencing** Outline the major steps in the nitrogen cycle.
   c. **Predicting** What might happen in a community if all the nitrogen-fixing bacteria died?

Writing in Science

Comic Strip Choose one of the cycles discussed in this section. Then draw a comic strip with five panels that depicts the important events in the cycle. Remember that the last panel must end with the same event that begins the first panel.

Section 3

Biogeography

Reading Preview

Key Concepts

- How has the movement of the continents affected the distribution of species?
- What are three ways that dispersal of organisms occurs?
- What factors can limit the dispersal of a species?

Key Terms

- biogeography
- continental drift
- dispersal
- exotic species
- climate

Target Reading Skill

Relating Cause and Effect As you read, identify three causes of dispersal. Write the information in a graphic organizer like the one below.

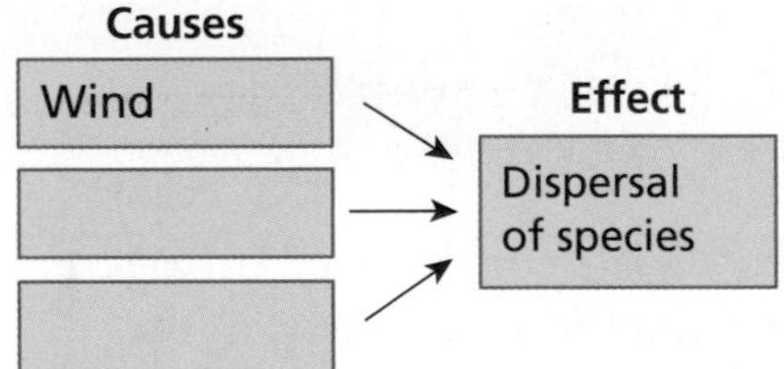

Lab zone Discover Activity

How Can You Move a Seed?

1. Place a few corn kernels at one end of a shallow pan.
2. Make a list of ways you could move the kernels to the other side of the pan. You may use any of the simple materials your teacher has provided.
3. Now try each method. Record whether each was successful in moving the kernels across the pan.

Think It Over

Predicting How might seeds be moved from place to place?

Imagine how European explorers must have felt when they saw Australia for the first time. Instead of familiar grazing animals such as horses and deer, they saw animals that looked like giant rabbits with long tails. Peering into eucalyptus trees, the explorers saw bearlike koalas. And who could have dreamed up an egg-laying animal with a beaver's tail, a duck's bill, and thick fur? You can see why people who heard the first descriptions of the platypus accused the explorers of lying!

As the explorers had learned, different species live in different parts of the world. The study of where organisms live is called **biogeography.** The word *biogeography* is made up of three Greek word roots: *bio,* meaning "life"; *geo,* meaning "Earth"; and *graphy*, meaning "description of." Together, these root words tell what biogeographers do—they describe where living things are found on Earth.

Koala in a eucalyptus tree in Australia ▶

FIGURE 10
Continental Drift
The movement of the continents is one factor affecting the distribution of organisms. **Interpreting Maps** *How has Australia's location changed?*

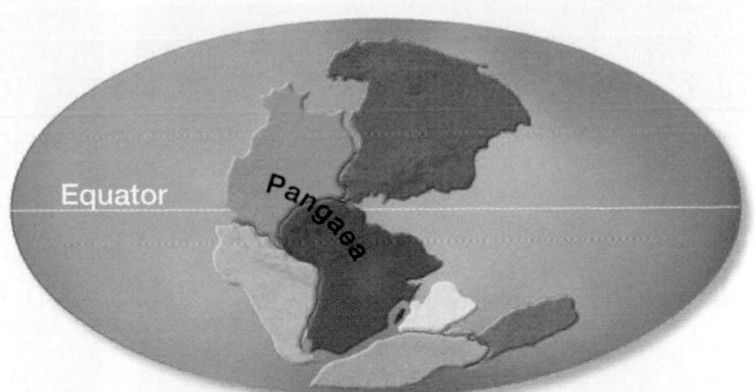

225 Million Years Ago

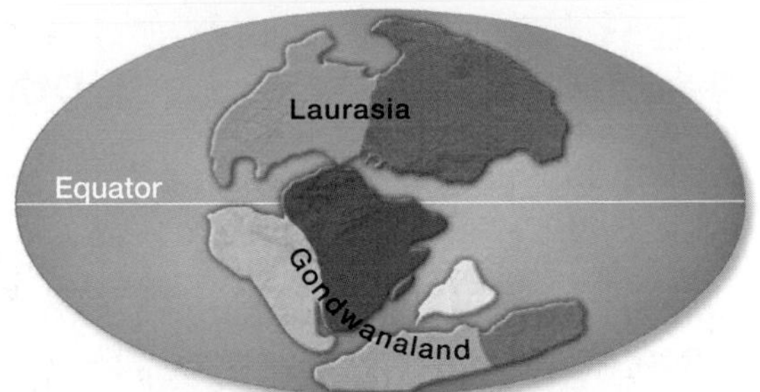

180–200 Million Years Ago

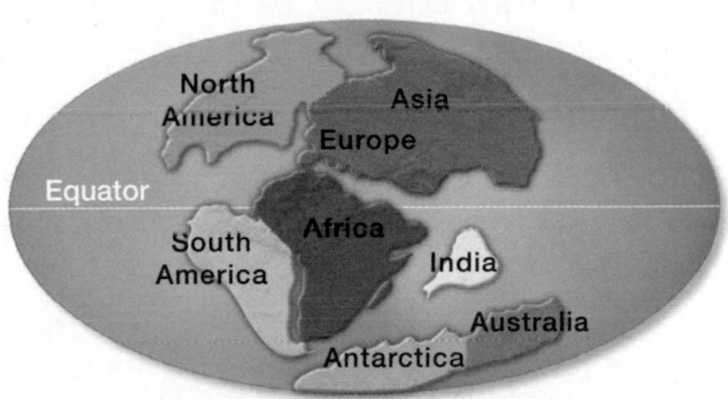

135 Million Years Ago

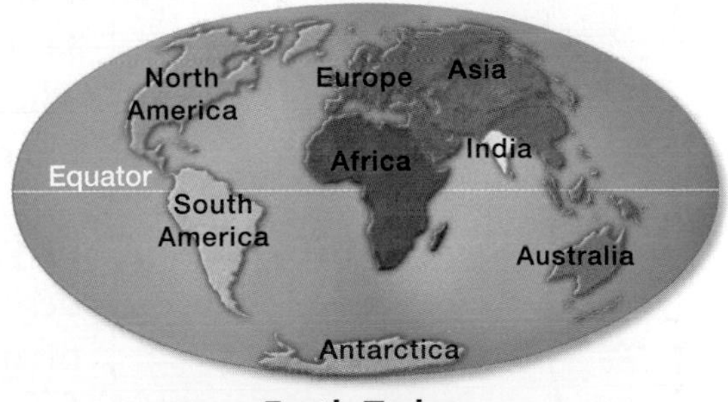

Earth Today

Continental Drift
In addition to studying where species live, biogeographers also try to understand what led to the worldwide distribution of species that exists today. **One factor that has affected how species are distributed is the motion of Earth's continents.** The continents are parts of huge blocks of solid rock, called plates, that make up Earth's surface. Scientists have found that the plates have been moving very slowly for millions of years. As the plates move, the continents move with them in a process called **continental drift.**

Figure 10 shows how much the continents have moved over time. About 225 million years ago, all of today's continents were part of one large landmass now called Pangaea. But after millions of years of slow drifting, they have moved to their present locations.

Continental drift has had a great impact on the distribution of species. Consider Australia, for example. Millions of years ago Australia drifted away from the other landmasses. Organisms from other parts of the world could not reach the isolated island. Kangaroos, koalas, and other unique species flourished in this isolation.

What was Pangaea?

Means of Dispersal
The movement of organisms from one place to another is called **dispersal.** Organisms may be dispersed in several different ways. **Dispersal can be caused by wind, water, or living things, including humans.**

Wind and Water Many animals move into new areas on their own. But plants and small organisms need assistance to move from place to place. Wind can disperse seeds, the spores of fungi, tiny spiders, and other small, light organisms. Similarly, water transports objects that float, such as coconuts and leaves. Small animals may get a free ride to a new home on top of these floating rafts.

For: Continental Drift activity
Visit: PHSchool.com
Web Code: cfp-1015

FIGURE 11
Means of Dispersal
Berry seeds can be dispersed by animals, such as cedar waxwings (top left), that eat berries and leave seeds in their wastes. The spores of puffball mushrooms (top center) and the seeds of milkweed plants (top right) are usually dispersed by wind.
Inferring *What are two ways that seeds disperse?*

Other Living Things Organisms may also be dispersed by other living things. For example, a bird may eat berries in one area and deposit the seeds elsewhere in its wastes. And if your dog or cat has ever come home covered with sticky plant burs, you know another way seeds can get around.

Humans are also important to the dispersal of organisms. As people move around the world, they take organisms with them. Sometimes this dispersal is intentional, as when Europeans who explored Central and South America in the 1500s took corn and tomato plants back to Europe. Sometimes it is unintentional, as when insects are carried from one location to another by an airplane passenger. An organism that is carried into a new location by people is referred to as an **exotic species.**

What are two ways that an animal can disperse a species?

Limits to Dispersal

With all these means of dispersal, you might expect to find the same species everywhere in the world. Of course, that's not so. **Three factors that limit dispersal of a species are physical barriers, competition, and climate.**

Physical Barriers Barriers such as water, mountains, and deserts are hard to cross. These features can limit the movement of organisms. For example, once Australia became separated from the other continents, the ocean acted as a barrier to dispersal. Organisms could not easily move to or from Australia.

Competition When an organism enters a new area, it must compete for resources with the species already there. To survive, the organism must find a unique niche. Existing species may outcompete the new species. In this case, competition is a barrier to dispersal. Sometimes, however, new species outcompete the existing species. The existing species may be displaced.

Climate The typical weather pattern in an area over a long period of time is the area's **climate.** Climate differences can limit dispersal. For example, conditions at the top of the mountain shown in Figure 12 are very different from those at the base. The base of the mountain is warm and dry. Low shrubs and cactuses grow there. Higher up, the climate becomes cooler and wetter, and larger trees such as oaks and firs grow. Near the top of the mountain, it is very cold and windy. Only short plants can grow in this area.

Places with similar climates tend to have species that occupy similar niches. For example, most continents have a large area of flat, grassy plains. So these continents have organisms that occupy the niche of "large, grazing mammal." In North America, the large, grazing mammals of the grasslands are bison. In Africa, they are wildebeests and antelopes. And in Australia, they are kangaroos.

How does the climate at the base of a mountain differ from the climate at the top?

FIGURE 12
Climate Differences and Dispersal
The climate changes dramatically as you move up a tall mountain. Climate determines the distribution of species on different parts of the mountain.

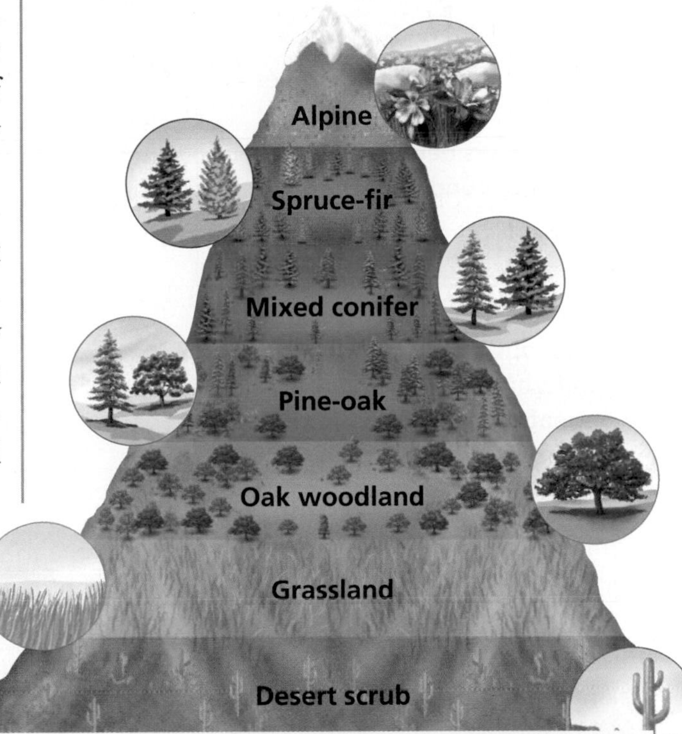

Section 3 Assessment

Target Reading Skill

Relating Cause and Effect Refer to your graphic organizer about means of dispersal to help you answer Question 2 below.

Reviewing Key Concepts

1. a. **Defining** What is continental drift?
   b. **Explaining** How has continental drift affected the dispersal of organisms?
   c. **Relating Cause and Effect** How can continental drift explain why unique species are often found on islands?
2. a. **Listing** What are three ways in which organisms can be dispersed?
   b. **Explaining** What role do humans play in the dispersal of species?
   c. **Predicting** Do you think the role of humans in the dispersal of species will increase or decrease in the next 50 years? Defend your answer.
3. a. **Identifying** What are three factors that can limit the dispersal of a species?
   b. **Applying Concepts** Suppose that a new species of insect were introduced to your area. How might competition limit its dispersal?

Lab zone At-Home Activity

Sock Walk Take an adult family member on a "sock walk" to learn about seed dispersal. Each person should wear a thick white sock over one shoe. Take a short walk through woods, a field, or a park. Back home, observe how many seeds you collected. Then plant the socks in pans of soil. Place the pans in a sunny spot and water them regularly. How many species did you successfully disperse?

Section 4

Biomes

Reading Preview

Key Concepts

- What are the six major biomes found on Earth?
- What factors determine the type of biome found in an area?

Key Terms

- biome • canopy • understory
- desert • grassland • savanna
- deciduous tree
- coniferous tree • tundra
- permafrost

Target Reading Skill

Comparing and Contrasting As you read, compare and contrast the different biomes by completing a table like the one below.

Characteristic	Tropical Rain Forest	Tundra
Temperature	Warm all year	
Precipitation		
Typical Organisms		

Lab zone **Discover Activity**

How Much Rain Is That?

The table shows the typical amount of precipitation that falls each year in four locations. With your classmates, you will create a full-sized bar graph on a wall to represent these amounts.

Location	Precipitation (cm)
Mojave Desert	15
Illinois Prairie	70
Great Smoky Mountains	180
Costa Rican Rain Forest	350

1. Using a meter stick, measure a strip of adding-machine paper 15 centimeters long. Label this strip "Mojave Desert."
2. Repeat Step 1 for the other locations. Label each strip.
3. Follow your teacher's instructions on hanging your strips.

Think It Over

Developing Hypotheses What effect might the amount of precipitation have on the types of species that live in a location?

Congratulations! You and your classmates have been selected to take part in an around-the-world scientific expedition. On this expedition you will collect data on the climate and typical organisms of each of Earth's biomes. A **biome** is a group of land ecosystems with similar climates and organisms.

The ecologists leading your expedition have agreed to focus on six major biomes. **The six major biomes that most ecologists study are the rain forest, desert, grassland, deciduous forest, boreal forest, and tundra.**

Be sure to pack a variety of clothing for your expedition. You will visit places ranging from steamy tropical jungles to frozen Arctic plains. **It is mostly the climate—temperature and precipitation—in an area that determines its biome.** This is because climate limits the species of plants that can grow in an area. In turn, the species of plants determine the kinds of animals that live there.

Hurry up and pack—it's almost time to go!

Ecosystems and Biomes

Video Preview
▶ Video Field Trip
Video Assessment

Rain Forest Biomes

The first stop on your expedition is a rain forest. This biome is living up to its name—it's pouring! Fortunately, you remembered to pack a raincoat. After just a short shower, however, the sun reappears. Surprisingly, though, very little sunlight reaches you through the thick leaves above.

Plants are everywhere in the rain forest. Some plants, such as the ferns, flowers, and vines hanging from tree limbs, even grow on other plants! And animals are flying, creeping, and slithering all around you.

Temperate Rain Forests When you hear the term *rain forest,* you probably think of a warm, humid, "jungle" in the tropics. But there is another type of rain forest. The northwestern coast of the United States receives more than 300 centimeters of rain a year. Huge trees grow there, including cedars, redwoods, and Douglas firs. However, it is difficult to classify this region. Many ecologists refer to this ecosystem as a temperate rain forest. The term *temperate* means having moderate temperatures.

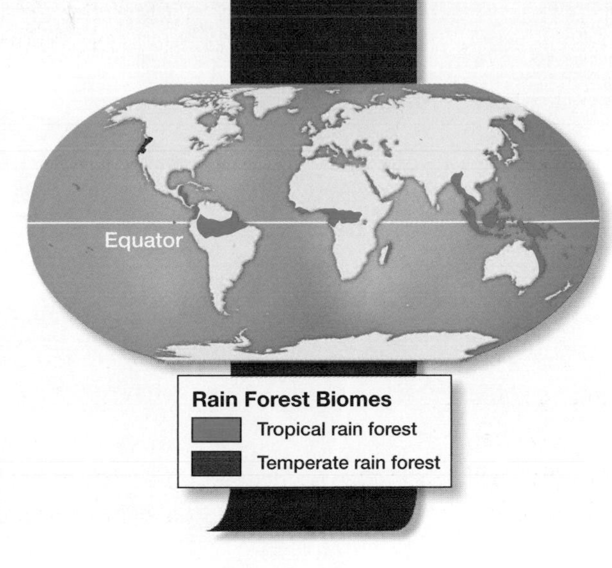

◀ Pileated woodpecker

FIGURE 13
Temperate Rain Forest
Temperate rain forests receive a great deal of rain and have moderate temperatures. Mule deer are commonly found in the Olympic Rain Forest in Washington State.
Interpreting Maps *Where is one temperate rain forest located?*

◀ Orangutan

▲ Bromeliad

Tropical Rain Forests As you can see on the map, tropical rain forests are found in regions close to the equator. The climate is warm and humid all year long, and there is a lot of rain. Because of these climate conditions, an astounding variety of plants grow in tropical rain forests. In fact, scientists studying a 100-square-meter area of one rain forest identified 300 different kinds of trees!

Trees in the rain forest form several distinct layers. The tall trees form a leafy roof called the **canopy.** A few giant trees poke out above the canopy. Below the canopy, a second layer of shorter trees and vines form an **understory.** Understory plants grow well in the shade formed by the canopy. The forest floor is nearly dark, so only a few plants live there.

The abundant plant life in tropical rain forests provides habitats for many species of animals. Ecologists estimate that millions of species of insects live in tropical rain forests. These insects serve as a source of food for many reptiles, birds, and mammals. Many of these animals are, in turn, food sources for other animals. Although tropical rain forests cover only a small part of the planet, they probably contain more species of plants and animals than all the other biomes combined.

What is the climate of the tropical rain forest?

FIGURE 14
Tropical Rain Forest
Tropical rain forests are wet, warm biomes that contain an amazing variety of plants and other organisms. In the large photo, a river winds through the lush Indonesian rain forest.

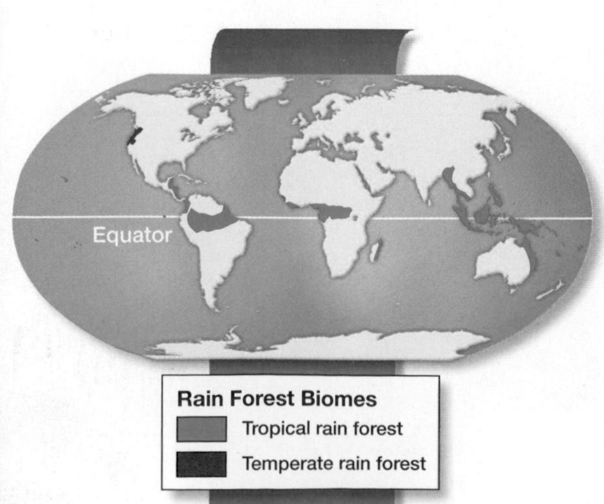

Desert Biomes

The next stop on your expedition is a desert. It couldn't be more different from the tropical rain forest you just left. You step off the bus into the searing summer heat. At midday, it is too hot to walk outside in the desert.

A **desert** is an area that receives less than 25 centimeters of rain per year. The amount of evaporation in a desert is greater than the amount of precipitation. Some of the driest deserts may not receive any precipitation in a year! Deserts often undergo large shifts in temperature during the course of a day. A scorching hot desert like the Namib Desert in Africa cools rapidly each night when the sun goes down. Other deserts, such as the Gobi in central Asia, are cooler, and even experience freezing temperatures in the winter.

Organisms that live in the desert must be adapted to the lack of rain and extreme temperatures. For example, the stem of a saguaro cactus has folds that work like the pleats in an accordion. The stem expands to store water when it is raining. Gila monsters can spend weeks at a time in their cool underground burrows. Many other desert animals are most active at night when the temperatures are cooler.

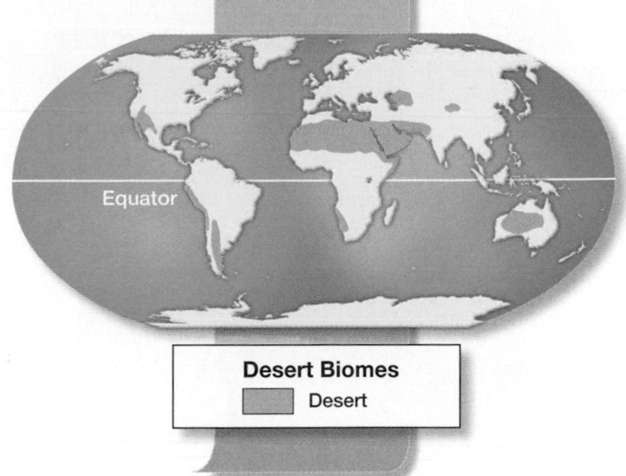

FIGURE 15
Desert
The Mojave Desert in the southwestern United States is a typical hot desert.
Making Generalizations *Describe the climate conditions of a typical desert.*

Lab zone Try This Activity

Desert Survival

Use a hand lens to carefully observe a small potted cactus. **CAUTION:** *Be careful of the spines.* With a pair of scissors, carefully snip a small piece from the tip of the cactus. Observe the inside of the plant. Note any characteristics that seem different from those of other plants.

Observing How is the inside of the cactus different from the outside? Suggest how the features you observe might be adaptations to its desert habitat.

FIGURE 16
Savanna
Migrating wildebeest make their way across a vast Kenyan savanna. A savanna is one type of grassland biome—an area populated mostly by grasses and other non-woody plants.

Grassland Biomes

The next stop on the expedition is a grassy plain called a prairie. Temperatures here are more comfortable than they were in the desert. The breeze carries the scent of soil warmed by the sun. This rich soil supports grasses as tall as you. Startled by your approach, sparrows dart into hiding places among the waving grass stems.

Although this prairie receives more rain than a desert, it does not get enough rain for trees to grow. Ecologists classify prairies, which are generally found in the middle latitudes, as grasslands. A **grassland** is an area that is populated mostly by grasses and other non-woody plants. Most grasslands receive 25 to 75 centimeters of rain each year. Fires and droughts are common in this biome. Grasslands that are located closer to the equator than prairies are known as savannas. A **savanna** receives as much as 120 centimeters of rain each year. Scattered shrubs and small trees grow on savannas along with grass.

Grasslands are home to many of the largest animals on Earth—herbivores such as elephants, bison, antelopes, zebras, rhinoceroses, giraffes, and kangaroos. Grazing by these large herbivores helps to maintain the grasslands. They keep young trees and bushes from sprouting and competing with the grass for water and sunlight.

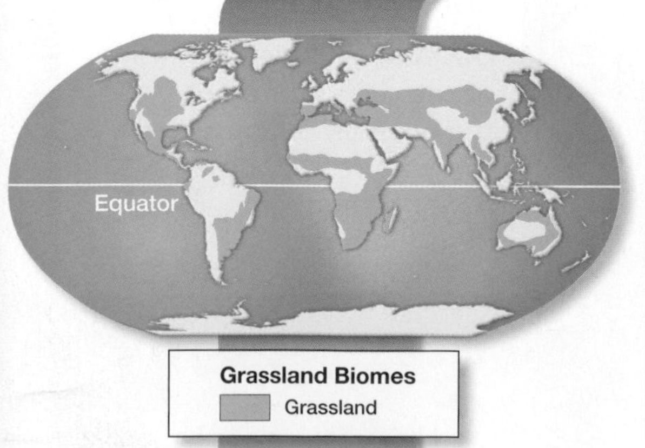

What type of grassland usually receives more rainfall, a prairie or a savanna?

Deciduous Forest Biomes

Your trip to the next biome takes you to another forest. It is now late summer. Cool mornings here give way to warm days. Several members of the expedition are busy recording the numerous plant species. Others are looking through their binoculars, trying to identify the songbirds. You step carefully to avoid a small salamander.

You are now visiting a deciduous forest biome. Many of the trees in this forest are **deciduous trees** (dee SIJ oo us), trees that shed their leaves and grow new ones each year. Oaks and maples are examples of deciduous trees. Deciduous forests receive enough rain to support the growth of trees and other plants, at least 50 centimeters per year. Temperatures in the deciduous forest vary greatly during the year. The growing season usually lasts five to six months.

The variety of plants in a deciduous forest creates many different habitats. Different species of birds live in different parts of the forest, eating the insects and fruits in their specific areas. Mammals such as chipmunks and skunks live in deciduous forests. In a North American deciduous forest you might also see wood thrushes, white-tailed deer, and black bears.

If you were to return to this biome in the winter, you would not see much wildlife. Many of the bird species migrate to warmer areas. Some of the mammals hibernate, or enter a state of greatly reduced body activity similar to sleep. Animals that hibernate rely on fat stored in their bodies during the winter months.

Reading Checkpoint What are deciduous trees?

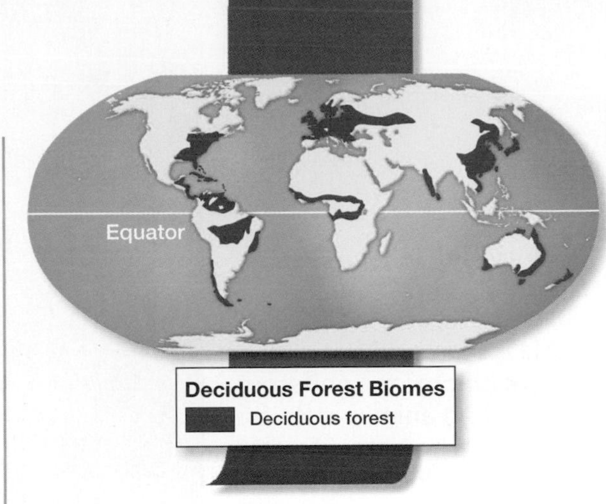

FIGURE 17
Deciduous Forest
This forest is a beautiful example of a deciduous forest in autumn. Most of the trees in a deciduous forest have leaves that change color and drop each autumn.
Comparing and Contrasting *How do deciduous forests differ from rain forests?*

▼ Southern flying squirrel

▼ Red fox

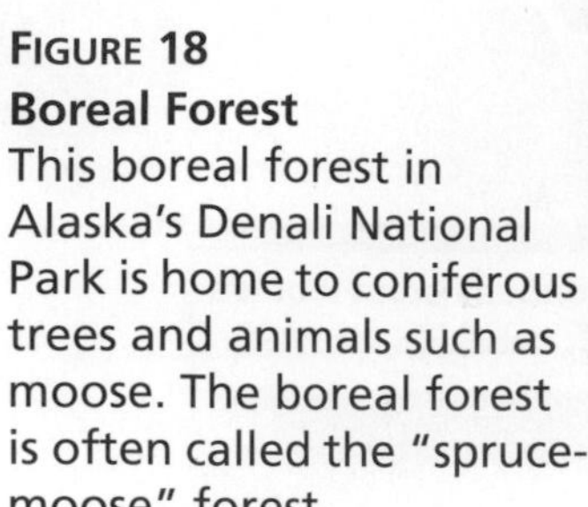

FIGURE 18
Boreal Forest
This boreal forest in Alaska's Denali National Park is home to coniferous trees and animals such as moose. The boreal forest is often called the "spruce-moose" forest.

Boreal Forest Biomes

Now the expedition heads north into a colder climate. The expedition leaders claim they can identify the next biome, a boreal forest, by its smell. When you arrive, you catch a whiff of the spruce and fir trees that blanket the hillsides. Feeling the chilly early fall air, you pull a jacket and hat out of your bag.

Boreal Forest Plants Most of the trees in the boreal forest are **coniferous trees** (koh NIF ur us), trees that produce their seeds in cones and have leaves shaped like needles. The boreal forest is sometimes referred to by its Russian name, the *taiga* (TY guh). Winters in these forests are very cold. The snow can reach heights well over your head! Even so, the summers are rainy and warm enough to melt all the snow.

Tree species in the boreal forest are well-adapted to the cold climate. Since water is frozen for much of the year, trees in the boreal forest must have adaptations that prevent water loss. Fir, spruce, hemlock, and other coniferous trees all have thick, waxy needles that prevent water from evaporating.

Boreal Forest Animals Many of the animals of the boreal forest eat the seeds produced by the coniferous trees. These animals include red squirrels, insects, and birds such as finches and chickadees. Some herbivores, such as snowshoe hares, moose, and beavers, eat tree bark and new shoots. The variety of herbivores in the boreal forest supports many large predators, including wolves, bears, great horned owls, and lynxes.

How are needles an advantage to trees in the boreal forest?

Lab zone Skills Activity

Inferring

Observe the map that shows the locations of boreal forests. Where are most boreal forests located? Why are there no boreal forests in the Southern Hemisphere?

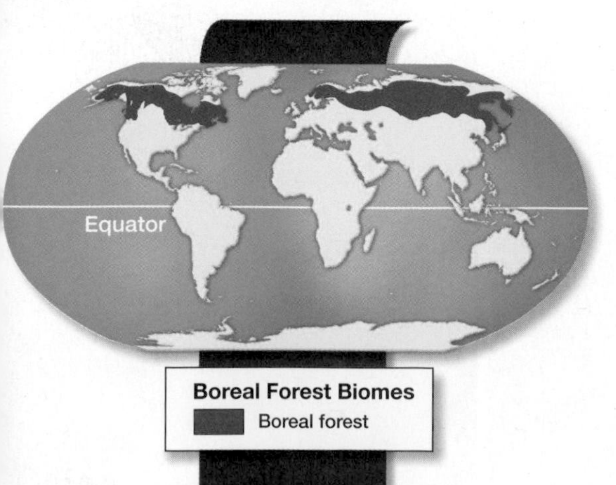

Tundra Biomes

As you arrive at your next stop, the driving wind gives you an immediate feel for this biome. The **tundra** is an extremely cold and dry biome. Expecting deep snow, many are surprised to learn that the tundra may receive no more precipitation than a desert.

Most of the soil in the tundra is frozen all year. This frozen soil is called **permafrost.** During the short summer, the top layer of soil thaws, but the underlying soil remains frozen. Because rainwater cannot soak into the permafrost, there are many shallow ponds and marshy areas on the tundra in the summer.

Equator

Tundra Biomes

Tundra

Tundra Plants Plants of the tundra include mosses, grasses, shrubs, and dwarf forms of a few trees, such as willows. Most of the plant growth takes place during the long days of the short summer season. North of the Arctic Circle, the sun does not set during midsummer.

Tundra Animals In summer, the animals you might remember most are insects. Insect-eating birds take advantage of the plentiful food and long days by eating as much as they can. But when winter approaches, these birds migrate south. Mammals of the tundra include caribou, foxes, wolves, and Arctic hares. The mammals that remain on the tundra during the winter grow thick fur coats. What can these animals find to eat on the tundra in winter? The caribou scrape snow away to find lichens. Wolves follow the caribou and look for weak members of the herd to prey upon.

Reading Checkpoint **What is permafrost?**

FIGURE 19
Tundra
Although it is frozen and seemingly barren in winter, the tundra in Alaska explodes with color in autumn.
Relating Cause and Effect *Why are there no tall trees on the tundra?*

Musk ox ▲

FIGURE 20
Mountains
Mountains, such as these in Banff National Park in Canada, are not part of any major biome. They do support ecosystems, however. **Classifying** *Why can't a mountain be considered part of one specific biome?*

▲ A pika gathering mountain plants for food

Go Online
active art

For: Earth's Biomes activity
Visit: PHSchool.com
Web Code: cep-5024

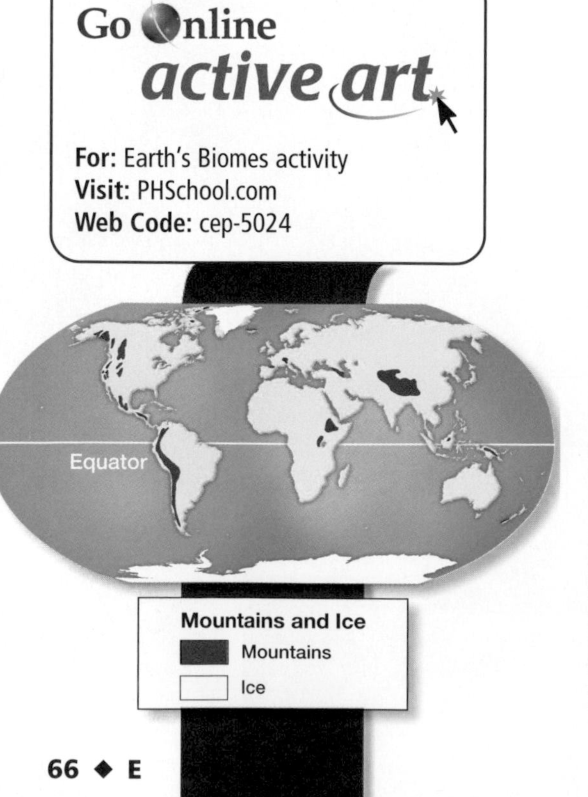

Mountains and Ice

Some areas of land are not part of any major biome. These areas include mountain ranges and land that is covered with thick sheets of ice.

You read in Section 3 that the climate of a mountain changes from its base to its summit. If you were to hike all the way up a tall mountain, you would pass through a series of biomes. At the base, you might find grasslands. As you climbed, you might pass through deciduous forest and then boreal forest. As you neared the top, your surroundings would resemble the treeless tundra.

Other places are covered year-round with thick ice sheets. Most of the island of Greenland and the continent of Antarctica fall into this category. Organisms that are adapted to life on ice include emperor penguins, polar bears, and leopard seals.

What are two landmasses that are covered year-round with ice?

Math Analyzing Data

Biome Climates

An ecologist collected climate data from two locations. The graph shows the monthly average temperatures in the two locations. The total yearly precipitation in Location A is 250 cm. In Location B, the total yearly precipitation is 14 cm.

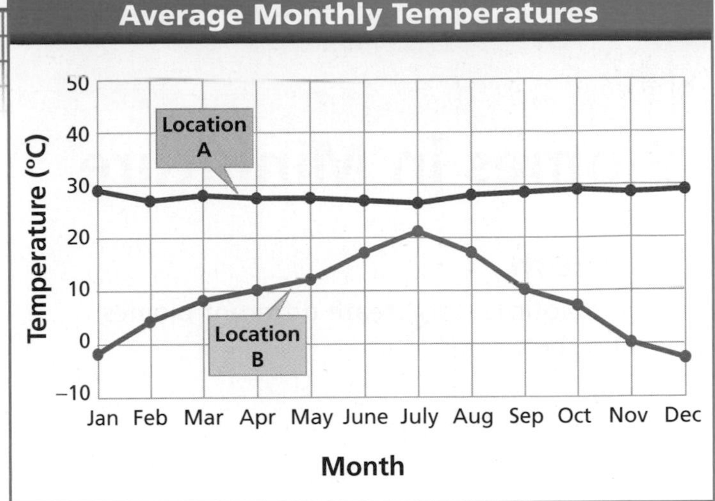

1. **Reading Graphs** What variable is plotted on the horizontal axis? On the vertical axis?
2. **Interpreting Data** Look over the graph. How would you describe the temperature over the course of a year in Location A? In Location B?
3. **Drawing Conclusions** Given the precipitation and temperature data for these locations, in which biome would you expect each to be located? Explain your answers.
4. **Predicting** What would you expect a temperature graph for your biome to look like? Draw a temperature graph for the biome in which you live.

Section 4 Assessment

Target Reading Skill Comparing and Contrasting Use the information in your table about biomes to help you answer Question 1 below.

Reviewing Key Concepts

1. a. **Listing** What are the six major biomes found on Earth?
   b. **Comparing and Contrasting** How are the three forest biomes (rain forests, deciduous forests, and boreal forests) alike? How are they different?
   c. **Inferring** What biome might you be in if you were standing on a bitterly cold, dry plain with only a few, short plants scattered around?
2. a. **Reviewing** What two factors are most important in determining an area's biome?
   b. **Relating Cause and Effect** If deserts and tundras receive similar amounts of rainfall, why are these two biomes so different?
   c. **Applying Concepts** Why would hiking up a tall mountain be a good way to observe how climate determines an area's biome?

Writing in Science

Firsthand Account Choose one of the biomes and write a journal entry detailing the observations you made during your expedition. Include descriptions of sights, sounds, and smells you experienced as well as specific details about the organisms you observed. Conclude your journal entry with a surprising fact you learned about the biome while visiting.

Lab zone **Skills Lab**

Biomes in Miniature

Problem

What abiotic factors create different biomes around the world?

Skills Focus

observing, making models

Materials

- scissors
- clear plastic wrap
- index card
- lamp
- tape
- empty, clean cardboard milk carton
- stapler
- about 30 rye grass seeds
- 10 impatiens seeds
- 5 lima bean seeds
- sandy soil or potting soil

Procedure

1. Your teacher will assign your group a biome. You will also observe the other groups' model biomes. Based on the chart below, predict how well you think each of the three kinds of seeds will grow in each set of conditions. Record these predictions in your notebook. Then copy the data table on the facing page four times, once for each biome.
2. Staple the spout of the milk carton closed. Completely cut away one of the four sides of the carton. Poke a few holes in the opposite side for drainage, and then place that side down.
3. Fill the carton to 3 centimeters from the top with the type of soil given in the table. Divide the surface of the soil into three sections by making two lines in it with a pencil.
4. In the section near the spout, plant the impatiens seeds. In the middle section, plant the lima bean seeds. In the third section, scatter the rye grass seeds on the surface.
5. Water all the seeds well. Then cover the open part of the carton with plastic wrap.
6. On an index card, write the name of your biome, the names of the three types of seeds in the order you planted them, and the names of your group members. Tape the card to the carton. Put the carton in a warm place where it will not be disturbed.
7. Once the seeds sprout, provide your biome with light and water as specified in the chart. Keep the carton covered with plastic wrap except when you add water.
8. Observe all the model biomes daily for at least one week. Record your observations.

Growing Conditions

Biome	Soil Type	Hours of Light per Day	Watering Instructions
Forest	Potting soil	1–2 hours of direct light	Let the surface dry; then add water.
Desert	Sandy soil	5–6 hours of direct light	Let the soil dry to a depth of 2.5 cm below the surface.
Grassland	Potting soil	5–6 hours of direct light	Let the surface dry; then add water.
Rain forest	Potting soil	No direct light; indirect light for 5–6 hours	Keep the surface of the soil moist.

Data Table			
Name of Biome:			
Day	Impatiens	Lima Beans	Rye Grass
1			
2			
3			
4			
5			
6			
7			

Analyze and Conclude

1. **Observing** In which model biome did each type of seed grow best? In which model biome did each type of seed grow least well?
2. **Making Models** In this experiment, how did you model the following abiotic factors: sunlight, water, and temperature?
3. **Inferring** How was each type of seed affected by the soil type, amount of light, and availability of water?
4. **Classifying** Why do you think that ecologists who study biomes often focus on identifying the key abiotic factors and typical plants in an area?
5. **Communicating** Write a paragraph explaining how your miniature biomes modeled real-life biomes. Which features of real-life biomes were you able to model well? Which features of real-life biomes were more difficult to model?

Design an Experiment

Write a plan for setting up a model rain forest or desert terrarium. Include typical plants found in that biome. *Obtain your teacher's approval before carrying out your investigation.*

Section 5 Aquatic Ecosystems

Reading Preview

Key Concept

- What are the two major types of aquatic ecosystems?

Key Terms

- estuary
- intertidal zone
- neritic zone

Target Reading Skill

Outlining As you read, make an outline about the different types of aquatic ecosystems. Use the red headings for the main ideas and the blue headings for the supporting ideas.

Aquatic Ecosystems

I. Freshwater ecosystems
  A. Streams and rivers
  B.
II. Marine ecosystems
  A.

Lab zone Discover Activity

Where Does It Live?

1. The organism in the photo lives in a pond. Look carefully at its body.
2. Think about how the organism might move around and how it might eat.

Think It Over

Observing Make a list of the organism's features that might help it survive in its habitat. For each feature, describe how it is suited to its function.

No worldwide expedition could be complete without exploring Earth's waters. Since almost three quarters of Earth's surface is covered with water, don't be surprised at how much there is to see. Many living things make their homes in and near the water. **Your travels will take you to two types of aquatic, or water-based, ecosystems: freshwater ecosystems and marine (or saltwater) ecosystems.**

All aquatic ecosystems are affected by the same abiotic factors: sunlight, temperature, oxygen, and salt content. Sunlight is an especially important factor in aquatic ecosystems. Sunlight is necessary for photosynthesis in the water just as it is on land. However, because water absorbs sunlight, there is only enough light for photosynthesis near the surface or in shallow water. The most common producers in aquatic ecosystems are algae rather than plants.

FIGURE 21
A River Ecosystem
Streams and rivers are freshwater ecosystems in which the water flows in a current. The bear and gulls are enjoying the plentiful supply of fish in this river.

Freshwater Ecosystems

Even though most of Earth's surface is covered with water, only a tiny fraction is fresh water. Freshwater ecosystems include streams, rivers, ponds, and lakes. On this part of your expedition, you'll find that freshwater ecosystems provide habitats for an amazing variety of organisms, from microscopic algae to huge bears.

FIGURE 22
A Pond Ecosystem
Ponds and lakes are freshwater ecosystems characterized by still water. Pickerelweed and herons are typical pond organisms.
Interpreting Photographs *How is the heron well-suited to its* ◀ *aquatic environment?*

Streams and Rivers Your first stop is a mountain stream. Where the stream begins, the cold, clear water flows rapidly. Animals that live here are adapted to the strong current. For example, insects and other small animals have hooks or suckers that help them cling to rocks. Trout have streamlined bodies that allow them to swim despite the rushing water. Few plants or algae can grow in this fast-moving water. Instead, first-level consumers rely on leaves and seeds that fall into the stream.

As the stream flows along, other streams join it. The current slows, and the water becomes cloudy with soil. The slower-moving water is warmer and contains less oxygen. This larger stream might now be called a river. Different organisms are adapted to life in a river. Plants take root among the pebbles on the river bottom. These producers provide food for young insects and homes for frogs and their tadpoles. These consumers, in turn, provide food for many larger consumers.

Ponds and Lakes Your next stop is a pond. Ponds and lakes are bodies of standing, or still, fresh water. Lakes are generally larger and deeper than ponds. Ponds are often shallow enough that sunlight can reach the bottom even in the center of the pond, allowing plants to grow there. In large ponds and most lakes, however, algae floating at the surface are the major producers.

Many animals are adapted for life in the still water. Along the shore of the pond, you observe dragonflies, turtles, snails, and frogs. Sunfish live in the open water, feeding on insects and algae from the surface. Scavengers such as catfish live near the pond bottom. Bacteria and other decomposers also feed on the remains of other organisms.

What are two abiotic factors that affect organisms in a stream?

FIGURE 23
Marine Ecosystems
The ocean is home to a number of different ecosystems. Factors such as water temperature and the amount of sunlight determine what types of organisms can live in each zone.

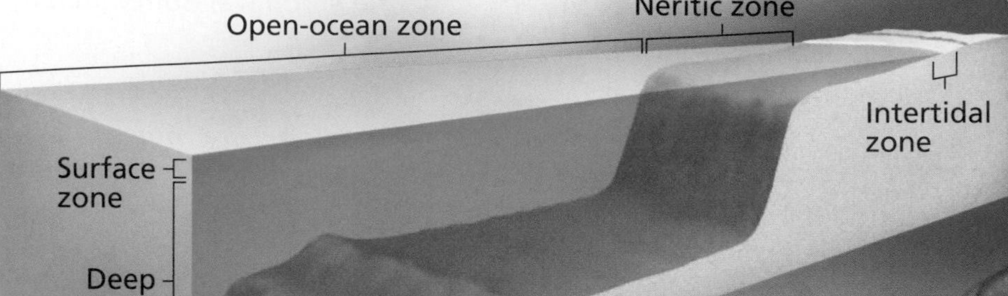

Marine Ecosystems

The expedition now heads to the coast to explore some marine ecosystems. On your way, you'll pass through an estuary. An **estuary** (ES choo ehr ee), is found where the fresh water of a river meets the salt water of the ocean. Algae and plants such as marsh grasses provide food and shelter for numerous animals, including crabs, worms, clams, and fish. Many animals use the calm waters of estuaries for breeding grounds.

Intertidal Zone Next, you take a walk along the rocky shoreline. Here, between the highest high-tide line and the lowest low-tide line, is the **intertidal zone.** Organisms here must be able to survive pounding waves and the sudden changes in water levels and temperature that occur with high and low tides. You observe animals such as barnacles and sea stars clinging to the rocks. Others, such as clams and crabs, burrow in the sand.

Neritic Zone Now it's time to set out to sea. The edge of a continent extends into the ocean for a short distance, like a shelf. Below the low-tide line is a region of shallow water called the **neritic zone** (nuh RIT ik), which extends over the continental shelf.

Because sunlight passes through the shallow water of the neritic zone, photosynthesis can occur. As a result, this zone is particularly rich in living things. Many large schools of fish, such as sardines, feed on algae. In warm ocean waters, coral reefs may form. Coral reefs provide living homes to a wide variety of other organisms.

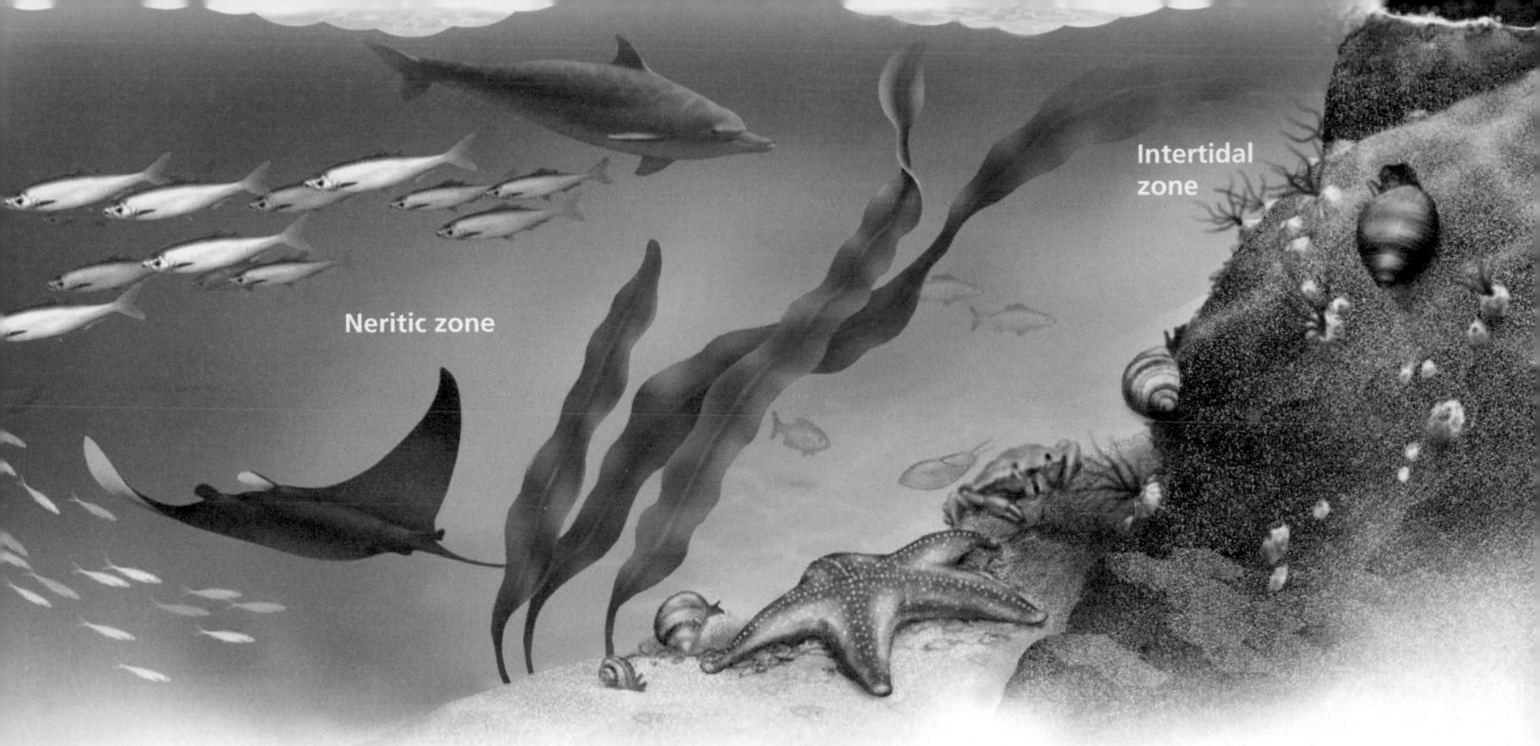
Intertidal zone
Neritic zone

The Open Ocean Out in the open ocean, light penetrates only to a depth of a few hundred meters. Algae carry out photosynthesis in this region of the open ocean, which is known as the surface zone. Marine animals, such as tuna, swordfish, and some whales, depend on the algae for food.

The deep zone is located below the surface zone. The deep zone is almost totally dark. Most animals in this zone feed on the remains of organisms that sink down from the surface zone. The deepest parts of the deep zone are home to bizarre-looking animals, such as giant squid whose eyes glow in the dark.

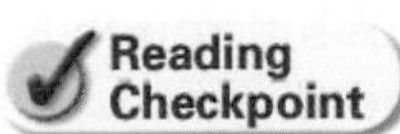

Reading Checkpoint **What are two differences between the surface zone and the deep zone?**

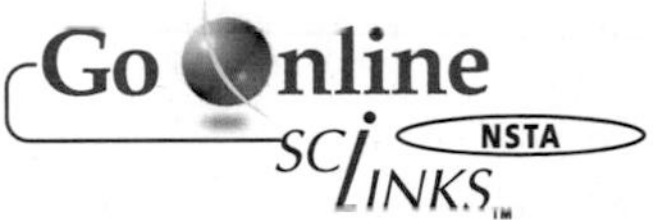

Go Online SCiLINKS NSTA
For: Links on aquatic ecosystems
Visit: www.SciLinks.org
Web Code: scn-0525

Section 5 Assessment

Target Reading Skill **Outlining** Use the information in your outline about aquatic ecosystems to help you answer the questions below.

Reviewing Key Concepts

1. a. **Reviewing** Name two major types of aquatic ecosystems.
   b. **Explaining** Why is sunlight an important abiotic factor in all aquatic ecosystems?
   c. **Predicting** Would you expect to find many organisms living at the bottom of a deep lake? Explain.

Lab zone At-Home **Activity**

Aquatic Photos Find photos of two different aquatic ecosystems. Take notes on the similarities and differences between the ecosystems and the organisms that live in them. Then explain those characteristics to a family member.

Change in a Tiny Community

Problem

How does a pond community change over time?

Skills Focus

observing, classifying

Materials

- hay solution
- pond water
- small baby-food jar
- wax pencil
- plastic dropper
- microscope slide
- coverslip
- microscope

Procedure

1. Use a wax pencil to label a small jar with your name.
2. Fill the jar about three-fourths full with hay solution. Add pond water until the jar is nearly full. Examine the mixture, and record your observations in your notebook.
3. Place the jar in a safe location out of direct sunlight where it will remain undisturbed. Always wash your hands thoroughly with soap after handling the jar or its contents.
4. After two days, examine the contents of the jar, and record your observations.
5. Use a plastic dropper to collect a few drops from the surface of the solution in the jar. Make a slide following the procedures in the box at the right. **CAUTION:** *Slides and coverslips are fragile, and their edges are sharp. Handle them carefully.*
6. Examine the slide under a microscope, using both low and high power and following the procedures in the box at the right. Draw each type of organism you observe. Estimate the number of each type in your sample. The illustration below shows some of the organisms you might see.
7. Repeat Steps 5 and 6 with a drop of solution taken from the side of the jar beneath the surface.
8. Repeat Steps 5 and 6 with a drop of solution taken from the bottom of the jar. When you are finished, follow your teacher's directions about cleaning up.
9. After 3 days, repeat Steps 5 through 8.
10. After 3 more days, repeat Steps 5 through 8 again. Then follow your teacher's directions for returning the solution.

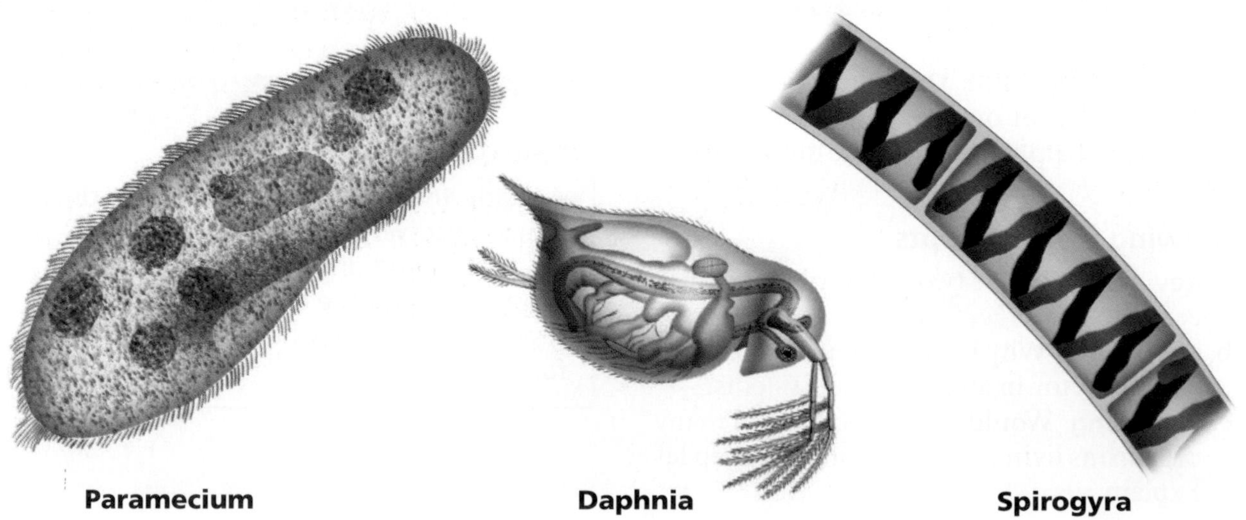

Paramecium **Daphnia** **Spirogyra**

Making and Viewing a Slide

A. Place one drop of the solution to be examined in the middle of a microscope slide. Place one edge of a coverslip at the edge of the drop, as shown in the photo. Gently lower the coverslip over the drop. Try not to trap any air bubbles.

B. Place the slide on the stage of a microscope so the drop is over the opening in the stage. Adjust the stage clips to hold the slide.

C. Look from the side of the microscope, and use the coarse adjustment knob to move the low-power objective close to, but not touching, the coverslip.

D. Look through the eyepiece, and use the coarse adjustment knob to raise the body tube and bring the slide into view. Use the fine adjustment knob to bring the slide into focus.

E. To view the slide under high power, look from the side of the microscope, and revolve the nosepiece until the high-power objective clicks into place just over, but not touching, the slide.

F. While you are looking through the eyepiece, use the fine adjustment knob to bring the slide into focus.

Analyze and Conclude

1. **Classifying** Identify as many of the organisms you observed as possible. Use the diagrams on the facing page and any other resources your teacher provides.
2. **Observing** How did the community change over the period of time that you made your observations?
3. **Inferring** What biotic and abiotic factors may have influenced the changes in this community? Explain.
4. **Developing Hypotheses** Where did the organisms you observed in the jar come from?
5. **Communicating** Based on what you have observed in this lab, write a paragraph that explains why ecosystems change gradually over time. Be sure to discuss the important factors that lead to changes in ecosystems.

Design an Experiment

Write a hypothesis about what would happen if you changed one biotic or abiotic factor in this activity. Design a plan to test your hypothesis. *Obtain your teacher's permission before carrying out your investigation.*

Chapter 2 Study Guide

The BIG Idea

Cycles of Matter and Energy In ecosystems, matter cycles between organisms and the environment. Energy from sunlight is not recycled, but moves through organisms in food chains.

1 Energy Flow in Ecosystems

Key Concepts

- Each organism in an ecosystem fills the energy role of producer, consumer, or decomposer.
- The movement of energy through an ecosystem can be shown in diagrams called food chains and food webs.
- As you move up an energy pyramid, each level has less energy available than the level below.

Key Terms

producer
consumer
herbivore
carnivore
omnivore
scavenger
decomposer
food chain
food web
energy pyramid

2 Cycles of Matter

Key Concepts

- The processes of evaporation, condensation, and precipitation make up the water cycle.
- In ecosystems, the processes by which carbon and oxygen are recycled are linked. Producers, consumers, and decomposers play roles in recycling carbon and oxygen.
- Nitrogen cycles from the air to the soil, into living things, and back into the air.

Key Terms

water cycle
evaporation
condensation
precipitation
nitrogen fixation

3 Biogeography

Key Concepts

- One factor that has affected how species are distributed is the motion of Earth's continents.
- Dispersal can be caused by wind, water, or living things, including humans.
- Three factors that limit dispersal of a species are physical barriers, competition, and climate.

Key Terms

biogeography
continental drift
dispersal
exotic species
climate

4 Biomes

Key Concepts

- The six major biomes that most ecologists study are the rain forest, desert, grassland, deciduous forest, boreal forest, and tundra.
- It is mostly the temperature and precipitation in an area that determine its biome.

Key Terms

biome
canopy
understory
desert
grassland
savanna
deciduous tree
coniferous tree
tundra
permafrost

5 Aquatic Ecosystems

Key Concept

- There are two types of aquatic ecosystems: freshwater and marine (or saltwater) ecosystems.

Key Terms

estuary
intertidal zone
neritic zone

Review and Assessment

For: Self-Assessment
Visit: PHSchool.com
Web Code: cea-5020

Organizing Information

Sequencing Copy the cycle diagram about the nitrogen cycle onto a separate sheet of paper. Then complete it. (For more on Sequencing, see the Skills Handbook.)

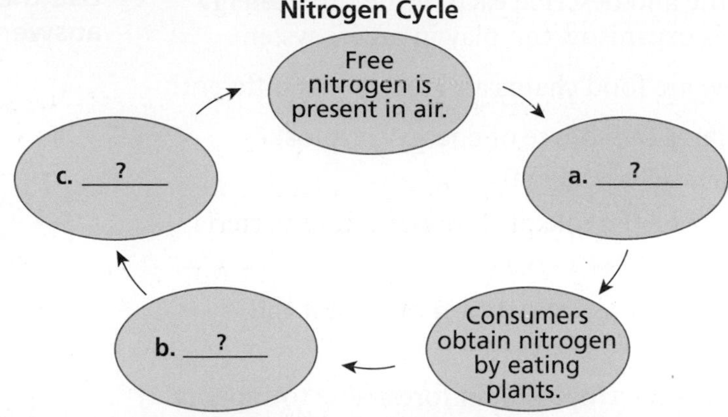

Reviewing Key Terms

Choose the letter of the best answer.

1. Which of the following organisms are typical decomposers?
   a. grasses and ferns
   b. mushrooms and bacteria
   c. mice and deer
   d. lions and snakes
2. A diagram that shows how much energy is available at each feeding level in an ecosystem is a(n)
   a. food chain. **b.** food web.
   c. water cycle. **d.** energy pyramid.
3. When drops of water in a cloud become heavy enough, they fall to Earth as
   a. condensation. **b.** evaporation.
   c. permafrost. **d.** precipitation.
4. Organisms may be dispersed in all the following ways *except* by
   a. wind.
   b. water.
   c. temperature.
   d. other organisms.
5. Much of Canada is covered in fir and spruce forests. The winter is cold and long. What is this biome?
   a. tundra
   b. boreal forest
   c. deciduous forest
   d. grassland

If the statement is true, write *true*. If it is false, change the underlined word or words to make the statement true.

6. An organism that eats the remains of dead organisms is called a(n) herbivore.
7. The study of where organisms live is called continental drift.
8. Precipitation and temperature are the two major abiotic factors that determine what types of plants can grow in an area.

Writing in Science

Encyclopedia Entry Write a half-page encyclopedia entry about life in the desert. Describe at least two plants and animals that live in the desert. Focus on the adaptations that allow these organisms to thrive in the harsh environment.

Ecosystems and Biomes
Video Preview
Video Field Trip
▶ Video Assessment

Review and Assessment

Checking Concepts

9. Name and describe each of the three energy roles organisms can play in an ecosystem.
10. How are food chains and food webs different?
11. What is the source of energy for most ecosystems? Explain.
12. Describe the role of nitrogen-fixing bacteria in the nitrogen cycle.
13. Explain how competition can affect the dispersal of species.
14. Why is the tropical rain forest able to support so many species?
15. In which biome would you find large herbivores such as elephants and zebras? Explain.
16. Which abiotic factors are important to aquatic ecosystems?

Thinking Critically

17. **Inferring** Polar bears are very well adapted to life around the Arctic Ocean. Their white fur camouflages them in the snow. They can withstand freezing temperatures for a long time. They can swim and hunt in very cold water. Is the distribution of polar bears limited by physical barriers, competition, or climate? Explain your answer.
18. **Comparing and Contrasting** How are the temperate rain forest and the tropical rain forest similar? How are they different?
19. **Predicting** A chemical spill has just killed off all the algae in a part of the surface zone in the open ocean. How will this accident affect the food webs in that part of the surface zone?
20. **Classifying** Which organisms in the illustration are producers? Consumers?

Applying Skills

Use the diagram of a food web below to answer Questions 21–24.

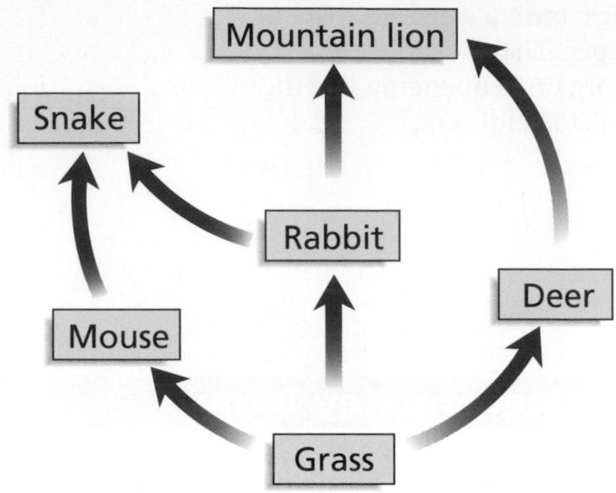

21. **Interpreting Diagrams** Which organism in this food web fills the role of producer?
22. **Classifying** Specify whether each consumer in this food web is a first-level, second-level, or third-level consumer.
23. **Inferring** Which level of the food web contains the greatest amount of available energy?
24. **Predicting** If a disease were to kill most of the rabbits in this area, predict how the snakes, deer, and mountain lions would be affected.

Lab zone Chapter Project

Performance Assessment Create a report, poster, or other product that clearly presents your data and conclusions from your decomposition experiment. In your notebook, compare your results to your predictions about the different waste materials in the compost mixture. Were you surprised by any of your results? Based on what you have learned from your project and those of your classmates, make a list of the ideal conditions for decomposition.

Standardized Test Prep

Test-Taking Tip

Interpreting a Diagram

When answering questions about diagrams, examine the diagram carefully, including labels. Ask yourself what the diagram is about and what it shows you. Make sure that you understand the meaning of any arrows. For example, the arrows in the diagram below indicate the direction of energy flow from producers to consumers in a food chain.

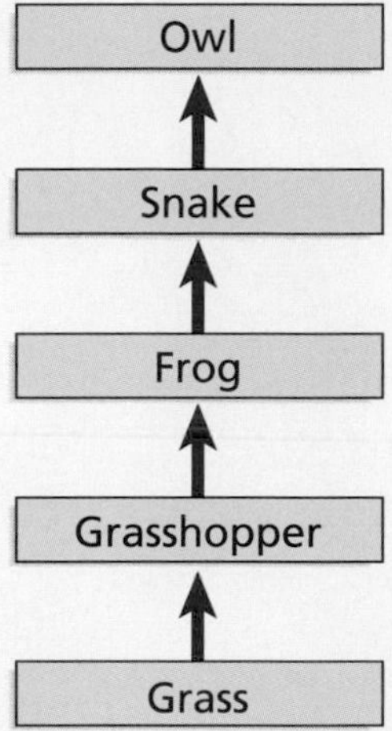

Sample Question

In the food chain shown in the diagram, which of the following organisms obtains its energy directly from the frog?

A the grass **B** the grasshopper
C the snake **D** the owl

Answer

The correct answer is **C**. By looking at the arrows in the diagram, you can see that the energy flows in this food chain directly from the frog to the snake.

Choose the letter of the best answer.

1. You are in an area in Maryland where the fresh water of the Chesapeake Bay meets the Atlantic Ocean. What type of habitat are you in?
A a neritic zone **B** an intertidal zone
C an estuary **D** the tundra

2. Which pair of terms could apply to the same organism?
F carnivore and producer
G decomposer and consumer
H scavenger and herbivore
J carnivore and consumer

3. You and your classmates have just set up a terrarium in a jar using gravel, moist soil, leafy plants, and mosses. The day after the jar was sealed, you noticed water droplets on the inside of the jar. What process caused the water droplets to form?
A evaporation **B** condensation
C precipitation **D** surface runoff

Use the energy pyramid diagram below and your knowledge of science to answer Questions 4 and 5.

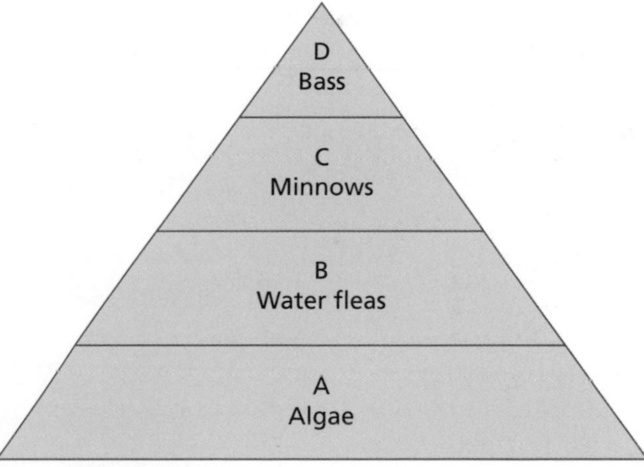

4. Which organisms are the producers in this ecosystem?
F algae **G** minnows
H water fleas **J** bass

5. At which level of this energy pyramid is the LEAST energy available?
A level A **B** level B
C level C **D** level D

Constructed Response

6. Explain how the processes by which carbon and oxygen cycle through the atmosphere are interrelated.

Chapter 3

Living Resources

The BIG Idea

Environment and Resources

What are the main types of environmental issues?

Chapter Preview

Coral reefs are the most diverse ecosystems in the ocean. ▶

Living Resources

▶ Video Preview
Video Field Trip
Video Assessment

Lab zone™ Chapter **Project**

Variety Show

In this chapter's project, you will become an ecologist as you study the diversity of life in a small plot of land. Keep in mind that the area you will study has just a tiny sample of the huge variety of organisms that live on Earth.

Your Goal To observe the diversity of organisms in a plot of land

To complete this project, you must

- stake out a 1.5 meter-by-1.5 meter plot of ground
- keep a record of your observations of the abiotic conditions
- identify the species of organisms you observe
- follow the safety guidelines in Appendix A

Plan It! Look for a location for your plot. With your teacher's approval, stake out a square plot measuring 1.5 meters on each side. Prepare a notebook in which to record your observations, including the date, time, air temperature, and other weather conditions. Also include places for drawings or photographs of the organisms in your plot.

Section 1

Environmental Issues

Reading Preview

Key Concepts

- What are the general categories of environmental issues?
- How do decision makers balance different needs and concerns?

Key Terms

- natural resource
- renewable resource
- nonrenewable resource
- pollution
- environmental science

Target Reading Skill

Identifying Main Ideas As you read the Types of Environmental Issues section, write the main idea in a graphic organizer like the one below. Then write three supporting details that give examples of the main idea.

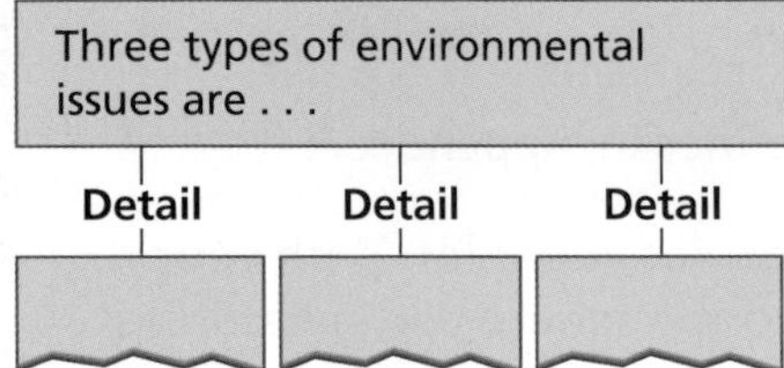

Lab zone Discover Activity

How Do You Decide?

1. On a sheet of paper, list the three environmental issues you think are most important today.
2. Next to each issue you have listed, write the reason you think it is important.
3. Form a group with three other classmates. Share your lists. Decide as a group which one of the issues on your lists is the most important.

Think It Over

Forming Operational Definitions Based on your group's discussion, how would you define *environmental issue?*

Here's a riddle for you: What is bigger than the United States and Mexico combined; is covered with more than two kilometers of ice; is a unique habitat for many animals; and is a source of oil, coal, and iron? The answer is Antarctica. Some people think of Antarctica as a useless, icy wasteland. But there are unique wildlife habitats in Antarctica. There are also valuable minerals beneath its thick ice.

Now the question is, What is the best use of Antarctica? Many people want access to its rich deposits of minerals and oil. Others worry that mining will harm its delicate ecosystems. Some people propose building hotels, parks, and ski resorts. But others feel that Antarctica should remain undeveloped. It is not even clear who should decide Antarctica's fate.

In 1998, 26 nations agreed to ban mining and oil exploration in Antarctica for at least 50 years. As resources become more scarce elsewhere in the world, the debate will surely continue.

1000 B.C.
About 50 million

A.D. 1
About 285 million

Types of Environmental Issues

The debate about Antarctica's future is just one environmental issue that people face today. **Environmental issues fall into three general categories: resource use, population growth, and pollution.** Because these three types of issues are interconnected, they are very difficult to study and solve.

Resource Use Anything in the environment that is used by people is called a **natural resource.** Some natural resources are renewable. **Renewable resources** are either always available or are naturally replaced in a relatively short time. Renewable resources include sunlight, wind, fresh water, and trees. Some people think that renewable resources can never be used up. This is not true for some renewable resources. For example, if people cut down trees faster than they can grow back, the supply of this resource will decrease and could possibly run out.

Natural resources that are not replaced in a useful time frame are called **nonrenewable resources.** As nonrenewable resources such as coal or oil are used, the supply decreases.

Population Growth Figure 1 shows how the human population has changed in the last 3,000 years. You can see that the population grew very slowly until about A.D. 1650. Around that time, improvements in medicine, agriculture, and waste disposal began to enable people to live longer. The human population has been growing faster and faster since then. However, scientists do not expect the population to grow as rapidly in the future.

When a population grows, the demand for resources also grows. Has your town ever experienced a water shortage? If so, you might have noticed that people have been asked to restrict their water use. This sometimes happens in areas with fast-growing populations. The water supplies in such areas were designed to serve fewer people than they now do, so shortages sometimes occur during unusually warm or dry weather.

A.D. 2000
About 6 billion

FIGURE 1
Human Population Growth
More than 6 billion people now live on Earth.
Making Generalizations
How has the human population changed over the past 1,000 years?

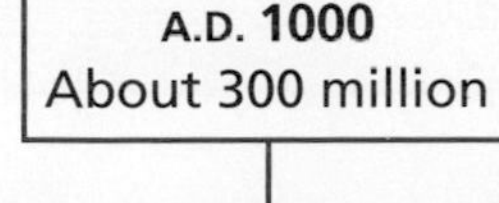

For: Links on the environment
Visit: www.SciLinks.org
Web Code: scn-0531

Pollution The contamination of Earth's land, water, or air is called **pollution.** Pollution can be caused by a variety of factors, including chemicals, wastes, noise, heat, and light. Pollution can destroy wildlife and cause human health problems.

Pollution can be related to resource use. As you probably know, the burning of gasoline releases pollutants into the air. With more cars on the road, more gasoline is used, so more pollutants are released into the air.

Pollution can also be related to population growth. For example, as populations grow, and more people need to be fed, more fertilizers and other chemicals may be used to produce that food. As these chemicals run off the land, they can pollute bodies of water.

What are three factors that can cause pollution?

Science and History

Making a Difference

Can one individual change the way people think? The leaders featured in this timeline have influenced the way that many people think about environmental issues.

1890 John Muir
The actions of John Muir, a nature writer from California, lead to the establishment of Yosemite National Park.

1903 Theodore Roosevelt
President Theodore Roosevelt establishes the first National Wildlife Refuge on Pelican Island, Florida, to protect the brown pelican.

1905 Gifford Pinchot
Forestry scientist Gifford Pinchot is appointed the first director of the United States Forest Service. His goal is to manage forests scientifically to meet current and future lumber needs.

1880 1900 1920

Making Environmental Decisions

Dealing with environmental issues means making decisions. These decisions can be made at personal, local, national, or global levels. Your decision to walk to your friend's house rather than ride in a car is made at a personal level. A town's decision about how to dispose of its trash is made at a local level. A decision about whether the United States should allow oil drilling in a wildlife refuge is a decision made on a national level. Decisions about how to protect Earth's atmosphere are made on a global level.

Every decision has some impact on the environment. Your personal decisions of what to eat or how to travel have a small impact. But when the personal decisions of millions of people are combined, they have a huge impact on the environment.

Writing in Science

Research and Write Find out more about one of the people featured in this timeline. Write a short biography of the person's life that explains how he or she became involved in environmental issues. What obstacles did the person overcome to accomplish his or her goal?

1962 Rachel Carson
Biologist Rachel Carson writes *Silent Spring*, which describes the harmful effects of pesticides on the environment. The book raises awareness of how human activities can affect the environment.

1969 Marjory Stoneman Douglas
At the age of 79, journalist Marjory Stoneman Douglas founds Friends of the Everglades. This grassroots organization is dedicated to preserving the unique Florida ecosystem. She continued to work for the Everglades until her death in 1998.

1949 Aldo Leopold
A Sand County Almanac is published shortly after the death of its author, Aldo Leopold. This classic book links wildlife management to the science of ecology.

1977 Wangari Maathai
Biologist Wangari Maathai founds the Green Belt Movement. This organization encourages restoring forests in Kenya and in other African nations.

1940 1960 1980

FIGURE 2
Resource Use
Decisions about undeveloped land must weigh the costs and benefits. Some benefits of parks are shown here.

Scenic Benefit The park is a beautiful and peaceful place where we can hike and bird watch.

Economic Benefit The trees and other resources of the park provide jobs for loggers and builders.

Balancing Different Needs Lawmakers work with many groups to make environmental decisions. One such group is environmental scientists. **Environmental science** is the study of natural processes in the environment and how humans can affect them. But the data provided by environmental scientists are only part of the decision-making process.

Environmental decision making requires a delicate balance between the needs of the environment and the needs of people. **To help balance the different opinions on an environmental issue, decision makers weigh the costs and benefits of a proposal.**

Types of Costs and Benefits Costs and benefits are often economic. Will a proposal provide jobs? Will it cost too much money? But costs and benefits are not only measured in terms of money. For example, suppose a state must decide whether to allow logging in a park. Removing trees changes the ecosystem, which is an ecological cost. However, by providing jobs and needed wood, logging has an economic benefit.

It is also important to consider the short-term and long-term costs and benefits of an environmental decision. A plan's short-term costs might be outweighed by its long-term benefits.

Weighing Costs and Benefits Once you have identified the potential costs and benefits of a decision, you must analyze them. Consider the costs and benefits of drilling for oil in Antarctica. There would be many costs. It would be very expensive to set up a drilling operation in such a cold and distant place. Transporting the oil would also be difficult and costly. An oil spill in the seas around Antarctica could harm the fish, penguins, and seals there.

Recreational Benefit The park rivers are great places for us to fish in.

Ecological Benefit The park contains habitats for many animals, plants, and other organisms.

On the other hand, there would be benefits to drilling for oil in Antarctica. Oil drilling would provide a new supply of oil for heat, electricity, and transportation. If the worldwide supply of oil were larger, the price might drop, making oil available to more people. The plan would also create many new jobs. Would the benefits of drilling for oil in Antarctica outweigh the costs? This is the kind of question lawmakers must ask before they make environmental decisions.

Reading Checkpoint What are two types of costs and benefits?

Section 1 Assessment

Target Reading Skill Identifying Main Ideas Use your graphic organizer about types of environmental issues to help you answer Question 1 below.

Reviewing Key Concepts

1. a. **Identifying** What are the three main types of environmental issues?
   b. **Explaining** Why is population growth an environmental issue?
   c. **Relating Cause and Effect** How might a growing population affect the supply of trees, a renewable resource? Explain your answer.
2. a. **Reviewing** Why is weighing costs and benefits useful for decision makers?
   b. **Classifying** Name one economic cost and one noneconomic cost of drilling for oil in Antarctica. List one benefit of drilling in Antarctica.
   c. **Making Judgments** Suppose you were a world leader faced with the question of drilling in Antarctica. What decision would you make? Give reasons for your decision.

Writing in Science

Persuasive Letter Write a letter to the editor expressing your viewpoint on whether people should be allowed to use powerboats on a lake in your town. Your letter should clearly show how you weighed the costs and benefits to arrive at your viewpoint.

Lab zone **Skills Lab**

Recycling Paper

Problem

Is paper a renewable resource?

Skills Focus

observing, predicting

Materials

- newspaper
- microscope
- water
- eggbeater
- square pan
- screen
- plastic wrap
- mixing bowl
- heavy book
- microscope slide

Procedure

1. Tear off a small piece of newspaper. Place it on a microscope slide and examine it under a microscope. Record your observations.
2. Tear a sheet of newspaper into pieces about the size of postage stamps. Place the pieces in the mixing bowl. Add enough water to cover the newspaper. Cover the bowl and let the mixture stand overnight.
3. The next day, add more water to cover the paper if necessary. Use the eggbeater to mix the wet paper until it is smooth. This thick liquid is called paper pulp.
4. Place the screen in the bottom of the pan. Pour the pulp onto the screen, spreading it out evenly. Then lift the screen above the pan, allowing most of the water to drip into the pan.
5. Place the screen and pulp on several layers of newspaper to absorb the rest of the water. Lay a sheet of plastic wrap over the pulp. Place a heavy book on top of the plastic wrap to press more water out of the pulp.
6. After 30 minutes, remove the book. Carefully turn over the screen, plastic wrap, and pulp. Remove the screen and plastic wrap. Let the pulp sit on the newspaper for one or two more days to dry. Replace the newspaper layers if necessary.
7. When the pulp is dry, observe it closely. Record your observations.

Analyze and Conclude

1. **Observing** What kind of structures did you observe when you examined torn newspaper under a microscope?
2. **Inferring** What are these structures made of? Where do they come from?
3. **Predicting** What do you think happens to the structures you observed when paper is recycled? How do you think this affects the number of times paper can be recycled?
4. **Communicating** Based on what you learned in this lab, do you think paper should be classified as a renewable or nonrenewable resource? Defend your answer with evidence and sound reasoning.

Design an Experiment

Using procedures like those in this lab, design an experiment to recycle three different types of paper, such as shiny magazine paper, paper towels, and cardboard. *Obtain your teacher's permission before carrying out your investigation.* How do the resulting papers differ?

Section 2

Forests and Fisheries

Reading Preview

Key Concepts

- How can forests be managed as renewable resources?
- How can fisheries be managed for a sustainable yield?

Key Terms

- clear-cutting
- selective cutting
- sustainable yield
- fishery
- aquaculture

Target Reading Skill

Using Prior Knowledge Before you read, write what you know about forests and ocean resources in a graphic organizer like the one below. As you read, write what you learn.

What You Know
1. Forests provide people with lumber and paper. 2.

What You Learned
1. 2.

Lab zone Discover Activity

What Happened to the Tuna?

1. Use the data in the table to make a line graph. Label the axes of the graph and add a title. (To review graphing, see the Skills Handbook.)
2. Mark the high and low points on the graph.

Think It Over

Inferring Describe the changes in the tuna population during this period. Can you suggest a reason for these changes?

Year	Western Atlantic Bluefin Tuna Population
1970	218,000
1975	370,000
1980	67,000
1985	58,000
1990	46,000
1995	63,000
2000	67,000

At first glance, an oak tree and a bluefin tuna may not seem to have much in common. One is a plant and the other is an animal. One lives on land and the other lives in the ocean. However, oak trees and tuna are both living resources. People use oak trees to make furniture, lumber, and cork. Tuna are a source of food for people.

Every day you use many different products that are made from living organisms. In this section, you will read about two major types of living resources: forests and fisheries.

Forest Resources

Forests contain many valuable resources. Many products are made from the fruits, seeds, and other parts of forest plants. Some of these products, such as maple syrup, rubber, and nuts, come from living trees. Other products, such as lumber and wood pulp for making paper, require cutting trees down. Coniferous trees, including pine and spruce, are used for construction and for making paper. Hardwoods, such as oak, cherry, and maple, are used for furniture because of their strength and beauty.

Trees and other plants produce oxygen that organisms need to survive. They also absorb carbon dioxide and many pollutants from the air. Trees help prevent flooding and control soil erosion. Their roots absorb rainwater and hold the soil together.

◀ Newspapers ready for recycling

Managing Forests

There are about 300 million hectares of forests in the United States. That's nearly a third of the nation's area! Many forests are located on public land. Others are owned by individuals or by private timber and paper companies. Forest industries in the United States provide jobs for more than 1 million people.

Because new trees can be planted to replace trees that are cut down, forests can be renewable resources. The United States Forest Service and environmental organizations work with forestry companies to conserve forest resources. They try to develop logging methods that maintain forests as renewable resources.

For: Logging Methods activity
Visit: PHSchool.com
Web Code: cep-5032

Logging Methods There are two major methods of logging: clear-cutting and selective cutting. **Clear-cutting** is the process of cutting down all the trees in an area at once. Cutting down only some trees in a forest and leaving a mix of tree sizes and species behind is called **selective cutting.**

FIGURE 3
Logging Methods
Clear-cutting involves cutting down all the trees in an area at once.
Interpreting Diagrams *What is selective cutting?*

Each logging method has advantages and disadvantages. Clear-cutting is usually quicker and cheaper than selective cutting. It may also be safer for the loggers. In selective cutting, the loggers must move the heavy equipment and logs around the remaining trees in the forest. But selective cutting is usually less damaging to the forest environment than clear-cutting. When an area of forest is clear-cut, the ecosystem changes. After clear-cutting, the soil is exposed to wind and rain. Without the protection of the tree roots, the soil is more easily blown or washed away. Soil washed into streams may harm the fish and other organisms that live there.

Sustainable Forestry Forests can be managed to provide a sustainable yield. A **sustainable yield** is an amount of a renewable resource such as trees that can be harvested regularly without reducing the future supply. Sustainable forestry works sort of like a book swap: as long as you donate a book each time you borrow one, the total supply of books will not be affected. Planting a tree to replace one that was cut down is like donating a book to replace a borrowed one.

In sustainable forestry, after trees are harvested, young trees are planted. Trees must be planted frequently enough to keep a constant supply. Different species grow at different rates. Forests containing faster-growing trees, such as pines, can be harvested and replanted every 20 to 30 years. On the other hand, some forests containing hardwood trees, such as hickory, oak, and cherry, may be harvested only every 40 to 100 years. One sustainable approach is to log small patches of forest. This way, different sections of forest can be harvested every year.

Certified Wood The Forest Stewardship Council is an international organization dedicated to sustainable forest management. This organization oversees certification of forests that are well managed and provide good working conditions for workers. Once a forest is certified, its wood may carry a "well-managed" label. This label allows businesses and individuals to select wood from forests that are managed for sustainable yields.

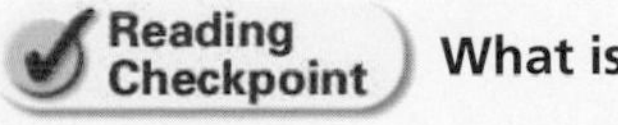

What is a sustainable yield?

FIGURE 4
Sustainable Forestry
Sustainable forestry practices include the planting of young trees after mature trees have been harvested.

Lab zone Skills Activity

Calculating

In a recent year, the total catch of fish in the world was 112.9 million metric tons. Based on the data below, calculate the percent of this total each country caught.

Country	Catch (millions of metric tons)
China	24.4
Japan	6.8
United States	5.6
Peru	8.9

Fisheries

An area with a large population of valuable ocean organisms is called a **fishery.** Some major fisheries include the Grand Banks off Newfoundland, Georges Bank off New England, and Monterey Canyon off California. Fisheries like these are valuable renewable resources.

Until recently, fisheries seemed like an unlimited resource. The waters held such huge schools of fish. And fish reproduce in incredible numbers. A single codfish can lay as many as 9 million eggs in a single year! But people have discovered that this resource has limits. After many years of big catches, the number of sardines off the California coast suddenly declined. The same thing happened to the huge schools of cod off the New England coast. What caused these changes?

The fish were caught faster than they could breed, so the population decreased. This situation is known as overfishing. Scientists estimate that 70 percent of the world's major fisheries have been overfished. But if fish populations recover, a sustainable yield can again be harvested. **Managing fisheries for a sustainable yield includes strategies such as setting fishing limits, changing fishing methods, developing aquaculture techniques, and finding new resources.**

Fishing Limits Laws can ban the fishing of certain species. Laws may also limit the number or size of fish that can be caught or require that fish be within a certain range of sizes. These laws ensure that young fish survive long enough to reproduce and that all of the largest adult fish aren't caught. If a fishery has been severely overfished, however, the government may ban fishing completely until the populations recover.

FIGURE 5
Fisheries
Even though fisheries are renewable resources, they must be managed for sustainable yields, or the supply of fish may run out.

Fishing Methods Today many fishing crews use nets with a larger mesh size that allow small, young fish to escape. In addition, many other fishing practices are regulated by laws. Some fishing methods have been outlawed. These methods include poisoning fish with cyanide and stunning them by exploding dynamite underwater. These techniques harm all the fish in an area rather than targeting certain fish.

Aquaculture The practice of raising fish and other water-dwelling organisms for food is called **aquaculture.** The fish may be raised in artificial ponds or bays. Salmon, catfish, and shrimp are farmed in this way in the United States.

However, aquaculture is not a perfect solution. The artificial ponds and bays often replace natural habitats such as salt marshes. Maintaining the farms can cause pollution and spread diseases into wild fish populations.

FIGURE 6
Aquaculture
Aquaculture is helping to meet the demand for fish. This fish farm in Hawaii raises tilapia.
Applying Concepts *What costs and benefits does aquaculture involve?*

New Resources Today about 9,000 different fish species are harvested for food. More than half the animal protein eaten by people throughout the world comes from fish. One way to help feed a growing human population is to fish for new species. Scientists and chefs are working together to introduce people to deep-water species such as monkfish and tile fish, as well as easy-to-farm freshwater fish such as tilapia.

What is aquaculture?

Section 2 Assessment

Target Reading Skills **Using Prior Knowledge** Review your graphic organizer and revise it based on what you just learned in the section.

Reviewing Key Concepts

1. a. **Reviewing** Why are forests considered renewable resources?
   b. **Comparing and Contrasting** How does the clear-cutting logging method differ from selective cutting?
   c. **Developing Hypotheses** You are walking in a clear-cut section of forest a few days after a heavy rainstorm. A nearby stream is very muddy and has many dead fish. What might have happened?
2. a. **Listing** What are four ways fisheries can be managed for a sustainable yield?
   b. **Explaining** What are two kinds of laws that regulate fishing? How can they help ensure the health of a fishery?
   c. **Predicting** What might happen to a fish population over time if all the largest fish in the population were caught? Explain.

Lab zone At-Home Activity

Renewable Resource Survey With a family member, conduct a "Forest and Fishery" survey of your home. Make a list of all the things that are made from either forest or fishery products. Then ask other family members to predict how many items are on the list. Are they surprised by the answer?

Lab zone **Skills Lab**

Tree Cookie Tales

Problem

What can tree cookies reveal about the past? A tree cookie is a slice of a tree trunk that contains clues about the tree's age, past weather conditions, and fires that occurred during its life.

Skills Focus

observing, inferring, interpreting data

Materials

- tree cookie
- metric ruler
- hand lens
- colored pencils
- calculator (optional)

Procedure

1. Your teacher will give you a "tree cookie." Use a hand lens to examine your tree cookie. Draw a simple diagram of your tree cookie. Label the bark, tree rings, and center, or pith.
2. Notice the light-colored and dark-colored rings. The light ring results from fast springtime growth. The dark ring, where the cells are smaller, results from slower summertime growth. Each pair of light and dark rings represents one year's growth, so the pair is called an annual ring. Observe and count the annual rings.
3. Compare the spring and summer portions of the annual rings. Identify the thinnest and thickest rings.
4. Measure the distance from the center to the outermost edge of the last summer growth ring. This is the radius of your tree cookie. Record your measurement.
5. Measure the distance from the center to the outermost edge of the tenth summer growth ring. Record your measurement.
6. Examine your tree cookie for any other evidence of its history, such as damaged bark or burn marks. Record your observations.

Analyze and Conclude

1. **Inferring** How old was your tree? How do you know?
2. **Calculating** What percent of the tree's growth took place during the first ten years of its life? (*Hint:* Divide the distance from the center to the tenth growth ring by the radius. Then multiply by 100. This gives you the percent of growth that occurred during the tree's first ten years.)
3. **Observing** How did the spring rings compare to the summer rings for the same year? Suggest a reason.
4. **Interpreting Data** Why might the annual rings be narrower for some years than for others?
5. **Communicating** Using evidence from your tree cookie, write a paragraph that summarizes the history of the tree. Be sure to include as much detail as possible in your summary.

Design an Experiment

Suppose you had cookies from two other trees of the same species that grew near your tree. Write a plan for verifying the interpretations you made in this lab. *Obtain your teacher's permission before carrying out your investigation.*

Section 3

Biodiversity

Reading Preview

Key Concepts

- In what ways is biodiversity valuable?
- What factors affect an area's biodiversity?
- Which human activities threaten biodiversity?
- How can biodiversity be protected?

Key Terms

- biodiversity
- keystone species
- gene
- extinction
- endangered species
- threatened species
- habitat destruction
- habitat fragmentation
- poaching
- captive breeding

Target Reading Skill

Building Vocabulary After you read this section, reread the paragraphs that contain definitions of Key Terms. Use all the information you have learned to write a meaningful sentence using each Key Term.

Lab zone Discover Activity

How Much Variety Is There?

1. You will be given two cups of seeds and two paper plates. The seeds in cup A represent the trees in a section of tropical rain forest. The seeds in cup B represent the trees in a section of deciduous forest.
2. Pour the seeds from cup A onto a plate. Sort the seeds by type. Count the different types of seeds. This number represents the number of different kinds of trees in that forest.
3. Repeat Step 2 with the seeds in cup B.
4. Share your results with your class. Use the class results to calculate the average number of different kinds of trees in each type of forest.

Think It Over

Inferring How do the variety of trees in the two forests differ? Can you suggest any advantages of having a wide variety of species?

No one knows exactly how many species live on Earth. As you can see in Figure 7, more than 1.5 million species have been identified so far. The number of different species in an area is called its **biodiversity.** It is difficult to estimate the total biodiversity on Earth because many areas of the planet have not been thoroughly studied. Some experts think that the deep oceans alone could contain 10 million new species! Protecting biodiversity is a major environmental issue today.

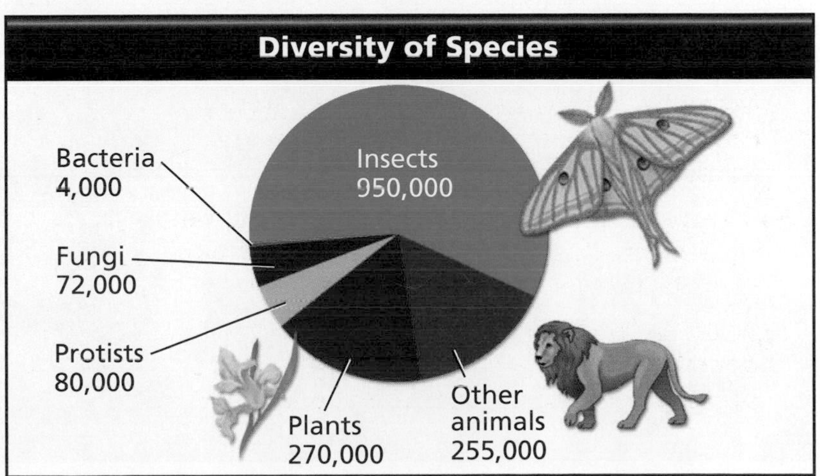

FIGURE 7
Organisms of many kinds are part of Earth's biodiversity.
Interpreting Data *Which group of organisms has the greatest number of species?*

The Value of Biodiversity

Perhaps you are wondering why biodiversity is important. Does it matter whether there are 50 or 5,000 fern species in some faraway rain forest? Is it necessary to protect every one of these species?

There are many reasons why preserving biodiversity is important. The simplest reason to preserve biodiversity is that wild organisms and ecosystems are a source of beauty and recreation. **In addition, biodiversity has both economic value and ecological value within an ecosystem.**

Economic Value Many plants, animals, and other organisms are economically valuable for humans. In addition to providing people with food, these organisms supply raw materials for clothing, medicine, and other products. No one knows how many other useful species have not yet been identified.

The ecosystems in which organisms live are economically valuable, too. For example, many companies now run wildlife tours in rain forests, savannas, mountain ranges, and other locations. This ecosystem tourism, or ecotourism, is an important source of jobs and money for such nations as Brazil, Costa Rica, and Kenya.

FIGURE 8
Economic Value of Biodiversity
The biodiversity in rainforests and other ecosystems can have great economic value. Rain forest organisms are a source of many products, including latex paints. Ecosystem tourism in countries such as Costa Rica provides many jobs for local people.

FIGURE 9
Ecological Value of Biodiversity
These sea stars in the Pacific Ocean near Washington and this sea otter near the California coast are both keystone species in their ecosystems. If the population of a keystone species drops too far, the entire ecosystem can be disrupted.
Relating Cause and Effect *How do sea otters help keep their ecosystem in balance?*

Ecological Value All the species in an ecosystem are connected to one another. Species may depend on each other for food and shelter. A change that affects one species will surely affect all the others.

Some species play a particularly important role in their ecosystems. A **keystone species** is a species that influences the survival of many other species in an ecosystem. For example, the sea stars in Figure 9 prey mostly on the mussels that live in tide pools. When researchers removed the sea stars from an area, the mussels began to outcompete many of the other species in the tide pool. The sea star predators had kept the population of mussels in check, allowing other species to live. When the sea stars disappeared, the balance in the ecosystem was destroyed.

The sea otter in Figure 9 is another keystone species. In the 1800s, hunters killed most of the sea otters on the Pacific coast for fur. With the sea otters nearly extinct, the sea urchins they preyed on reproduced uncontrollably. The huge population of sea urchins ate all of the kelp. When sea otters were reintroduced into the ecosystem, they preyed on the sea urchins. With fewer sea urchins, the kelp population began to recover.

What is a keystone species?

For: More on biodiversity
Visit: PHSchool.com
Web Code: ced-5033

Figure 10
Land and Ocean Ecosystems

Three factors that affect the biodiversity of an ecosystem are area, climate, and niche diversity. **Making Generalizations** *Which factor is most likely responsible for the biodiversity of coral reefs? Of tropical rain forests?*

Although tropical rain forests make up only 7% of Earth's land area, they are home to more than 50% of the world's species.

Factors Affecting Biodiversity

Biodiversity varies from place to place on Earth. **Factors that affect biodiversity in an ecosystem include area, climate, and diversity of niches.**

Area Within an ecosystem, a large area will contain more species than a small area. For example, suppose you were counting tree species in a forest. You would find far more tree species in a 100-square-meter area than in a 10-square-meter area.

Climate In general, the number of species increases from the poles toward the equator. The tropical rain forests of Latin America, southeast Asia, and central Africa are the most diverse ecosystems in the world. These forests cover only about 7 percent of Earth's land surface but contain more than half of the world's species.

The reason for the great biodiversity in the tropics is not fully understood. Many scientists hypothesize that it has to do with climate. For example, tropical rain forests have fairly constant temperatures and large amounts of rainfall throughout the year. Many plants in these regions grow year-round. This continuous growing season means that food is always available for other organisms.

Earth's Ocean Ecosystems

Coral reefs 1%

Although coral reefs make up less than 1% of Earth's oceans, they are home to about 20% of the world's saltwater fish species.

Niche Diversity Coral reefs make up less than 1 percent of the oceans' area. But reefs are home to 20 percent of the world's saltwater fish species. Coral reefs are the second most diverse ecosystems in the world. Found only in shallow, warm waters, coral reefs are often called the rain forests of the sea. A reef supports many different niches for organisms that live under, on, and among the coral. This enables more species to live in the reef than in a more uniform habitat, such as a flat sandbar.

Gene Pool Diversity

Just as the diversity of species is important within an ecosystem, diversity is also important within a species. The organisms in a healthy population have a diversity of traits. Traits such as color, size, and ability to fight disease are determined by genes. **Genes** are the structures in an organism's cells that carry its hereditary information.

Organisms receive a combination of genes from their parents. Genes determine an organism's characteristics, from its size and appearance to its ability to fight disease.

The organisms in one species share many genes. But each organism also has some genes that differ from those of other individuals. These individual differences make up the total gene "pool" of that species.

Species that lack a diverse gene pool are less able to adapt to changes in the environment. For example, some food crops have little diversity. A fungus once wiped out much of the corn crop in the United States. Fortunately, some wild varieties of corn have genes that make them resistant to the fungus. Scientists were able to use some of those wild varieties to breed corn that could fight off the fungus. A species with a diverse gene pool is better able to survive such challenges.

Lab zone Try This Activity

Grocery Gene Pool

With a parent or other adult, visit a supermarket or produce market in your area. Choose one type of fruit or vegetable, such as apples or potatoes. Make a list of all the different varieties of that fruit or vegetable the store sells. Note any differences in appearance between the varieties.

Inferring Judging from the appearance of the different varieties, do you think your fruit or vegetable has a diverse gene pool? Explain.

Reading Checkpoint What do an organism's genes determine?

Figure 11
Genetic Diversity
Diverse genes give these potatoes their rainbow of colors. Having a diverse gene pool helps a species fight disease and adapt to changes in its environment.

Extinction of Species

The disappearance of all members of a species from Earth is called **extinction.** Extinction is a natural process. But in the last few centuries, the number of species becoming extinct has increased dramatically.

Once the size of a population drops below a certain level, the species may not be able to recover. For example, in the 1800s, there were millions of passenger pigeons in the United States. People hunted the birds, killing many hundreds of thousands. This was only part of the total population. But the remaining birds could not reproduce enough to sustain the population. Only after 1914, when the species became extinct, did people realize that the species could not survive without its enormous numbers.

FIGURE 12
Endangered Species

A broad range of species and habitats are represented on the endangered list in the United States.

California Tiger Salamander ▲
Towns have replaced much of this salamander's habitat. The salamanders that remain are in danger of being run over by cars or washed down storm drains.

◀ **Tennessee Purple Coneflower**
These daisy-like plants grow only in cedar forests in central Tennessee. Conservation organizations and landowners are working together to protect these plants.

◀ **Grizzly Bear**
This omnivore needs a large area to obtain enough food. Shrinking wilderness areas have limited its numbers.

Species in danger of becoming extinct in the near future are called **endangered species.** Species that could become endangered in the near future are called **threatened species.** Threatened and endangered species are found on every continent and in every ocean.

Some endangered or threatened species are well-known animals, such as the tiger or China's giant panda. Others are little known, such as hutias, rodents that live on only a few Caribbean islands. Ensuring that these species survive is one way to protect Earth's biodiversity.

Reading Checkpoint **How has the number of species becoming extinct changed in the last few centuries?**

▲ **Schaus Swallowtail Butterfly**
Threatened by habitat loss and pesticide pollution in the Florida Keys, this butterfly was nearly wiped out by Hurricane Andrew in 1992.

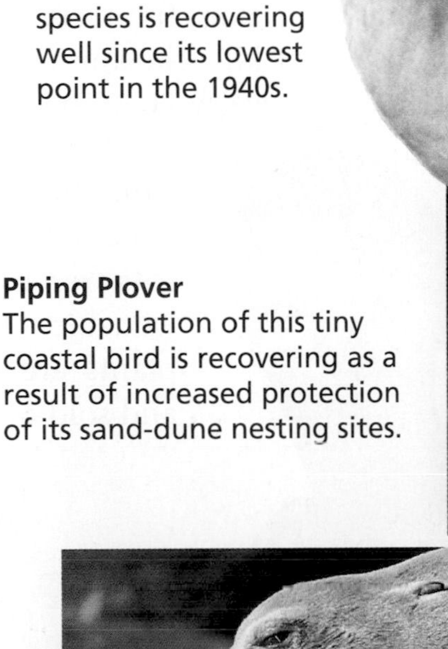

Whooping Crane ▶
Threatened by habitat destruction and disease, about half of the remaining whooping cranes are in zoos. The species is recovering well since its lowest point in the 1940s.

◀ **Piping Plover**
The population of this tiny coastal bird is recovering as a result of increased protection of its sand-dune nesting sites.

Steller's Sea Lion ▶
Overfishing has led to a decline in this mammal's sources of food. Other factors may also be threatening this species.

Living Resources

Video Preview
▶Video Field Trip
Video Assessment

Causes of Extinction

A natural event, such as an earthquake or a volcanic eruption, can damage an ecosystem, wiping out populations or even species. **Human activities can also threaten biodiversity. These activities include habitat destruction, poaching, pollution, and the introduction of exotic species.**

Habitat Destruction The major cause of extinction is **habitat destruction,** the loss of a natural habitat. This can occur when forests are cleared to build towns or create grazing land. Plowing grasslands or filling in wetlands greatly changes those ecosystems. Some species may not be able to survive such changes to their habitats.

Breaking larger habitats into smaller, isolated pieces, or fragments, is called **habitat fragmentation.** For example, building a road through a forest disrupts habitats. This makes trees more vulnerable to wind damage. Plants may be less likely to disperse their seeds successfully. Habitat fragmentation is also very harmful to large mammals. These animals usually need large areas of land to find enough food to survive. They may not be able to obtain enough resources in a small area. They may also be injured trying to cross to another area.

Poaching The illegal killing or removal of wildlife from their habitats is called **poaching.** Many endangered animals are hunted for their skin, fur, teeth, horns, or claws. Hunters sell the animals they kill. The animal parts are then used for making medicines, jewelry, coats, belts, and shoes.

People illegally remove organisms from their habitats to sell them as exotic pets. Tropical fish, tortoises, and parrots are very popular pets, making them valuable to poachers. Endangered plants are sometimes illegally dug up and sold as houseplants or medicines.

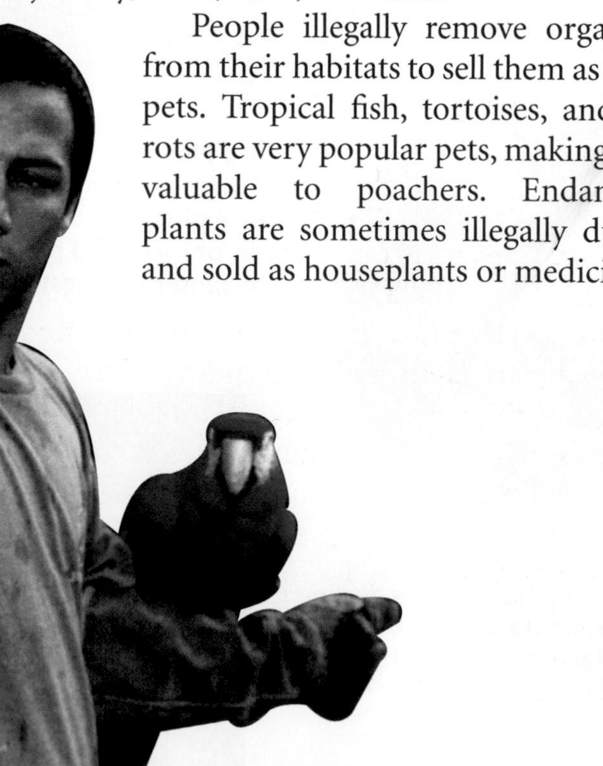

FIGURE 13
Poaching
These scarlet macaws at a zoo in Costa Rica were rescued from poachers who were exporting macaws illegally as pets. Zoo employees will help restore the birds to full health so they can be released back into their habitats.
Inferring *Why are there laws against removing endangered species from their habitats?*

Math Analyzing Data

California Peregrine Falcon Recovery

The peregrine falcon, the world's fastest bird of prey, was nearly extinct in the United States in 1970. The pesticide DDT was weakening peregrine eggshells, so the eggs rarely hatched. In 1972, the United States banned DDT. Use the graph to answer questions about the peregrine population in California.

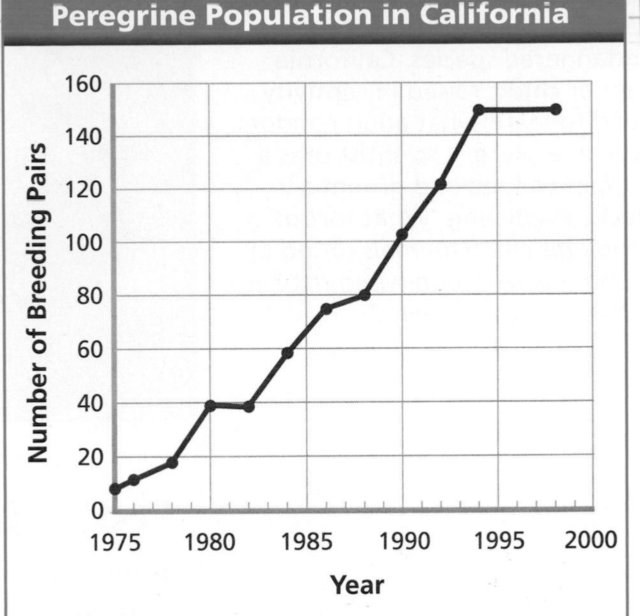

1. **Reading Graphs** What variable is plotted on the *x*-axis? What variable is plotted on the *y*-axis?
2. **Interpreting Data** How did California's peregrine population change from 1976 to 1998?
3. **Inferring** Why do you think the peregrine population grew fairly slowly at first?
4. **Predicting** What might this graph have looked like if DDT had not been banned?

Pollution Some species are endangered because of pollution. Substances that cause pollution, called pollutants, may reach animals through the water they drink or air they breathe. Pollutants may also settle in the soil. From there, they are absorbed by plants and build up in other organisms through the food chain. Pollutants may kill or weaken organisms or cause birth defects.

Exotic Species Introducing exotic species into an ecosystem can threaten biodiversity. When European sailors began visiting Hawaii hundreds of years ago, rats from their ships escaped onto the islands. Without any predators in Hawaii, the rats multiplied quickly. They ate the eggs of the nene goose. To protect the geese, people brought the rat-eating mongoose from India to help control the rat population. Unfortunately, the mongooses preferred eating eggs to rats. With both the rats and the mongoose eating its eggs, the nene goose is now endangered.

What is poaching?

FIGURE 14
Kudzu
Kudzu is an exotic species that was introduced to the United States from Japan in 1876. It can grow up to 30 centimeters a day, so its vines can quickly strangle native trees and shrubs. It can also take over abandoned structures, such as this house in Georgia.

FIGURE 15
Captive Breeding
Captive breeding programs use a scientific approach to protect endangered species. California condor chicks raised in captivity need to learn what adult condors look like. Here, a scientist uses a puppet to feed and groom a chick. **Predicting** *What sort of problems could animals raised by humans come upon when they are released into the wild?*

Protecting Biodiversity

Some people who work to preserve biodiversity focus on protecting individual endangered species. Others try to protect entire ecosystems, such as the Great Barrier Reef in Australia. **Three successful approaches to protecting biodiversity are captive breeding, laws and treaties, and habitat preservation.**

Captive Breeding **Captive breeding** is the mating of animals in zoos or wildlife preserves. Scientists care for the young, and then release them into the wild when they are grown.

Captive breeding was the only hope for the California condor, the largest bird in North America. Condors became endangered due to habitat destruction, poaching, and pollution. By 1984, there were only 15 California condors. Scientists captured all the condors and brought them to zoos to breed. Today, there are more than 200 California condors. Though successful, this program has cost more than $20 million. You can see the drawback of captive breeding.

FIGURE 16
A Protected Species
Laws against selling products made from endangered species have helped protect animals such as these ocelots. These small cats were once hunted nearly to extinction for their fur.

Laws and Treaties Laws can help protect individual species. In the United States, the Endangered Species Act prohibits trade in products made from threatened or endangered species. This law also requires the development of plans to save endangered species. American alligators and green sea turtles have begun to recover as a result of this law.

The most important international treaty protecting wildlife is the Convention on International Trade in Endangered Species. This treaty lists more than 800 threatened and endangered species that cannot be traded for profit. Treaties like this are difficult to enforce. Even so, this treaty has helped to protect many endangered species, including African elephants.

Habitat Preservation The most effective way to preserve biodiversity is to protect whole ecosystems. Protecting whole ecosystems saves not only endangered species, but also the species they depend upon and those that depend upon them.

Beginning in 1872 with Yellowstone National Park, the world's first national park, many countries have set aside wildlife habitats as parks and refuges. In addition, private organizations have purchased millions of hectares of endangered habitats throughout the world. Today, there are about 7,000 nature parks, preserves, and refuges in the world.

To be most effective, reserves must have the characteristics of diverse ecosystems. For example, they must be large enough to support the populations that live there. The reserves must contain a variety of niches. And of course, it is still necessary to keep the air, land, and water clean, control poaching, and remove exotic species.

FIGURE 17
Habitat Preservation
Preserving whole habitats is an effective way to protect biodiversity. Habitat preservation is the aim of national parks such as Yellowstone.

What is the most effective way to preserve biodiversity?

Section 3 Assessment

Target Reading Skill Building Vocabulary Use your sentences to help answer the questions.

Reviewing Key Concepts

1. a. **Listing** What are two ways in which biodiversity is valuable?
   b. **Problem Solving** What economic reasons could you give people in the rain forest for preserving the ecosystem?
2. a. **Identifying** What are three factors that affect the biodiversity in an ecosystem?
   b. **Explaining** How does each of these factors affect biodiversity?
   c. **Developing Hypotheses** Would you expect to find great biodiversity in the tundra biome? Why or why not?
3. a. **Listing** Name four human activities that can threaten biodiversity.
   b. **Applying Concepts** Black bears are roaming through a new housing development in search of food, even though the housing development is still surrounded by forest. How can you account for the bears' behavior?
4. a. **Reviewing** What are three approaches to protecting biodiversity?
   b. **Relating Cause and Effect** For each approach to protecting biodiversity, list at least one factor that might limit its success.
   c. **Making Judgments** List some ways in which those limitations might be dealt with.

Lab zone At-Home Activity

Species Refuges Obtain a map of your community or state. With a family member, identify any city, state, or national parks, reserves, or refuges in your area. Choose one location and find out whether there are endangered or threatened species living there. Then prepare a five-minute presentation for your class on what you learned.

Section 4

Integrating Health

The Search for New Medicines

Reading Preview

Key Concepts

- What is one reason why medical researchers want to protect biodiversity?
- Why are many rain forest plants sources of medicines?

Key Term

- taxol

Target Reading Skill

Asking Questions Before you read, preview the red headings. In a graphic organizer like the one below, ask a *what, how,* or *why* question for each heading. As you read, write the answers to your questions.

The Search for New Medicines

Question	Answer
Why is biodiversity important to medicine?	Biodiversity is important to medicine because . . .

Lab zone Discover Activity

How Are Plant Chemicals Separated?

1. Using a black marking pen, draw a dot about 2 centimeters from the end of a strip of filter paper.
2. Pour a few centimeters of water into a clear plastic cup.
3. Tape the top edge of the filter paper strip to a pencil. Place the pencil across the top of the cup so that the ink dot hangs just below the water surface. If necessary, turn the pencil to adjust the length of the paper.
4. Observe what happens to the black dot.

Think It Over

Observing How many different colors of ink did you separate from the black ink? This process models one way of separating individual chemicals contained in plants.

You lace up your hiking boots and sling your collecting bag over your shoulder. It's time to head out for another day of searching in the cool, damp forest. Stepping carefully to avoid mud, you walk beneath giant evergreens. Their needle-covered branches form a thick roof above your head. Rotting logs covered with ferns, seedlings, and brightly colored fungi line your path. You scan the area for telltale signs of the object of your search. What are you searching for? A plant that can save lives!

This ancient forest is the temperate rain forest of the Pacific Northwest. Many of its giant trees are more than 200 years old. Like tropical rain forests, temperate rain forests are diverse ecosystems. They contain many species that are found nowhere else. Some of these species are rare or endangered, including the bull trout, Olympic salamander, and the life-saving plant you are looking for—the Pacific yew tree.

For: Links on medicines from plants
Visit: www.SciLinks.org
Web Code: scn-0534

Biodiversity and Medicine

People have always studied plants for their ability to heal wounds, fight diseases, and ease pain. For example, aspirin was originally made from the bark of the willow tree. The active chemical in aspirin can now be made in a laboratory.

Almost half of all medicines sold today contain chemicals originally found in wild organisms. For example, digitalis, a medication used to treat certain heart problems, comes from the leaves of the foxglove, a common garden plant. The study of another plant, the Madagascar rosy periwinkle, has produced two effective cancer treatments. From this flowering plant, researchers have produced vincristine, a medication for childhood leukemia, and vinblastine, a medication for Hodgkin's disease.

What other medicines exist undiscovered in Earth's forests, oceans, and other locations? **In 1995, the American Medical Association called for the protection of Earth's biodiversity. Their goal was to preserve the undiscovered medicines that may exist in nature.** Governments, scientists, and private companies are working together to find new species and study known species all over the world. They are working hard to find new sources of disease-fighting drugs.

Reading Checkpoint **From what plant was aspirin originally made?**

▼ **Foxglove:**
source of heart medication

FIGURE 18
Biodiversity and Medicine
Scientists study organisms to identify new sources of disease-fighting medicines. **Predicting** *How could the extinction of species affect the search for new medicines?*

▲ **Longsnout Seahorse:**
possible source of painkillers and cancer treatments

▲ **Madagascar Rosy Periwinkle:**
source of cancer treatments

FIGURE 19
Pacific Yew Tree
While studying the Pacific yew's resistance to disease and insects, scientists discovered taxol.
Developing Hypotheses *Why might Pacific yew trees need such strong resistance?*

The Story of Taxol

Plants in many ecosystems can produce chemicals that protect them from predators, parasites, and diseases. This ability results from the plants' adaptations to their environment. In rain forests, where so many organisms eat plants, plants have many adaptations that protect them. **Some protective chemicals that rain forest plants produce can also be used to fight human diseases.**

The Pacific Yew The Pacific yew tree grows in the temperate rain forest. It is unusually resistant to the many diseases and insects found there. Scientists began to study the bark of the Pacific yew to find out why it was so hardy. When they separated the various chemicals found in the bark, they discovered unusual crystals. These crystals are made from a chemical called **taxol,** the substance that protects the Pacific yew tree.

Taxol as a Cancer Treatment Scientists conducted experiments with taxol in the laboratory. The experiments showed that taxol crystals affect cancer cells in an unusual way. Typically, cancer cells grow and divide very rapidly. This quick growth forms a mass of cells called a tumor. When cancer cells are exposed to taxol, the taxol forms structures that look like tiny cages around each cancer cell. These structures prevent the cancer cells from dividing. As a result, the cancer cannot grow and spread.

After more research, doctors were ready to test taxol on cancer patients. The taxol treatments often were able to shrink certain types of tumors. Sometimes they even stopped the cancer from spreading in the body. Taxol is now used to treat thousands of cancer patients each year.

FIGURE 20
Cancer Survivors
These women are breast cancer survivors. Some of them probably received taxol as a treatment.

The Supply of Taxol As the demand for taxol rapidly grew, many scientists became concerned about the supply of Pacific yew trees. The bark of three Pacific yew trees was required to produce enough pure taxol for just one cancer patient's treatment. Without its bark, a yew cannot survive. Also, by the time researchers discovered taxol's value as a cancer-fighting drug, large portions of the temperate rain forests where yew trees grow were gone.

Today, the bark of the Pacific yew is no longer used in the manufacture of taxol. Chemists worked for many years to reproduce taxol's complex chemical structure in the laboratory, and they finally succeeded in the mid-1990s. This discovery ensured a good supply of taxol for the future. It also helped protect the remaining Pacific yew trees for future generations.

Why was it important for scientists to find a way to make taxol in the laboratory?

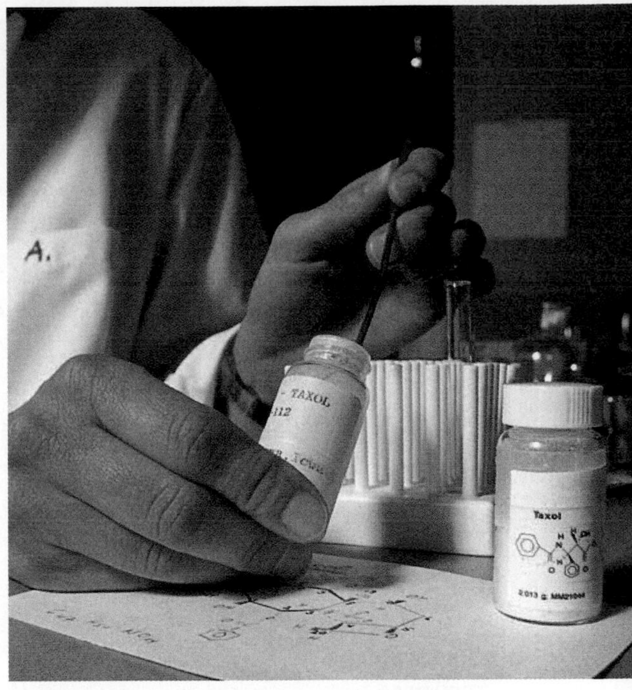

FIGURE 21
Supply of Taxol
Because of its complex chemical structure, it took scientists many years to create taxol in the laboratory.

Section 4 Assessment

Target Reading Skill Asking Questions Use the answers to the questions you wrote about the headings to help you answer the questions below.

Reviewing Key Concepts

1. a. **Reviewing** Why did the American Medical Association call for the protection of Earth's biodiversity?
   b. **Inferring** Do you think that scientists have identified all the wild plants that may have medical uses? Why or why not?
   c. **Predicting** Suppose many wild plants were to become extinct within a short time. What effect might this have on medical research? Explain your answer.
2. a. **Identifying** What adaptations of rain forest plants make them likely sources of medicines?
   b. **Explaining** What plant is the source of taxol, and what is the function of taxol in this plant?
   c. **Comparing and Contrasting** What is the effect of taxol on cancerous tumors? In what way is this effect similar to the function of taxol in the plant?

Writing in Science

News Report Suppose that you were a health news reporter at the time taxol became available as a cancer treatment. Write a two-paragraph news report about taxol. In the first paragraph, discuss the discovery of taxol. In the second paragraph, describe how taxol stops cancer from spreading.

Chapter 3 Study Guide

The BIG Idea

Environment and Resources Environmental issues include the use of renewable and nonrenewable resources, population growth, and pollution. Another major issue is the value of biodiversity to the economy and to ecosystems.

1 Environmental Issues

Key Concepts

- Environmental issues fall into three general categories: resource use, population growth, and pollution.
- To help balance the different opinions on an environmental issue, decision makers weigh the costs and benefits of a proposal.

Key Terms

natural resource
renewable resource
nonrenewable resource
pollution
environmental science

2 Forests and Fisheries

Key Concepts

- Because new trees can be planted to replace trees that are cut down, forests can be renewable resources.
- Managing fisheries for a sustainable yield includes setting fishing limits, changing fishing methods, developing aquaculture techniques, and finding new resources.

Key Terms

clear-cutting
selective cutting
sustainable yield
fishery
aquaculture

3 Biodiversity

Key Concepts

- Biodiversity has both economic value and ecological value within an ecosystem.
- Factors that affect biodiversity in an ecosystem include area, climate, and diversity of niches.
- Habitat destruction, poaching, pollution, and the introduction of exotic species can threaten biodiversity.
- Three successful approaches to protecting biodiversity are captive breeding, laws and treaties, and habitat preservation.

Key Terms

biodiversity
keystone species
gene
extinction
endangered species
threatened species
habitat destruction
habitat fragmentation
poaching
captive breeding

4 The Search for New Medicines

Key Concepts

- In 1995, the American Medical Association called for the protection of biodiversity to preserve medicines that may exist in nature.
- Some chemicals that rain forest plants produce can also be used to fight human diseases.

Key Term

taxol

Review and Assessment

For: Self-Assessment
Visit: PHSchool.com
Web Code: cea-5030

Organizing Information

Concept Mapping Copy the concept map about biodiversity onto a separate sheet of paper. Then complete it and add a title. (For more on Concept Mapping, see the Skills Handbook.)

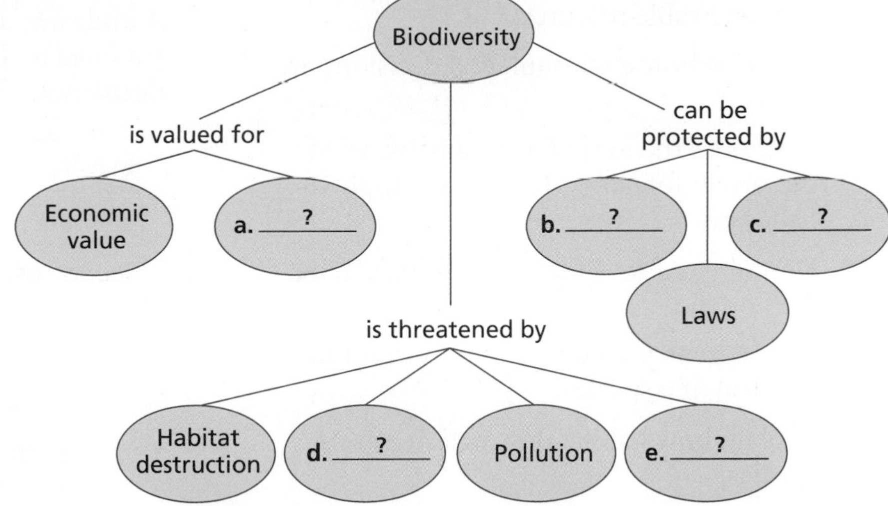

Reviewing Key Terms

Choose the letter of the best answer.

1. The contamination of Earth's air, land, or water is called
   a. extinction.
   b. aquaculture.
   c. pollution.
   d. habitat destruction.
2. The practice of raising fish for food is called
   a. aquaculture.
   b. overfishing.
   c. poaching.
   d. captive breeding.
3. The most diverse ecosystems in the world are
   a. coral reefs.
   b. deserts.
   c. grasslands.
   d. tropical rain forests.
4. If all members of a species disappear from Earth, that species is
   a. extinct.
   b. endangered.
   c. renewable.
   d. threatened.
5. The most effective way to preserve biodiversity is through
   a. habitat fragmentation.
   b. habitat destruction.
   c. habitat preservation.
   d. captive breeding.
6. Taxol, which originally came from Pacific yew trees, is a medicine that is used to fight
   a. heart disease. **b.** cancer.
   c. kidney disease. **d.** diabetes.

Writing in Science

Dialogue The salmon population in an area of the ocean has declined significantly. Fishers depend on catching salmon to make a living. Write a dialogue in which an environmental scientist and a fisher try to find a solution to the problem.

Living Resources

Video Preview
Video Field Trip
▶ Video Assessment

Review and Assessment

Checking Concepts

7. What is a renewable resource? What is a nonrenewable resource?
8. Describe how environmental decisions are made.
9. How does the idea of a sustainable yield pertain to forestry? How does it apply to fisheries?
10. Describe one way that overfishing can be prevented.
11. Why is gene pool diversity important to survival of a species?
12. Explain how habitat destruction affects species.
13. Describe the importance of biodiversity to drug research.

Thinking Critically

14. **Relating Cause and Effect** Explain how human population growth affects resource use and pollution.
15. **Comparing and Contrasting** Which logging method is shown below? Compare the effects of this method with those of selective cutting.

16. **Making Generalizations** Describe how an exotic species can threaten other species in an ecosystem.
17. **Predicting** How could the extinction of a species today affect your life in 20 years?
18. **Inferring** Why are many human medicines made from chemicals that come from plants?

Applying Skills

Use the table to answer Questions 19–23.

A study was done to identify the reasons why mammal and bird species become endangered or threatened. The data are shown in the table below.

Reason	Mammals	Birds
Poaching	31%	20%
Habitat loss	32%	60%
Exotic species	17%	12%
Other causes	20%	8%

19. **Graphing** Make a bar graph comparing the reasons why mammals and birds become endangered or threatened. Show reasons on the horizontal axis and percentages of animal groups on the vertical axis.
20. **Interpreting Data** What is the major reason that mammals become endangered or threatened? What is the main threat to birds?
21. **Predicting** Would stricter laws against poaching be likely to benefit mammal species or bird species more? Explain.
22. **Making Judgments** If you were on a committee formed to protect bird species in your state, what action would you recommend? Support your recommendation using the data in the table.
23. **Developing Hypotheses** Suggest two explanations for the differences between the data for mammals and birds.

Lab zone Chapter Project

Performance Assessment In your presentation, clearly describe the biodiversity you observed in your plot. You can use drawings, video, photos, or a computer for your presentation. Be sure to include the data you collected on abiotic factors as well.

Standardized Test Prep

Test-Taking Tip

Reading All the Answer Choices

Always read every answer choice before selecting the answer you think is correct. If you don't read all the answer choices, you may not notice another choice that is more complete and precise.

Sample Question

The major cause of extinction today is

A poaching.
B pollution.
C habitat destruction.
D introduction of exotic species.

Answer

The correct answer is **C. A, B,** and **D** are also causes of extinction, but **C**—habitat destruction—is the major cause.

Choose the letter of the best answer.

1. A disease kills most members of a plant species in an ecosystem. Several animal species feed on that plant species. After a time, the populations of those animal species decline. Which of the following inferences is valid?
A The ecosystem will soon recover.
B The plant species will become extinct.
C The plant species is a keystone species in that ecosystem.
D Several animal species in the ecosystem will eventually become extinct.

2. In some areas, foresters plant one tree for every tree they cut. This activity is an example of
F a nonsustainable approach to a nonrenewable natural resource
G a sustainable approach to a nonrenewable natural resource
H a nonsustainable approach to a renewable natural resource
J a sustainable approach to a renewable natural resource

The graph below shows how the population of one kind of fish, haddock, changed in Georges Bank between 1980 and 2000. Use the graph below to answer Questions 3 and 4.

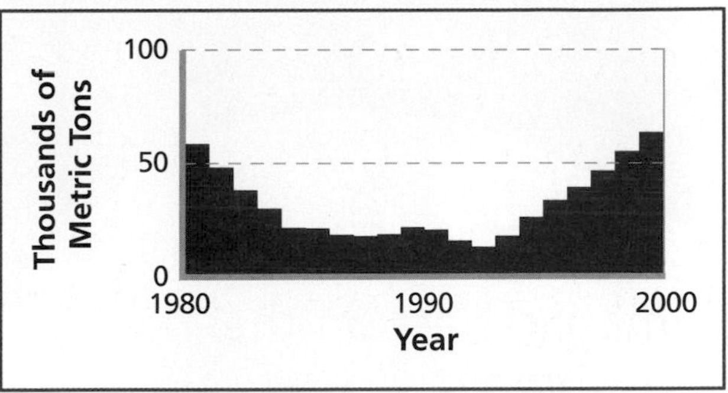

3. Which of the following statements is a valid interpretation of the graphed data?
A Overfishing of haddock began in 1990 and stopped in 2000.
B By 2000, the haddock population had recovered.
C The haddock population from 1980 to 1990 demonstrates the idea of sustainable use.
D The haddock population is decreasing and will probably continue to decrease.

4. Which of the following probably accounts for the trend shown between 1992 and 2000?
F laws regulating haddock fishing
G overfishing
H niche diversity
J habitat fragmentation

5. An environmental impact statement describes the possible effects that a project might have on the environment. Which of the following would be included in an environmental impact statement on drilling for oil in Antarctica?
A the costs of setting up a drilling operation
B the estimated amount of oil produced by the drilling operation
C the effect of oil spills on organisms living in Antarctica
D the effect of increased oil production on the economy

Constructed Response

6. Explain how people benefit when biodiversity is maintained and worldwide ecosystems contain a wide variety of organisms.

Chapter 4

Land, Water, and Air Resources

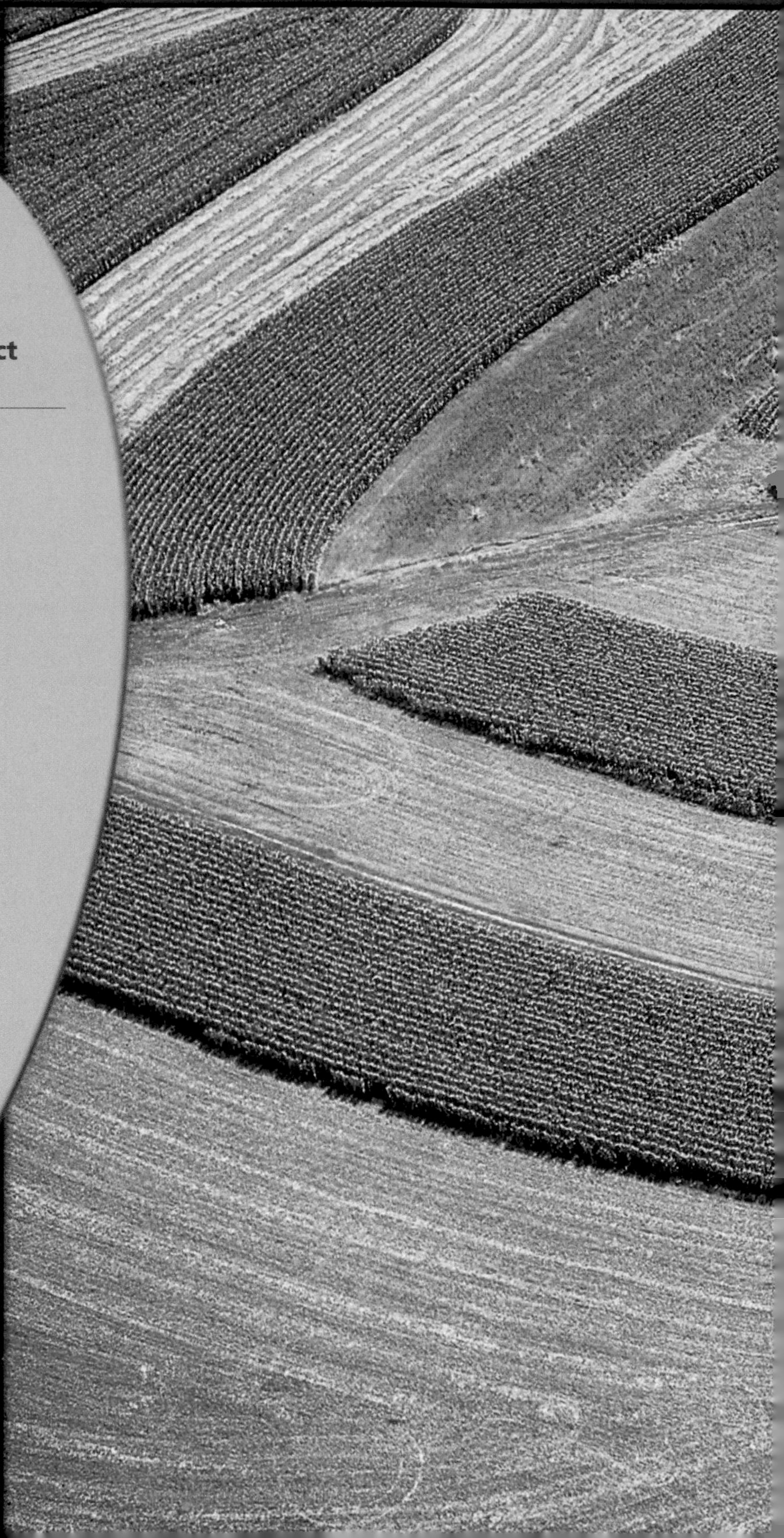

The BIG Idea

Human Impact on the Environment

How do human activities affect the environment?

Chapter Preview

The curved rows made by contour plowing help to conserve soil on hilly farms. ▶

Land, Water, and Air Resources

▶ Video Preview
Video Field Trip
Video Assessment

Lab zone™ Chapter **Project**

Design and Build a Product Package

The next time you're in the supermarket, look at all the different kinds of packages. There are plastic bottles, metal cans, cardboard boxes, paper wrappers, and more! Most of this packaging is eventually thrown away. In this project, you will create a less wasteful product package.

Your Goal To design and build a new package for an existing product that has the least possible packaging waste, but that protects the product

To complete this project, you must

- include a cutaway portion of the product's current package with each material labeled
- create a model of your new package
- test how well your new package protects the product and redesign it if necessary
- follow the safety guidelines in Appendix A

Plan It! Select a product package to study. Empty the package and clean it out. Then identify the materials from which the package is made. Determine how each of these materials protects the product. Decide whether each material could be eliminated or replaced without losing the package's protective function. Then start to sketch some ideas for your new product package.

Section 1

Conserving Land and Soil

Reading Preview

Key Concepts

- How do people use land?
- What is the structure of fertile soil?
- What kinds of problems occur when soil is not properly managed?

Key Terms

- development • litter
- topsoil • subsoil • bedrock
- erosion • nutrient depletion
- fertilizer • desertification
- drought • land reclamation

Target Reading Skill

Identifying Main Ideas As you read the "Types of Land Use" section, write the main idea in a graphic organizer like the one below. Then write three supporting details that give examples of the main idea.

Main Idea

Three uses that change the land are . . .

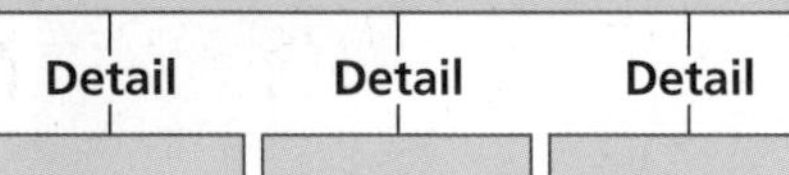

Lab zone Discover Activity

How Does Mining Affect the Land?

1. You will be given a pan filled with sand and soil that represents a mining site. There are at least ten deposits of "ore" (sunflower seeds) buried in your mining site.
2. Your goal is to locate and remove the ore from your site. You may use a pencil, a pair of tweezers, and a spoon as mining tools.
3. After you have extracted the chunks of ore, break them open to remove the "minerals" inside. **CAUTION:** *Do not eat the sunflower seeds.*
4. Observe your mining site and the surrounding area after your mining operations are finished.

Think It Over

Predicting How did mining change the land at your mining site? Predict whether it would be easy or difficult to restore the land to its original state. Explain.

Less than a quarter of Earth's surface is dry, ice-free land. Except for a small amount that forms when volcanoes erupt, new land cannot be created. All the people on Earth must share this limited amount of land to produce their food, build shelter, and obtain other resources. Land is a precious resource. As the American author Mark Twain once said about land, "They don't make it anymore."

▼ A dairy farm

Types of Land Use

People use land in many ways. **Three uses that change the land are agriculture, mining, and development.**

Agriculture Land is the source of most of the food that people eat. Crops such as wheat, rice, and potatoes require large areas of fertile land. But less than a third of Earth's land can be farmed. The rest is too dry, too wet, too salty, or too mountainous. To provide food for the growing population, new farmland is created by clearing forests, draining wetlands, and irrigating deserts. When people make these changes, organisms that depend on the natural ecosystem either find new homes or die off.

Not all agricultural land is used to grow food for people. Some land is used to grow food for livestock. Some animals, such as cows and horses, also require pasture or rangeland for grazing. And some land is used to grow crops other than food, such as cotton.

Mining Mining is the removal of nonrenewable resources from the land. Resources just below the surface are strip mined. Strip mining involves removing a strip of land to obtain minerals and then replacing the strip. Strip mines expose the soil, which can then be blown or washed away more easily. Strip-mined areas may remain barren for years before the soil becomes rich enough to support plant growth again.

For resources located deep underground, it is necessary to dig a tunnel, or shaft. The minerals are carried up through the shafts. This process is called underground mining.

Development People settled first in areas that had good soil and were near a source of fresh water. As populations grew, these settlements became towns and cities. People built more houses and paved roads. The construction of buildings, roads, bridges, dams, and other structures is called **development.**

In the United States, about a million hectares of farmland (an area half the size of New Jersey) are developed each year. Development not only reduces the amount of farmland, but can also destroy wildlife habitats.

Why isn't all land suitable for farming?

FIGURE 1
Development
Some of the land on Earth has been developed for the construction of houses.

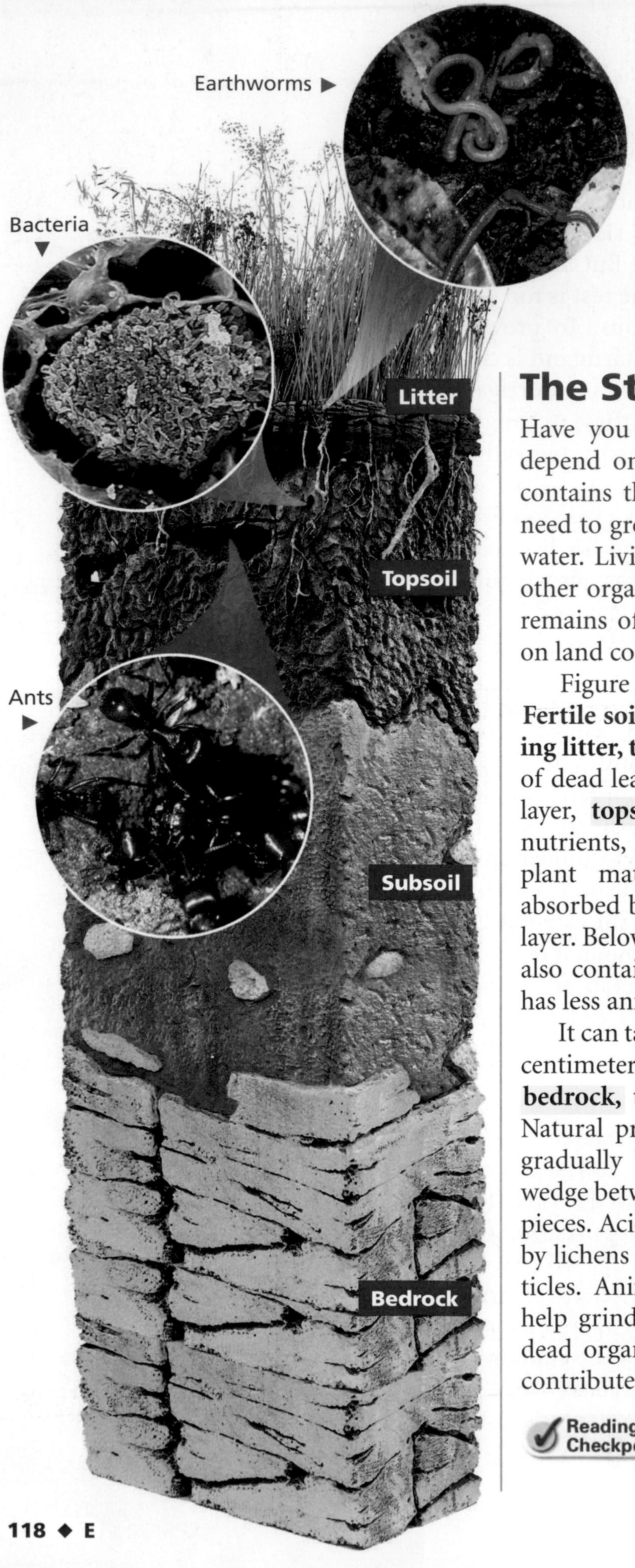

FIGURE 2
Soil Structure
Soil consists of several layers. Organisms such as ants, earthworms, and bacteria live mostly in the topsoil. **Applying Concepts** *In which layer are most plant roots located? What do the roots absorb there?*

The Structure of Soil

Have you ever thought about how much you depend on soil? You probably haven't. But soil contains the minerals and nutrients that plants need to grow. Soil also absorbs, stores, and filters water. Living in soil are the bacteria, fungi, and other organisms that break down the wastes and remains of living things. Without soil, most life on land could not exist.

Figure 2 shows the structure of fertile soil. **Fertile soil is made up of several layers, including litter, topsoil, and subsoil.** The very top layer of dead leaves and grass is called **litter.** The next layer, **topsoil,** is a mixture of rock fragments, nutrients, water, air, and decaying animal and plant matter. The water and nutrients are absorbed by the many plant roots located in this layer. Below the topsoil is the **subsoil.** The subsoil also contains rock fragments, water, and air, but has less animal and plant matter than the topsoil.

It can take hundreds of years to form just a few centimeters of new soil. All soil begins as **bedrock,** the rock that makes up Earth's crust. Natural processes such as freezing and thawing gradually break apart the bedrock. Plant roots wedge between rocks and break them into smaller pieces. Acids in rainwater and chemicals released by lichens slowly break the rock into smaller particles. Animals such as earthworms and moles help grind rocks into even smaller particles. As dead organisms break down, their remains also contribute to the mixture.

What is the first step in the process of soil creation?

Terracing ▲

Windbreaks ▲

Soil Management

Because rich topsoil takes so long to form, it is important to protect Earth's soil. **Poor soil management can result in three problems: erosion, nutrient depletion, and desertification. Fortunately, damaged soil can sometimes be restored.**

Erosion The process by which water, wind, or ice moves particles of rocks or soil is called **erosion.** Normally, plant roots hold soil in place. But when plants are removed during logging, mining, or farming, the soil is exposed, and erosion occurs more easily. Some farming methods that help reduce erosion are shown in Figure 3.

Nutrient Depletion Plants make their own food through photosynthesis. But plants also need nutrients such as the nitrogen, potassium, and phosphorus found in soil. Decomposers supply these nutrients to the soil as they break down the wastes and remains of organisms. But if a farmer plants the same crops in a field every year, the crops may use more nutrients than the decomposers can supply. The soil becomes less fertile, a situation called **nutrient depletion.**

When soil becomes depleted, farmers usually apply **fertilizers,** which include nutrients that help crops grow better. Farmers may choose other methods of soil management, however. Fields can be periodically left fallow, or unplanted. The unused parts of crops, such as cornstalks, can be left in the fields to decompose, adding nutrients to the soil. Farmers can also rotate crops. In crop rotation, a farmer alternates crops that use many nutrients with crops that use fewer nutrients or crops that restore nutrients.

FIGURE 3
Reducing Erosion
Terracing and windbreaks help prevent erosion. In terracing, hillsides are built up into a series of flat "terraces." The ridges of soil at the edges slow runoff and catch eroding soil (left). Windbreaks such as rows of trees block wind and help keep soil from eroding (right).

For: Links on erosion
Visit: www.SciLinks.org
Web Code: scn-0541

Desertification If the soil in a once-fertile area becomes depleted of moisture and nutrients, the area can become desert-like. The advance of desert-like conditions into areas that previously were fertile is called **desertification** (dih zurt uh fih KAY shun). In the past 50 years, desertification has occurred on about 5 billion hectares of land.

One cause of desertification is climate. For example, a **drought** is a period when less rain than normal falls in an area. During droughts, crops fail. Without plant cover, the exposed soil easily blows away. Overgrazing of grasslands by cattle and sheep also exposes the soil. In addition, cutting down trees for firewood can expose soil and cause desertification.

Desertification is a very serious problem. People cannot grow crops and graze livestock where desertification has occurred. As a result, people may face famine and starvation. In central Africa, where desertification is severe, millions of rural people are moving to the cities because they can no longer support themselves on the land.

Reading Checkpoint **What are three causes of desertification?**

FIGURE 4
Large areas of the world are at risk of desertification. One cause is overgrazing. Without grass to hold the soil in place, grasslands can become deserts.
Interpreting Maps *In which biome are most of the areas at risk of desertification located? (Hint:* Refer to *Chapter 2.)*

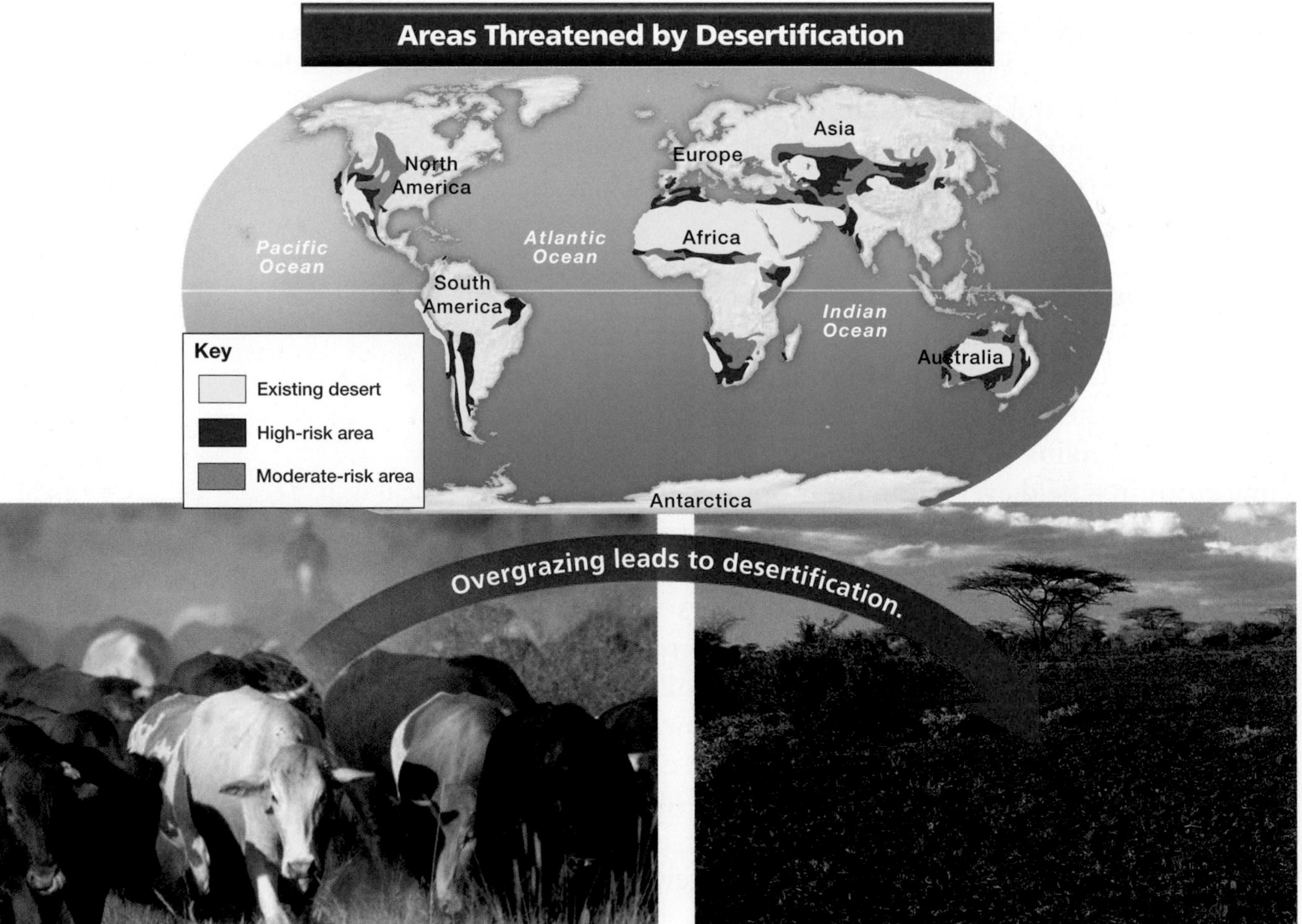

Land Reclamation Fortunately, it is often possible to restore land damaged by erosion or mining. The process of restoring an area of land to a more natural, productive state is called **land reclamation.** In addition to restoring land for agriculture, land reclamation can restore habitats for wildlife. Many different types of land reclamation projects are currently underway all over the world. But it is generally more difficult and expensive to restore damaged land and soil than it is to protect them in the first place.

Figure 5 shows an example of land reclamation. When the mining operation in the first scene was completed, the mine operators smoothed out the sides of the mining cuts. Then they carefully replaced the subsoil and topsoil that had been removed before mining. Finally, they planted grass and trees. The former mine is now becoming a wooded area.

FIGURE 5
Land Reclamation
It's hard to believe that this wooded area used to be an open mine. Thanks to land reclamation practices, many mining areas are being restored for other uses.

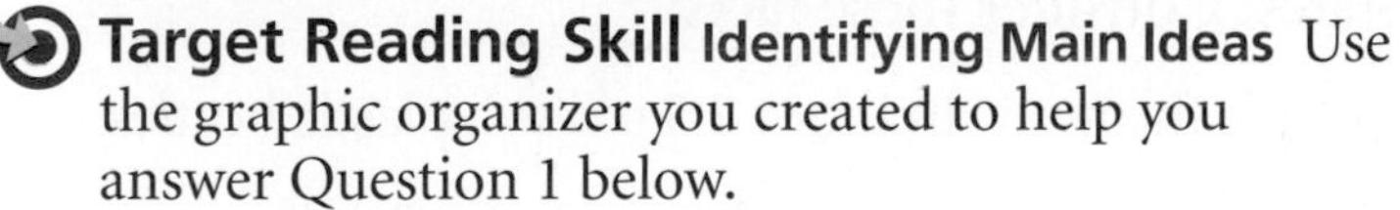

Section 1 Assessment

Target Reading Skill **Identifying Main Ideas** Use the graphic organizer you created to help you answer Question 1 below.

Reviewing Key Concepts

1. a. **Identifying** What are three ways that people use land?
   b. **Explaining** For each land use, describe how it changes the land.
   c. **Predicting** How would you expect each type of land use to change if the world's population were to continue to increase?
2. a. **Reviewing** Describe the different layers of fertile soil in order, from the surface downward.
   b. **Relating Cause and Effect** If large amounts of pesticides are applied to soil, the process of soil creation may be negatively affected. Why might this be the case?
3. a. **Listing** List three problems that can occur when soil is not properly managed.
   b. **Comparing and Contrasting** How are the causes of desertification related to erosion?
   c. **Developing Hypotheses** Suppose that a farmer's field is on a slight hill. How might this farmer reduce erosion of his field?

Writing in Science

Description Imagine that you are holding a lump of fertile soil in your hand. Write a paragraph describing its texture, appearance, smell, and anything else you would observe. Be sure to use a variety of adjectives in your paragraph.

Section 2

Waste Disposal and Recycling

Reading Preview

Key Concepts

- What are three methods of handling solid waste?
- What can people do to help control the solid waste problem?
- How can hazardous wastes be safely disposed of?

Key Terms

- municipal solid waste
- incineration
- leachate
- sanitary landfill
- recycling
- biodegradable
- composting
- hazardous waste

Target Reading Skill

Asking Questions Before you read, preview the red headings. In a graphic organizer like the one below, ask a *why, what,* or *how* question for each heading. As you read, write the answers to your questions.

The Problem of Waste Disposal

Question	Answer
What is the problem with waste disposal?	Each disposal method has . . .

Lab zone Discover Activity

What's in the Trash?

Your teacher will give you a trash bag. The items in the bag represent the most common categories of household waste in the United States.

1. Before you open the bag, predict what the two most common categories are.
2. Put on some plastic gloves. Open the bag and sort the trash items into categories based on what they are made of.
3. Count the number of trash items in each category. Construct a bar graph showing the number of pieces of trash in each category.

Think It Over

Interpreting Data Based on your graph, what are the two most common types of household waste? Was your prediction correct?

How much trash does your family throw away in a year? If it's your job to take the trash out, you might say that it's a large amount. Now imagine that amount multiplied by every family in the United States! Consider these facts:

- Every hour, people throw away about 2.5 million plastic bottles.
- Every day, the average person produces about 2 kilograms of trash.
- Every year, people throw away 2.8 million metric tons of plastic bags and 230 million automobile tires.

You can see why some people call the United States a "throw-away society"! Disposable products can be cheap and convenient. But they have created a big problem—what to do with all the trash.

The Problem of Waste Disposal

In their daily activities, people generate many types of waste, including used paper, empty packages, and food scraps. The waste materials produced in homes, businesses, schools, and other places in a community are called **municipal solid waste.** Other sources of solid waste include construction debris and certain agricultural and industrial wastes. **Three methods of handling solid waste are burning, burying, and recycling. Each method has advantages and disadvantages.**

Incineration The burning of solid waste is called **incineration** (in sin ur AY shun). Incineration has some advantages. The burning facilities, or incinerators, do not take up much space. They do not pose a risk of polluting groundwater. The heat produced by burning solid waste can be used to generate electricity. These "waste-to-energy" plants supply electricity to many homes in the United States.

Unfortunately, incinerators do have drawbacks. Even the best incinerators release some pollution into the air. And although incinerators reduce the volume of waste by as much as 90 percent, some waste still remains. This waste needs to be disposed of somewhere. Finally, incinerators are expensive to build.

FIGURE 6
Waste Disposal
Billions of tons of municipal solid waste are created in the United States each year. More than one third of that waste is paper.
Reading Graphs *What percentage of solid waste does food waste represent?*

For: Sanitary Landfill activity
Visit: PHSchool.com
Web Code: cep-5042

FIGURE 7
Sanitary Landfill
A well-designed sanitary landfill contains the waste and prevents it from polluting the surrounding land and water.

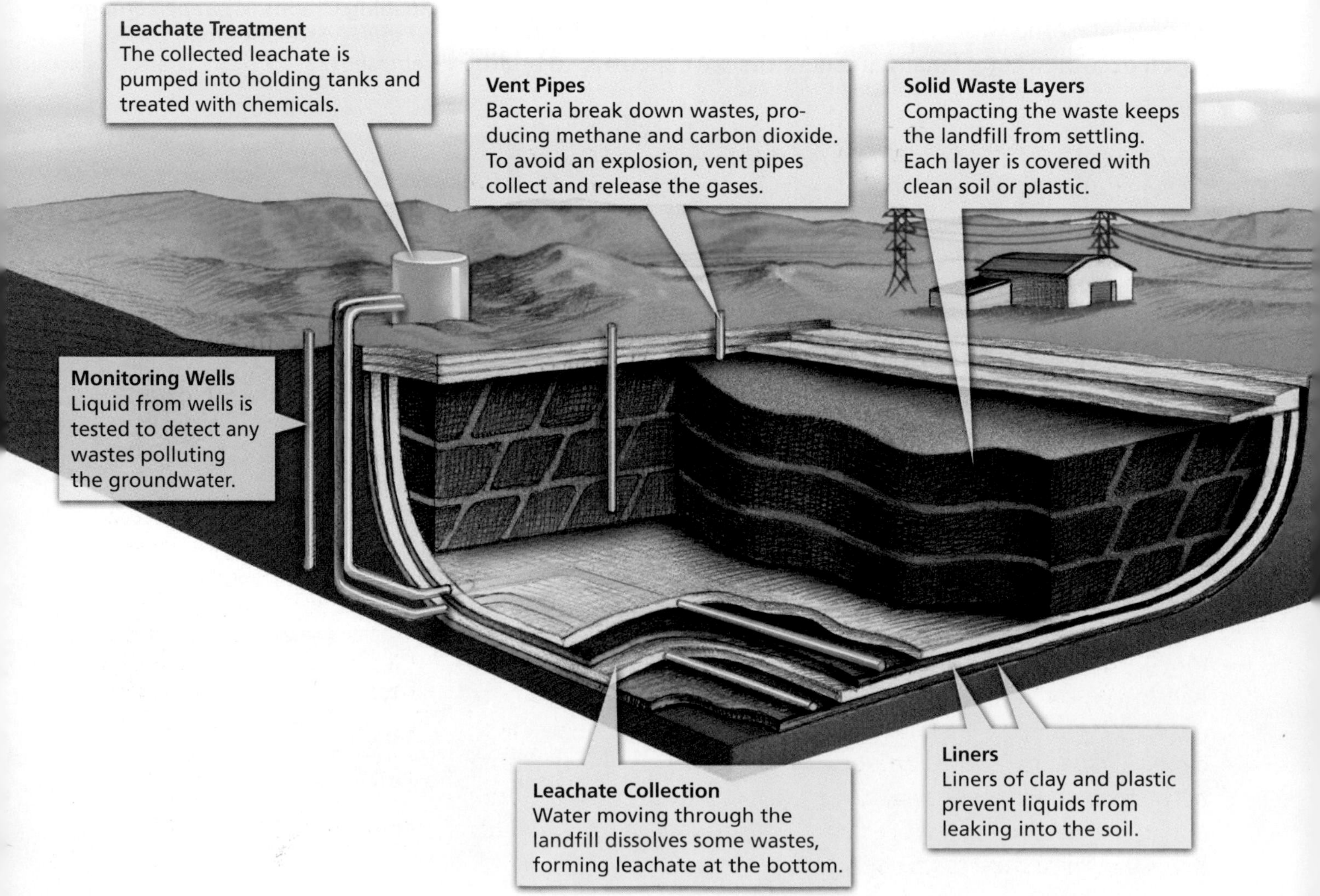

Landfills Until fairly recently, people usually disposed of waste in open holes in the ground. But these open dumps were dangerous and unsightly. Rainwater falling on a dump dissolved chemicals from the wastes, forming a polluted liquid called **leachate.** Leachate could run off into streams and lakes, or trickle down into the groundwater below the dump.

In 1976, the government banned open dumps. Now much solid waste is buried in landfills that are constructed to hold the wastes more safely. A **sanitary landfill** holds municipal solid waste, construction debris, and some types of agricultural and industrial waste. Figure 7 shows the parts of a well-designed sanitary landfill. Once a landfill is full, it is covered with a clay cap to keep rainwater from entering the waste.

However, even well-designed landfills still pose a risk of polluting groundwater. And while capped landfills can be reused in certain ways, including as parks and sites for sports arenas, they cannot be used for housing or agriculture.

What are two possible uses of a capped sanitary landfill?

Leachate Treatment
The collected leachate is pumped into holding tanks and treated with chemicals.

Vent Pipes
Bacteria break down wastes, producing methane and carbon dioxide. To avoid an explosion, vent pipes collect and release the gases.

Solid Waste Layers
Compacting the waste keeps the landfill from settling. Each layer is covered with clean soil or plastic.

Monitoring Wells
Liquid from wells is tested to detect any wastes polluting the groundwater.

Leachate Collection
Water moving through the landfill dissolves some wastes, forming leachate at the bottom.

Liners
Liners of clay and plastic prevent liquids from leaking into the soil.

FIGURE 8
Metal Recycling
Metal is a commonly recycled material. Here, crumpled aluminum cans ride up a conveyor belt in a recycling center. **Predicting** *Without recycling, what might eventually happen to the supply of aluminum?*

Recycling

The process of reclaiming raw materials and reusing them to create new products is called **recycling.** Recycling reduces the volume of solid waste by enabling people to use the materials in wastes again. While recycling uses some energy, it also saves the energy that would be needed to obtain and process raw materials.

As you know, matter in ecosystems is naturally recycled through the water cycle, carbon cycle, and other processes. Any material that can be broken down and recycled by bacteria and other decomposers is **biodegradable** (by oh dih GRAY duh bul). Unfortunately, many of the products people use today are not biodegradable. Plastic containers, metal cans, rubber tires, and glass jars are examples of products that do not naturally decompose. Instead, people have developed techniques to recycle the raw materials in these products.

A wide range of materials, including motor oil, tires, and batteries, can be recycled. Most recycling focuses on four major categories of products: metal, plastic, glass, and paper.

Metal In your classroom, you are surrounded by metal objects that can be recycled. Your desk, scissors, staples, and paper clips are probably made of steel. Another very common metal, aluminum, is used to make soda cans, house siding, window screens, and many other products.

Metals such as iron and aluminum can be recycled. Recycling metal saves money and causes less pollution than making new metal. With recycling, no ore needs to be mined, transported to factories, or processed. In addition, recycling metals helps conserve these nonrenewable resources.

Lab zone Skills Activity

Graphing

What happens to trash? Use the data in the table below to construct a circle graph of methods of municipal solid waste disposal in the United States. Give your circle graph a title. (For help making a circle graph, see the Skills Handbook.)

Method of Disposal	Percentage of Waste
Landfills	56%
Recycling	27%
Incineration	17%

FIGURE 9
Plastic Recycling
Plastic bottles can be recycled and made into many products, including polyester fleece for jackets.

Plastic When oil is refined to make gasoline and other petroleum products, solid materials called resins are left over. Resins can be heated, stretched, and molded into plastic products. Common plastic products that can easily be recycled include milk jugs, detergent containers, and soda bottles. When these products are recycled, they take on very different forms: as fleece jackets, carpeting, park benches, shower stalls, floor tiles, trash cans, fiber filling for sleeping bags, or even dock pilings!

Glass Glass is made from sand, soda ash, and limestone mixed together and heated. Glass is one of the easiest products to recycle because glass pieces can be melted down over and over to make new glass containers. Recycled glass is also used to make fiberglass, bricks, tiles, and the reflective paints on road signs.

Recycling glass is less expensive than making glass from raw materials. Because the recycled pieces melt at a lower temperature than the raw materials, less energy is required. Recycling glass also reduces the environmental damage caused by mining for soda and limestone.

Paper It takes about 17 trees to make one metric ton of paper. Paper mills turn wood into a thick liquid called pulp. Pulp is spread out and dried to produce paper. Pulp can also be made from old newspapers and old used paper. The paper must be washed to remove the inks and dyes. Then the paper is mixed with more water and other chemicals to form pulp.

Most paper products can only be recycled a few times. Recycled paper is not as smooth or strong as paper made from wood pulp. Each time paper is recycled to make pulp, the new paper is rougher, weaker, and darker.

What are three reasons to recycle glass?

Lab zone Try This Activity

It's in the Numbers

Plastic bottles and other plastic products usually have a number inside a triangle indicating the type of plastic they are made of. Plastics must be sorted by type before they can be recycled.

Sort the plastic products your teacher gives you into groups according to their recycling numbers.

Classifying Compare and contrast the pieces in each group with one another and with the pieces in other groups. Describe the characteristics of each group.

Is Recycling Worthwhile? Besides conserving resources, recycling also saves energy. For example, making aluminum products from recycled aluminum rather than from raw materials uses about 90 percent less energy overall. For certain materials, recycling is usually worthwhile.

But recycling is not a complete answer to the solid waste problem. For some cities, recycling is not cost-effective. Scientists have not found good ways to recycle some materials, such as plastic-coated paper and plastic foam. Some recycled products, such as low-quality recycled newspaper, have few uses. And all recycling processes require energy and create pollution. The value of recycling must be judged on a case-by-case basis.

What People Can Do

The good news is that there are ways individuals can help control the solid waste problem. **These are sometimes called the "three R's"—reduce, reuse, and recycle.** *Reduce* refers to creating less waste in the first place. For example, you can use a cloth shopping bag rather than a disposable paper or plastic bag. *Reuse* refers to finding another use for an object rather than discarding it. For example, you could refill plastic drink bottles with drinking water instead of buying new bottles of water.

As you have read, *recycle* refers to reclaiming raw materials to create new products. You can take the first step in the recycling process by recycling at home and by encouraging others to recycle. You can also make an effort to buy products made from recycled materials. This makes it more profitable for companies to use recycled materials in their products.

Another way to reduce the amount of solid waste your family produces is to start a compost pile. **Composting** is the process of helping biodegradable wastes to decompose naturally. The moist, dark conditions in a compost pile allow natural decomposers to break down waste more quickly. Compost piles can be used to recycle grass clippings, raked leaves, and some food wastes. Compost is an excellent natural fertilizer for plants.

FIGURE 10
Composting
Many kinds of food and yard waste can be composted.
Interpreting Photographs *How does composting help reduce household waste?*

Category: Toxic
Example: Chlorine

Category: Explosive
Example: Nitroglycerin

Category: Flammable
Example: Kerosene

FIGURE 11
Hazardous Materials
Vehicles transporting dangerous materials must use signs like these to alert people of the potential dangers of their loads.

Hazardous Wastes

Many people picture hazardous wastes as bubbling chemicals or oozing slime. But any material that can be harmful to human health or the environment if it is not properly disposed of is a **hazardous waste.**

Types of Hazardous Wastes Hazardous wastes are classified into four main categories. Toxic, or poisonous, wastes, can damage the health of humans and other organisms. Explosive wastes either react very quickly when exposed to air or water, or explode when they are dropped. Flammable wastes catch fire easily. Corrosive wastes can dissolve many materials.

Other wastes that require special disposal are radioactive wastes. Radioactive wastes give off radiation that can cause cancer and other diseases. Some radioactive waste can remain dangerous for thousands of years.

Health Effects A person can be exposed to hazardous wastes by breathing, eating, drinking, or touching them. Even short-term exposure to hazardous wastes can cause health problems such as skin irritation or breathing difficulties. Long-term exposure can cause diseases, such as cancer, damage to body organs, or death.

Disposal Methods It is difficult to dispose of hazardous wastes safely. Hazardous wastes are most often disposed of in carefully designed landfills. The landfills are lined and covered with clay and plastic. These materials prevent chemicals from leaking into the soil and groundwater. **Hazardous wastes that are not disposed of in carefully designed landfills may be incinerated or broken down by living organisms. Liquid wastes may be stored in deep rock layers.**

Scientists are still searching for methods that will provide safe, permanent disposal of radioactive wastes. Some radioactive wastes are currently stored in vaults dug hundreds of meters underground or in concrete and steel containers above ground.

Category: Corrosive
Example: Hydrochloric acid

Category: Radioactive
Example: Uranium

Disposal Sites It is even a challenge to decide where to build hazardous waste disposal facilities. In general, people would prefer to have a single large facility located in an area where few people live. However, it may be safer, cheaper, and easier to transport wastes to small local facilities instead.

Reducing Hazardous Waste The best way to manage hazardous wastes is to produce less of them in the first place. Industries are eager to develop safe alternatives to harmful chemicals. At home, you can find substitutes for some hazardous household chemicals. For example, use citronella candles instead of insect spray to repel insects.

What is the best way to manage hazardous wastes?

Section 2 Assessment

Target Reading Skill Asking Questions Use the answers to the questions you wrote about the headings to help you answer the questions below.

Reviewing Key Concepts

1. a. **Reviewing** Name three ways of dealing with solid waste.
   b. **Comparing and Contrasting** Describe one advantage and one disadvantage of each method.
   c. **Developing Hypotheses** Near a former open dump, there is a stream in which your older relatives used to fish. No one fishes there anymore, however, because there are no fish. What might have happened?
2. a. **Identifying** What is meant by the "three R's"?
   b. **Problem Solving** Give one example of how you could practice each of the "three R's."
3. a. **Listing** What are four ways to dispose of hazardous wastes safely?
   b. **Comparing and Contrasting** How do hazardous waste landfills differ from normal landfills?
   c. **Making Judgments** Do you think hazardous wastes should be treated and disposed of at one large central facility? Explain.

Lab zone At-Home Activity

Trash Weigh-In For one week, have your family collect its household trash in large bags. Do not include food waste. At the end of the week, hold a trash weigh-in. Multiply the total amount by 52 to show how much trash your family produces in a year. Can you come up with any ways to reduce your family trash load?

Lab zone **Skills Lab**

Waste, Away!

Problem

How do different kinds of landfills work?

Skills Focus

observing, making models

Materials

- measuring cup
- metric ruler
- soil
- small pebbles
- cheesecloth
- scissors
- plastic wrap
- water
- newspaper
- 5 rubber bands
- red food coloring
- tweezers
- heavy-duty plastic bag
- 12 small sponge cubes
- 3 transparent, wide-mouthed jars

Procedure

1. Read over the entire procedure to preview the three landfill systems you will model. Determine which parts of the models represent potential drinking water, rainfall, solid waste, leachate, and the landfill systems themselves. Write a prediction about the way each system will repond to the test you'll conduct in Part 2.

PART 1 Modeling Three Different Landfill Systems

2. Obtain three identical jars. Label them System 1, System 2, and System 3. Pour clean, clear water into each jar to a depth of 5 cm.
3. Add equal amounts of small pebbles to each jar. The pebbles should be just below the surface of the water.
4. For System 1, cover the pebble and water mixture with 2.5 cm of soil.
5. For System 2, hang a piece of cheesecloth in the jar about 5 cm above the waterline, as shown in the photograph. Hold the cheesecloth in place with a rubber band around the outside mouth of the jar. Gently pour a handful of small pebbles into the cheesecloth.
6. For System 3, suspend a plastic bag in the jar about 5 cm above the waterline. Hold the bag in place with a rubber band around the outside mouth of the jar. Gently pour a handful of small pebbles into the plastic bag.
7. Observe the water and pebbles at the bottom of each of the systems. Record your observations.

PART 2 Testing the Systems

8. Soak 12 identical sponge cubes in water tinted with red food coloring. Use tweezers to place four soaked sponge cubes onto the top surface in each jar.
9. Cover the sponge cubes in Systems 2 and 3 with a thin layer of soil. Leave the sponge cubes in System 1 uncovered.
10. Make a labeled drawing of each system. Explain what each part of each of the models represents.
11. Pour 150 mL of water over each system. Then cover each jar with plastic wrap, and hold the wrap in place with a rubber band. Let the systems stand overnight.
12. Observe each landfill system. Note especially any changes in the color or clarity of the "groundwater." Record your observations.

Analyze and Conclude

1. **Observing** Which part of each model represents the leachate? How well did each landfill system protect the groundwater from the leachate?
2. **Making Models** Identify which of your three models represent each of these three common types of landfills: a well-designed, or sanitary, landfill; a landfill with a poor design; and an open dump. Compare the way the three systems work.
3. **Predicting** If a community's landfill were not located immediately above its groundwater source, do you think its water supply would be completely protected? Explain.
4. **Communicating** Write a paragraph describing which landfill system would be safest for the environment. Use your observations to support your answer.

Design an Experiment

Solid waste can be compacted (crushed into smaller pieces), and the liquid in it can be removed before it is placed in a landfill. Does preparing the waste in this way make it safer for the environment? Write a hypothesis, and then use the ideas and procedures from this lab to design an experiment that tests your hypothesis. *Obtain your teacher's permission before trying your experiment.*

Section 3

Water Pollution and Solutions

Reading Preview

Key Concepts

- Why is fresh water a limited resource?
- What are the major sources of water pollution?
- How can water pollution be reduced?

Key Terms

- groundwater
- pollutant
- sewage
- pesticide
- sediment

Target Reading Skill

Previewing Visuals Before you read, preview Figure 13. Then write two questions that you have about the diagram in a graphic organizer like the one below. As you read, answer your questions.

Water Pollution

Q.	What are some household causes of water pollution?
A.	
Q.	

Lab zone Discover Activity

How Does the Water Change?

1. Shine a flashlight through a clear plastic cup of water.
2. Add six drops of milk to the water and stir.
3. Shine the flashlight through the cup again. Note any differences.

Think It Over

Observing Where in the cup of water is the milk located? Could you easily separate the milk from the water?

Most of Earth's surface is covered by some form of water. Oceans cover nearly three fourths of Earth's surface. Around the poles are vast sheets of ice. From space you cannot even see many parts of Earth because they are hidden behind clouds of tiny water droplets. There seems to be so much water—it's hard to believe that it is a scarce resource in much of the world.

Water—A Limited Supply

How can water be scarce when there is so much of it on Earth's surface? **The reason is that most of the water on Earth—about 97 percent—is salt water. Salt water cannot be used for drinking or for watering crops.** In addition, about three quarters of the fresh water on Earth is in the form of ice. Finally, the supplies of liquid fresh water that do exist are not always close to where people live. For example, many cities in the southwestern United States draw their drinking water from rivers hundreds of kilometers away. And about half the people in the United States use groundwater for their drinking water. **Groundwater** is the water stored in soil and rock beneath Earth's surface.

Renewing the Supply Fortunately, Earth's supply of fresh water is renewable. As you recall from Chapter 2, water continually moves between the atmosphere and Earth's surface in the water cycle. Even though fresh water is a renewable resource, there is not always enough of it in a given place at a given time.

Water Shortages Water shortages occur when people use water in an area faster than the water cycle can replace it. This is more likely to happen during a drought, when less rain than normal falls in an area. During a drought, people have to limit their water use. If a drought is severe, crops may die from lack of water.

Many places never receive enough rain to meet the water needs of their growing populations. These places must obtain water from distant sources or by other means. For example, cities in the desert nation of Saudi Arabia obtain more than half of their fresh water by removing salt from ocean water.

FIGURE 12
Fresh Water
Only fresh water can be used for drinking and household tasks.

What is groundwater?

Water Pollution

Since fresh water supplies are scarce, water pollution can be devastating. Substances that cause pollution are called **pollutants.** Some pollutants, such as iron and copper, make water unpleasant to drink or wash in. Other pollutants, such as mercury or benzene, can cause sickness or even death.

If you did the Discover activity, you saw that a few drops of milk quickly spread throughout a cup of water. You could not tell where the milk first entered the water. In the same way, pollutants can dissolve and move throughout a body of water. This is how pollution can affect areas far from its source.

Most water pollution is the result of human activities. **Wastes produced by households, agriculture, industry, mining, and other human activities can end up in water.**

Lab zone Try This **Activity**

Is There Tea There?

In this activity, you will see how difficult it can be to remove pollutants from water.

1. Pour some cooled herbal tea into a clear plastic cup. Observe the color of the tea.
2. Place a paper filter in a funnel. Fill it half way with crushed charcoal. Put the funnel on top of another clear plastic cup.
3. Slowly pour the tea into the funnel so it collects in the plastic cup.
4. Observe the filtered liquid.

Observing How successful were you in removing the pollutant (tea) from the water?

For: More on cleaning up oil spills
Visit: PHSchool.com
Web Code: ced-5043

Household Sewage The water and human wastes that are washed down sinks, toilets, and showers are called **sewage.** If sewage is not treated to kill disease-causing organisms, the organisms quickly multiply. People can become ill if they drink or swim in water containing these organisms.

Agricultural Wastes Animal wastes, fertilizers, and pesticides are also sources of pollution. Rain can wash animal wastes and fertilizers into ponds, where they cause algae to grow quickly. The algae soon cover the pond, blocking light from reaching plants in the pond and killing the plants.

Pesticides are chemicals that kill crop-destroying organisms. Because pesticides are usually spread over large, open areas, they can pollute bodies of water. Even low levels of chemicals in the water can build up to harmful concentrations as they move through the food chain.

Industry and Mining Wastes Some plants, mills, factories, and mines produce wastes that can pollute water. Chemicals and metal wastes can harm organisms that live in bodies of water. Animals that drink from polluted bodies of water or eat the organisms that live in them can also become ill.

Sediments Water that causes erosion picks up **sediments,** or particles of rock and sand. Sediments can cover up the food sources, nests, and eggs of organisms in bodies of water. Sediments also block sunlight, preventing algae and plants from growing. This affects organisms that rely on the algae and plants.

Heat A pollutant is usually thought of as an added material. But heat can also have a negative effect on a body of water. Some factories and power plants release water that has been used to cool machinery. This heated water can kill organisms living in the body of water into which it is released.

Oil and Gasoline One of the most dramatic forms of water pollution is an oil spill. You may have seen news reports showing beaches covered with sticky black oil, or volunteers cleaning oil from birds. It can take many years for an area to recover from an oil spill.

Another water pollution problem is caused by oil and gasoline that leak out of damaged underground storage tanks. The pollution can be carried far away from a leaking tank by groundwater.

Why is heat considered a water pollutant?

FIGURE 13
Water Pollution

Most water pollution is caused by human activities. **Interpreting Diagrams** *What are five specific sources of water pollution shown in the diagram?*

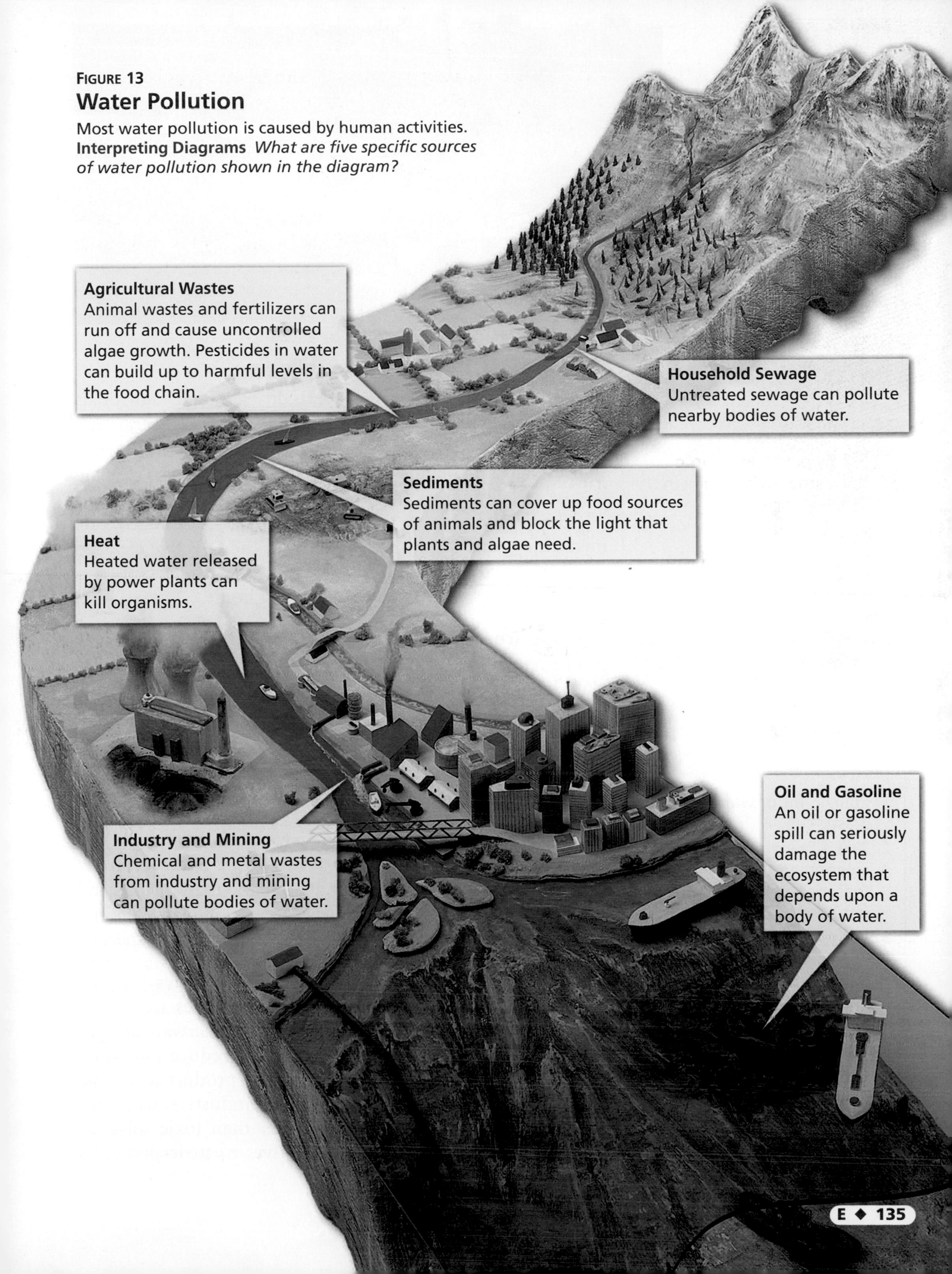

Agricultural Wastes
Animal wastes and fertilizers can run off and cause uncontrolled algae growth. Pesticides in water can build up to harmful levels in the food chain.

Household Sewage
Untreated sewage can pollute nearby bodies of water.

Sediments
Sediments can cover up food sources of animals and block the light that plants and algae need.

Heat
Heated water released by power plants can kill organisms.

Industry and Mining
Chemical and metal wastes from industry and mining can pollute bodies of water.

Oil and Gasoline
An oil or gasoline spill can seriously damage the ecosystem that depends upon a body of water.

FIGURE 14
Sewage Treatment
Riverbank State Park in New York City is a huge recreational complex built over a sewage treatment plant. **Problem Solving** *Why is this a good solution for a big city?*

Keeping Water Clean

By working together, government, industries, and individuals can improve water quality in the United States. Federal laws such as the Clean Water Act regulate the use of certain substances that can pollute water. State and local laws also regulate the use and cleanup of water pollutants.

The keys to keeping water clean are proper sewage treatment, the reduction of pollutants, and the effective cleanup of oil and gasoline spills. There are also some important ways that people can reduce water pollution at home.

Sewage Treatment Most communities treat wastewater before returning it to the environment. A typical treatment plant handles the waste in several steps. During primary treatment, the wastewater is filtered to remove solid materials. Then it is held in tanks where heavy particles settle out. During secondary treatment, bacteria in the system break down the wastes. Sometimes the water is then treated with chlorine to kill disease-causing organisms.

Some communities have come up with creative ways to deal with sewage treatment plants. In Figure 14, you can see Riverbank State Park in New York City. It is a park, marketplace, and sports facility built on top of a sewage treatment plant. The city now has a treatment plant and a park in half the usual space.

Reducing Pollutants Instead of releasing wastes into the environment, industries can recycle their wastes to recover useful materials. Once such programs are underway, companies often find they save money as well as reduce pollution. Other companies change their processes to produce less waste or less harmful waste. For example, some industries use natural fruit acids as cleaning agents rather than toxic solvents. Likewise, farmers are finding alternatives to toxic pesticides and fertilizers.

Lab zone Try This **Activity**

Getting Clean

In this activity you will see how Earth's fresh water is purified in the water cycle.

1. Pour 15 mL of water into a plastic cup.
2. Add a few drops of food coloring and half a teaspoon of sugar. Stir until the sugar is dissolved.
3. Put the cup in the sunlight in a place where it will not be disturbed.
4. Check on the cup twice a day until all the water has evaporated. Observe what remains in the cup.

Making Models What do the sugar and food coloring represent? What happens to the water in this activity?

Cleaning Up Oil and Gasoline Spills Oil is a pollutant that nature can handle in small amounts. Bacteria that break down oil live in the ocean. When oil is present, the bacteria multiply quickly as they feed on it. As the oil disappears, the bacteria population dies down. But in the case of a large spill, bacteria cannot clean up the spill fast enough. It takes the hard work of many scientists and volunteers to minimize environmental damage from large spills.

Gasoline or oil that leaks from an underground tank is hard to clean up. If the pollution has not spread far, the soil around the tank can be removed. But pollution that reaches groundwater may be carried far away. Groundwater can be pumped to the surface, treated, and then returned underground. This, however, can take many years.

What You Can Do It is easy to prevent water pollution at home. Some common household water pollutants are paints and paint thinner, motor oil, and garden chemicals. You can avoid causing water pollution by never pouring these chemicals down the drain. Instead, save these materials for your community's next hazardous waste collection day.

FIGURE 15
Cleaning Up Oil Spills
After an oil spill, a volunteer gently cleans oil from the feathers of a gannet, a large seabird.

Why are leaks from underground oil tanks hard to clean up?

Section 3 Assessment

Target Reading Skill Previewing Visuals Refer to your questions and answers about Figure 13 to help you answer Question 2 below.

Reviewing Key Concepts

1. a. **Reviewing** If most of Earth is covered with water, why is fresh water a scarce resource?
   b. **Calculating** If only 3 percent of the water on Earth is fresh water, and 75 percent of that fresh water is frozen, what percent of the water on Earth is liquid fresh water?
   c. **Predicting** A classmate suggests that the solution to water shortages is to melt some icebergs and transport the water to areas that need water. What are two problems with this plan?
2. a. **Listing** Name four types of human activities that can be sources of water pollution.
   b. **Relating Cause and Effect** Explain how a farmer spraying fields with pesticides can pollute a river miles away.
3. a. **Identifying** What are three ways that water pollution can be reduced?
   b. **Sequencing** List in order the steps of wastewater treatment.
   c. **Making Judgments** What kinds of laws do you think would result in the greatest reduction in water pollution? Explain.

Writing in Science

Dialogue Suppose that a sewage treatment and recreation complex like the one in Figure 14 has been proposed for your town. Write a one-page dialogue in which you and another person from your town debate whether this is a good idea. (*Hint:* The speakers must hold opposing viewpoints.) Be sure to support all opinions with specific details.

Section 4

Air Pollution and Solutions

Reading Preview

Key Concepts

- What are the causes of smog and acid rain?
- What are the causes of indoor air pollution?
- What is the key to reducing air pollution?

Key Terms

- emissions
- photochemical smog
- ozone
- temperature inversion
- acid rain
- radon

Target Reading Skill

Relating Cause and Effect As you read, identify three causes of air pollution. Write the information in a graphic organizer like the one below.

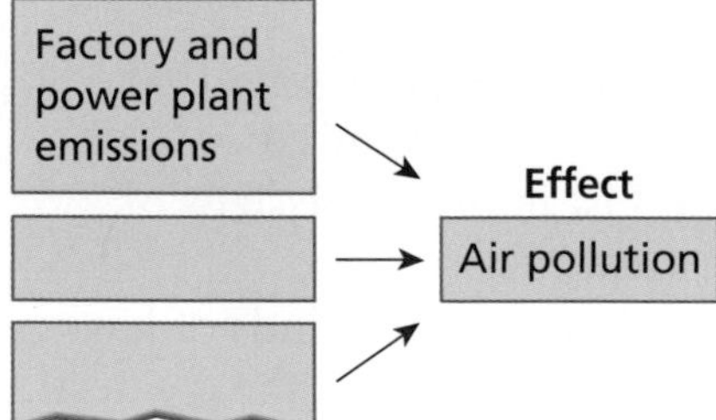

Lab zone Discover Activity

How Does the Scent Spread?

1. Choose a place to stand so that you and your classmates are evenly distributed around the room.
2. Your teacher will spray some perfume in one corner of the room.
3. Raise your hand when you first smell the perfume.

Think It Over

Inferring Describe the pattern you observed as people raised their hands. How do you think the scent traveled across the room?

You can't see, taste, or smell it, but you are surrounded by it. It's air, of course! But what is air? Air is a mixture of nitrogen, oxygen, carbon dioxide, water vapor, and other gases. Almost all living things depend on these gases to carry out their life processes. Recall from Chapter 2 that these gases cycle between the atmosphere and living things. These cycles guarantee that the air supply will not run out. But they don't guarantee that the air will be clean.

What causes air pollution? Perhaps you picture a smokestack belching thick, black smoke into the sky. Until the mid-1900s, in the United States, factories and power plants that burned coal produced most of the **emissions,** or pollutants that are released into the air. Today, there is a larger source of emissions: motor vehicles such as cars and trucks. There are some natural causes of air pollution, as well. For example, an erupting volcano sends an enormous load of pollutants into the atmosphere.

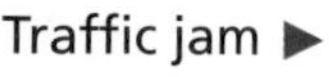

Traffic jam ▶

FIGURE 16
Temperature Inversion
Normally, pollutants rise into the atmosphere and blow away. But during a temperature inversion, a layer of warm air traps pollutants close to the ground.
Interpreting Photographs *What is the brownish haze?*

Smog

Have you ever heard a weather forecaster talk about a "smog alert"? A smog alert is a warning about a type of air pollution called photochemical smog. **Photochemical smog** is a thick, brownish haze formed when certain gases in the air react with sunlight. When the smog level is high, it settles as a haze over a city. Smog can cause eye and throat irritation and breathing problems. Exercising outdoors can make these problems worse.

Sources of Smog **The major sources of smog are the gases emitted by automobiles and trucks.** Burning gasoline in a car engine releases some gases into the air. These gases include hydrocarbons (compounds containing hydrogen and carbon) and nitrogen oxides. The gases react in the sunlight and produce a form of oxygen called **ozone.** Ozone, which is toxic, is the major chemical found in smog. Ozone can cause lung infections and damage the body's defenses against infection.

Temperature Inversion Normally, air close to the ground is heated by Earth's surface. As the air warms, it rises into the cooler air above it. Any pollutants in the air are carried higher into the atmosphere where they blow away from the place where they are produced.

Certain weather conditions cause a condition known as a temperature inversion. During a **temperature inversion,** a layer of warm air prevents the rising air from escaping. The polluted air is trapped and held close to Earth's surface. The smog becomes more concentrated and dangerous.

What is the major chemical found in smog?

For: More on air pollution
Visit: PHSchool.com
Web Code: ced-5044

FIGURE 17
Acid Rain
Acid rain can react with the stone in statues.
Inferring *Why do these statues look like they are melting?*

Acid Rain

Precipitation that is more acidic than normal because of air pollution is called **acid rain.** Acid rain can be in the form of snow, sleet, or fog as well as rain. **Acid rain is caused by the emissions from power plants and factories that burn coal and oil.** These fuels produce nitrogen oxides and sulfur oxides when they are burned. These gases react with water vapor in the air, forming nitric acid and sulfuric acid. The acids return to Earth's surface dissolved in precipitation.

As you can imagine, acid falling from the sky has some negative effects. When acid rain falls into a pond or lake, it changes the conditions there. Many fish, and particularly their eggs, cannot survive in more acidic water. When acid rain falls on plants, it can damage their leaves and stems. Acid rain that falls on the ground can also damage plants by affecting the nutrient levels in the soil. Whole forests have been destroyed by acid rain. Fortunately, some of the effects of acid rain are reversible. Badly damaged lakes have been restored by adding substances such as lime that neutralize the acid.

Acid rain doesn't just affect living things. The acid reacts with stone and metal in buildings and statues. Statues and stonework damaged by acid rain may look as if they are melting. Automobiles rust more quickly in areas with acid rain. These effects are not reversible.

How can acid rain affect nonliving things?

Lab zone Try This Activity

How Acid Is Your Rain?

In this activity you will test whether rain in your area is more or less acidic than lemon juice (citric acid).

1. Collect some rainwater in a clean plastic cup.
2. Indoors, dip a piece of pH paper into the cup. Compare the color of the paper to the chart on the package to find the pH. (The lower the pH of a substance, the more acidic it is.)
3. Pour a little lemon juice into a plastic cup. Repeat Step 2 with the lemon juice.

Measuring What is the pH of the rainwater? How does it compare to the pH of the lemon juice?

Indoor Air Pollution

You might think that you can avoid air pollution by staying inside. But in fact, the air inside buildings can be polluted, too. **Some substances that cause indoor air pollution, such as dust and pet hair, bother only those people who are sensitive to them. Other indoor air pollutants, such as toxic chemicals, can affect anyone.** Glues and cleaning supplies may give off toxic fumes. And cigarette smoke, even from another person's cigarette, can damage the lungs and heart.

Carbon Monoxide One particularly dangerous indoor air pollutant is carbon monoxide. Carbon monoxide is a colorless, odorless gas that forms when wood, coal, oil, or gas are incompletely burned. When carbon monoxide builds up in an enclosed space such as an apartment or house, it can be deadly. Any home heated by wood, coal, oil, or gas should have a carbon monoxide detector.

Radon Another indoor air pollutant that is difficult to detect is radon. **Radon** is a colorless, odorless gas that is radioactive. It is formed naturally by certain types of rocks underground. Radon can enter homes through cracks in basement walls or floors. Research indicates that breathing radon gas over many years may cause lung cancer and other health problems. But the level of radon necessary to cause these effects is unknown. To be safe, some homeowners have installed ventilation systems to prevent radon from building up in their homes.

Reading Checkpoint What is carbon monoxide?

FIGURE 18
Indoor Air Pollution
Air inside buildings can be polluted, too. **Observing** *How many sources of pollution can you spot in this room?*

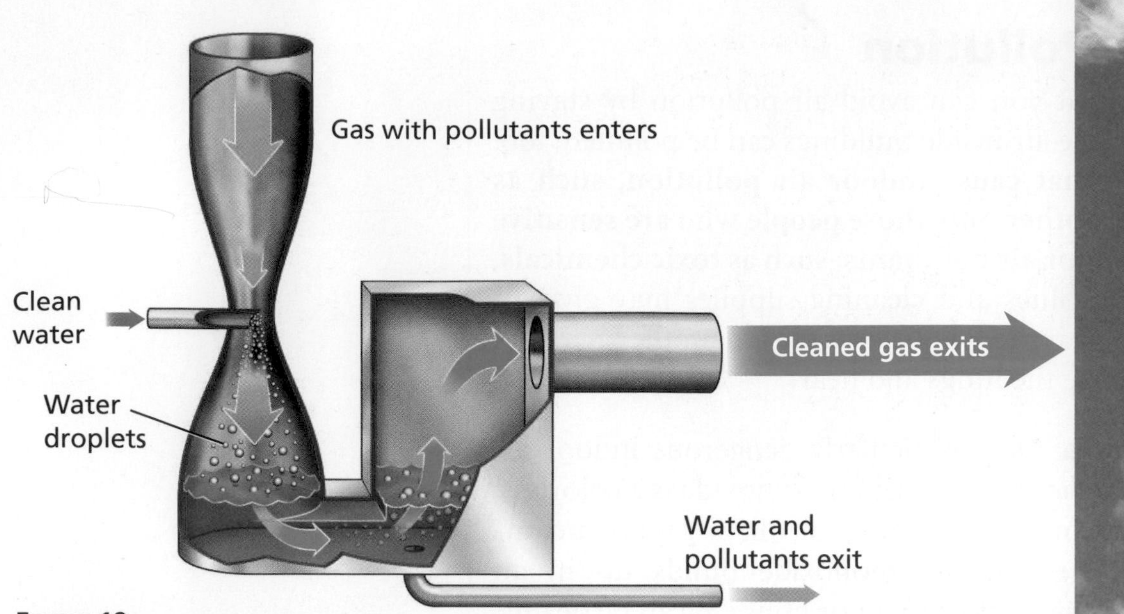

FIGURE 19
Controlling Factory Emissions
A smokestack scrubber removes pollutants such as sulfur dioxide from emissions. The dirty gas passes through a tube containing water droplets. Pollutants dissolve in the water, leaving clean gas to flow out of the chamber. The dirty water still must be properly disposed of. **Inferring** *Why aren't scrubbers a perfect solution to the emissions problem?*

Reducing Air Pollution

The key to reducing air pollution is to control emissions. In the United States, laws such as the Clean Air Act regulate the amount of certain pollutants that can be released into the air. These laws also encourage the development of new technology that reduces air pollution. But reducing emissions requires not only new technology but also the efforts of people like you.

Controlling Emissions From Factories At one time, industries dealt with emissions by building tall smokestacks. The stacks released wastes high in the air, where they could blow away. But the pollutants still ended up somewhere. Now factories place devices in the stacks to treat emissions. The device in Figure 19, called a scrubber, removes pollutants from emissions using a stream of water droplets. Pollutants dissolve in the water and fall into a container. The use of scrubbers explains why "smoke" from factories is white—it's not smoke, it's steam.

Controlling Emissions From Vehicles Cars and trucks now contain pollution-control devices. For example, a catalytic converter is a device that reduces emissions of carbon monoxide, hydrocarbons, and nitrogen oxides. This device causes the gases to react, forming less-harmful carbon dioxide and water.

Laws can ensure that people use pollution-control devices. For example, in many states, cars must pass emissions tests. The state of California's strict emissions-testing laws have helped reduce the smog problem in Los Angeles in recent years.

What You Can Do You may not think there is much you can do to reduce air pollution. But in fact, some small changes in people's behavior can make a big difference.

You can help reduce air pollution by reducing certain types of energy use. Much air pollution is a result of burning fuels to provide electricity and transportation. Using less energy conserves fuel resources and also reduces emissions. When you take public transportation, carpool, walk, or ride a bicycle, there is one fewer car on the road. This means there are fewer emissions that contribute to air pollution.

What are two things you can do to help reduce air pollution?

FIGURE 20
Reducing Air Pollution
Commuting to school or work by bicycle is one way to reduce the emissions that cause air pollution.

Section 4 Assessment

Target Reading Skill Relating Cause and Effect Refer to your graphic organizer about air pollution to help you answer Question 1 below.

Reviewing Key Concepts

1. a. **Reviewing** What causes smog? What causes acid rain?
   b. **Comparing and Contrasting** How are the causes of smog and acid rain similar? How are they different?
2. a. **Listing** Give four examples of indoor air pollutants.
   b. **Classifying** Which of the indoor air pollutants you listed bother only those people who are sensitive to them? Which can affect anyone?
   c. **Predicting** New homes today are better insulated and more airtight than older homes. How might this affect indoor air pollution problems?
3. a. **Identifying** What is the one key to the reduction of air pollution?
   b. **Applying Concepts** Use an example to explain how new technology can help reduce emissions.
   c. **Inferring** One bus produces more emissions than one car. Yet increasing the number of people who travel by bus results in fewer emissions overall. Explain.

Lab zone At-Home Activity

It's in the Air What solid particles are in your air? With a family member, set up two particle collectors. Smear petroleum jelly on the inside of two clean, empty glass jars. Place one inside your home and the other outside. Make sure both jars are in locations where they will not be disturbed. Predict what you will find if you leave the jars in place for a few days. Compare the solid particles in each jar. How similar are they? Can you identify any of the particles?

Lab zone **Design Your Own Lab**

How Does the Garden Grow?

Problem
How do pollutants affect seed growth?

Skills Focus
controlling variables, interpreting data, designing experiments

Suggested Materials
- 2 plastic petri dishes with lids
- wax pencil
- potting soil
- acid solution
- 20 radish seeds
- oil solution
- detergent solution
- salt solution
- day-old tap water
- masking tape
- 10-mL graduated cylinder
- metric ruler

Procedure 

PART 1 Observing the Effects of a Known Pollutant

1. Read all the steps of the lab. Write a hypothesis about how an acid solution might affect the growth of radish seeds. Then copy the data table into your notebook.
2. Write your initials on the lids of the petri dishes. Then write "Control" on one lid. Label the other lid "Acid Solution."
3. Fill each dish with potting soil. Do not pack down the soil.
4. Pour 10 mL of water into the control dish. Pour 10 mL of the acid solution into the pollutant dish. Lightly scatter ten seeds on the soil surface in each dish.
5. Cover each dish with the correct lid. Tape the lids firmly in place. Store the dishes where they will receive light and will not be moved. Wash your hands with soap.
6. Once a day for the next five days, observe the seeds (do not open the lids). Record your observations in the data table. Use a metric ruler to measure the length of any roots or shoots that develop. If you do not observe any change, record that observation.

PART 2 Observing the Effects of a Possible Pollutant

7. Using the procedures you followed in Part 1, design an experiment that tests the effect of a possible pollutant on the growth of radish seeds. (*Hint:* You may use one of the remaining solutions listed under Suggested Materials.) Be sure to write a hypothesis and control all necessary variables.
8. Submit your experimental plan to your teacher for review. After making any necessary changes, create a data table in which to record your observations. Then carry out your experiment.

Data Table

Date	Number of Seeds That Germinated		Condition of Seedlings	
	Control	Pollutant (Acid Solution)	Control	Pollutant (Acid Solution)

Analyze and Conclude

1. **Observing** In Part 1, how many seeds germinated each day in the control dish? In the pollutant dish? What was the total number of seeds that germinated in each dish?
2. **Controlling Variables** In Part 1, how did the preparation of the two petri dishes differ? How was this difference important to the investigation?
3. **Interpreting Data** In Part 1, did the seedlings grown under the two conditions differ? If so, how?
4. **Drawing Conclusions** In Part 1, did your results support your hypothesis? Explain.
5. **Designing Experiments** What was the manipulated variable in Part 2? What was the responding variable?
6. **Inferring** In Part 2, did the solution you chose act as a pollutant? Explain.
7. **Communicating** Write a paragraph explaining what the effect would be if the pollutant you investigated in Part 2 reached a vegetable garden or farm.

More to Explore

Do you think the pollutant you studied in Part 1 has the same effect on all types of plants? Explain your reasoning. How might you test your hypothesis?

Section 5

Integrating Earth Science

Global Changes in the Atmosphere

Reading Preview

Key Concepts

- How have human activities damaged the ozone layer?
- How might human activities be linked to global climate changes?

Key Terms

- ozone layer
- chlorofluorocarbon
- greenhouse effect
- global warming

Target Reading Skill

Outlining As you read, make an outline about global atmospheric changes that you can use for review. Use the red headings for the main ideas and the blue headings for the supporting ideas.

Global Changes in the Atmosphere

I. The thinning of the ozone layer
  A. The source of ozone
  B.
  C.
II. Global climate change
  A.
  B.

Lab zone Discover Activity

What Happens to the Beads?

1. Your teacher will give you beads that change color under certain conditions, along with two pipe cleaners and a small piece of T-shirt material.
2. Thread half of the beads on one pipe cleaner, twisting the ends together.
3. Repeat Step 2 with the remaining beads. Cover the beads on this pipe cleaner with the T-shirt fabric.
4. Take both sets of beads outdoors. After two minutes, go inside. Then remove the fabric covering. Immediately observe the two sets of beads and compare their colors.

Think It Over

Developing Hypotheses Was there any difference in color between the two sets of beads? Form a hypothesis to explain your observations.

It's the first day of vacation, and it's a perfect day for the beach. It's hot, and there's not a cloud in the sky. You've found the perfect spot to read your new book. But as you begin to read, the heat and the sound of the ocean start to make you sleepy. The next thing you know, you're waking up with your head in your book! You've been asleep for two hours! And the redness on your arms reminds you that you forgot to apply sunscreen. Ouch!

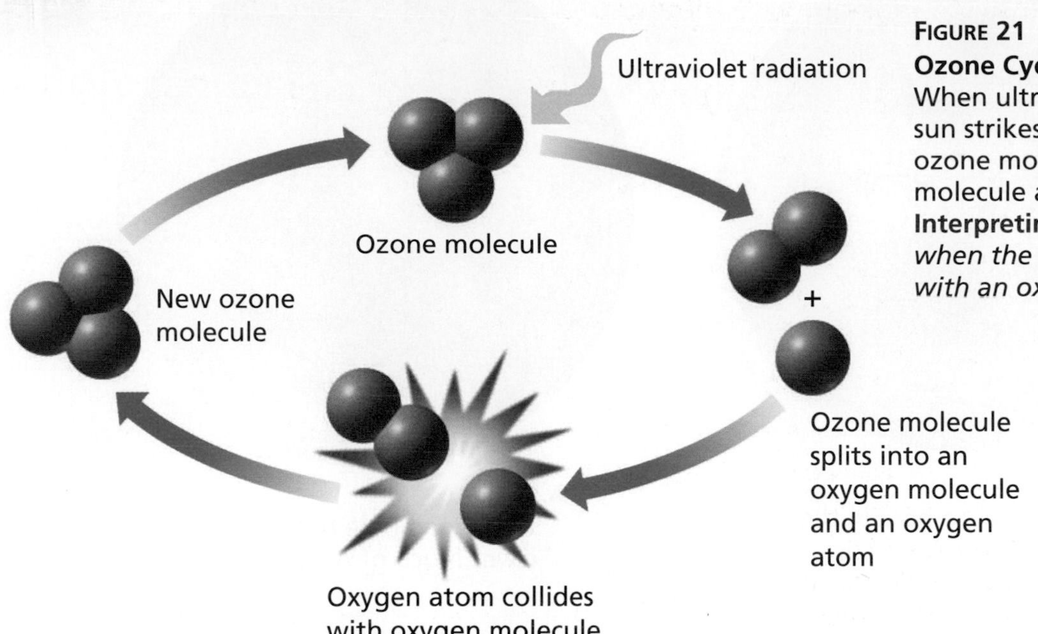

FIGURE 21
Ozone Cycle
When ultraviolet radiation from the sun strikes an ozone molecule, the ozone molecule splits into an oxygen molecule and a free oxygen atom.
Interpreting Diagrams *What happens when the free oxygen atom collides with an oxygen molecule?*

The Thinning of the Ozone Layer

If you have ever had a sunburn, you have experienced the painful effects of the sun's ultraviolet radiation. But did you know that such burns would be even worse without the protection of the ozone layer? The **ozone layer** is a layer of the upper atmosphere about 30 kilometers above Earth's surface. Actually, the concentration of ozone in this layer is very low—only a few parts per million. Yet even the small amount of ozone in the ozone layer protects people from the effects of too much ultraviolet radiation. These effects include sunburn, eye diseases, and skin cancer.

Since you read earlier that ozone is a pollutant, the fact that ozone can be helpful may sound confusing. The difference between ozone as a pollutant and ozone as a helpful gas is its location. Ozone close to Earth's surface in the form of smog is harmful. Higher in the atmosphere, where people cannot breathe it, ozone protects us.

The Source of Ozone Ozone is constantly being made and destroyed. When sunlight strikes an ozone molecule, the energy of the ultraviolet radiation is partly absorbed. This energy causes the ozone molecule to break apart into an oxygen molecule and an oxygen atom, as shown in Figure 21. The oxygen atom soon collides with another oxygen molecule. They react to form a new ozone molecule. Each time this cycle occurs, some ultraviolet energy is absorbed. That energy does not reach Earth's surface.

Math Skills

Calculating a Concentration

Levels of pollutants are often written as concentrations. A concentration is a ratio that compares the amount of one substance to the amount of another substance. For example, suppose that the concentration of ozone in part of the atmosphere is 3 parts per million. This means that there are 3 molecules of ozone in 1,000,000 molecules of air. This ratio can also be written in three other ways:

3 : 1,000,000

3 to 1,000,000

$$\frac{3}{1{,}000{,}000}$$

Practice Problems Express each of these concentrations in three different ways.

1. 7 parts per hundred
2. 25 parts per billion

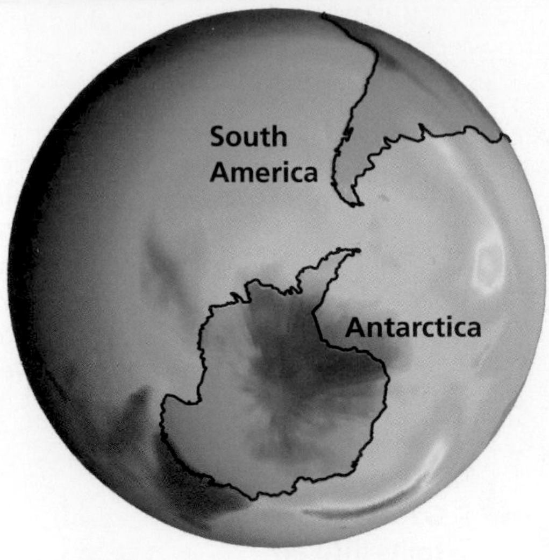

▲ **1979**
Scientists detect a hole in the ozone layer over Antarctica. (The bluish area represents the extent of the ozone hole.)

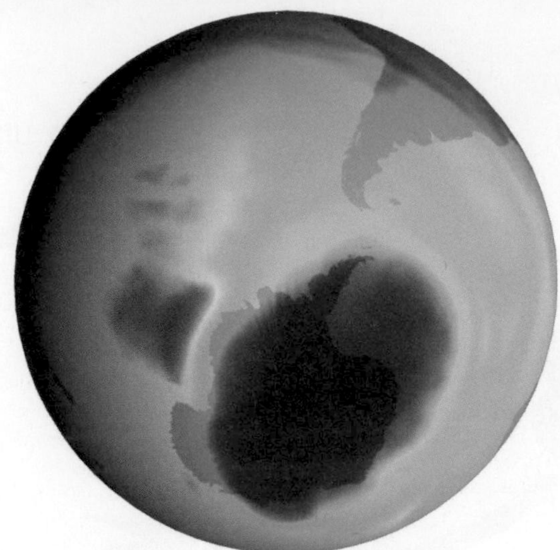
▲ **1986**
The ozone hole has grown to cover much of Antarctica.

FIGURE 22
Ozone Hole
The ozone hole was first detected over Antarctica in the 1970s. The hole has generally grown since then, though it varies a bit from year to year. In each of the globes, the blue area indicates the extent of the ozone hole in the spring of that year.
Observing *How would you describe the change in the ozone hole from 1979 to 2000?*

The Ozone Hole In the late 1970s, scientists observed that the ozone layer over Antarctica was growing thinner each spring. The amount of ozone in the ozone layer was decreasing, causing an area of severe ozone depletion, or an ozone hole. In Figure 22, you can see the size of the ozone hole in four selected years. In 2006, the hole was the largest ever, and in 2003, it was the second-largest ever.

What is to blame for the ozone hole? **Scientists determined that the major cause of the ozone hole is a group of gases called CFCs, which were used in many household products.** CFCs, or **chlorofluorocarbons,** are human-made gases that contain chlorine and fluorine. CFCs had been used in air conditioners, aerosol spray cans, and other products. High in the atmosphere, CFCs react with ozone molecules. The CFCs block the cycle in which ozone molecules absorb ultraviolet radiation. As a result, more ultraviolet light reaches Earth's surface.

What's Being Done In 1990, many nations signed an agreement to eventually ban the use of ozone-depleting substances, including CFCs. Most uses of CFCs were banned in 2000. Some uses of CFCs are still allowed, but compared to the 1970s, few CFCs now enter the atmosphere. Unfortunately, CFC molecules remain in the atmosphere for a long time. But scientists predict that if the ban on ozone-depleting substances is maintained, the ozone layer will gradually recover.

▲ **1993**
The ozone hole covers nearly all of Antarctica.

▲ **2000**
The ozone hole covers Antarctica and extends north over the tip of South America.

When scientists discovered that CFCs were harming the atmosphere, they immediately began to search for substitutes. Refrigerators and air conditioners were redesigned to use less harmful substances. Most spray cans were either replaced by pump sprays or redesigned to use other gases. Researchers developed new ways to make products such as plastic foam without using CFCs. As a result of this research and invention, far fewer CFCs now enter the atmosphere.

What do scientists predict will happen if the ban on CFCs is maintained?

Math Analyzing Data

Chlorine Levels

The line graph shows a scientist's measurements and predictions of how the ban on CFCs might affect chlorine levels in the atmosphere. The red line shows the levels of chlorine without the ban on CFCs. The blue line shows the levels with the ban on CFCs.

Chlorine Levels in the Atmosphere, 1970–2010

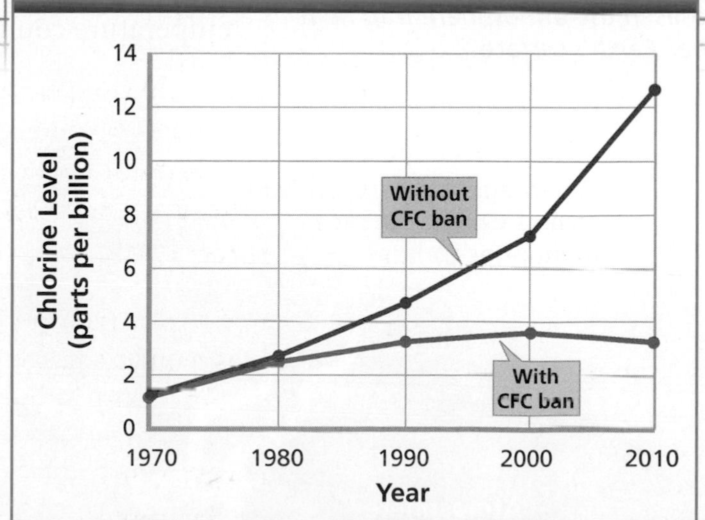

1. **Reading Graphs** What variable is plotted on the horizontal axis? What variable is plotted on the vertical axis?
2. **Interpreting Data** Which graphed line shows rising levels of chlorine? What trend does the other line show?
3. **Inferring** Why do the two lines start at the same point?
4. **Drawing Conclusions** How does the relationship between the two lines change?

For: Links on changes in climate
Visit: www. SciLinks.org
Web Code: scn-0545

Global Climate Change

Some changes to the atmosphere could affect the climate of the whole planet. To understand why, you need to know more about the atmosphere.

The Greenhouse Effect Think about the sun shining through a window on a cool day. The window lets light enter the room. The light strikes objects in the room and is converted to heat. The closed windows then trap the warm air inside, and the room becomes warmer.

In the atmosphere, water vapor, carbon dioxide, and certain other gases act like windows. These gases allow sunlight to reach Earth's surface, but they prevent some of the heat from escaping into space. The trapping of heat near Earth's surface is called the **greenhouse effect.** Without the greenhouse effect, Earth would be much colder—about 33 Celsius degrees colder, on average. All of Earth's water would be frozen!

Global Warming Since the 1800s, coal and oil have been the main sources of energy in many parts of the world. As you have read, burning these substances produces carbon dioxide. As a result, the amount of carbon dioxide in the atmosphere has increased from 280 parts per million to 385 parts per million. This amount is increasing more quickly every year.

Human activities that increase carbon dioxide levels may be intensifying the greenhouse effect. One theory, called **global warming,** predicts that the increase in carbon dioxide levels will cause the average temperature to continue to rise. Scientists have estimated that in this century, the average global temperature could rise several Celsius degrees.

FIGURE 23
Greenhouse Effect
When energy in the form of sunlight strikes Earth's surface, it changes to heat. Certain gases in the atmosphere trap some of the heat, preventing it from escaping back into space. This trapping of heat is known as the greenhouse effect. **Applying Concepts** *What gases in the atmosphere trap heat near Earth's surface?*

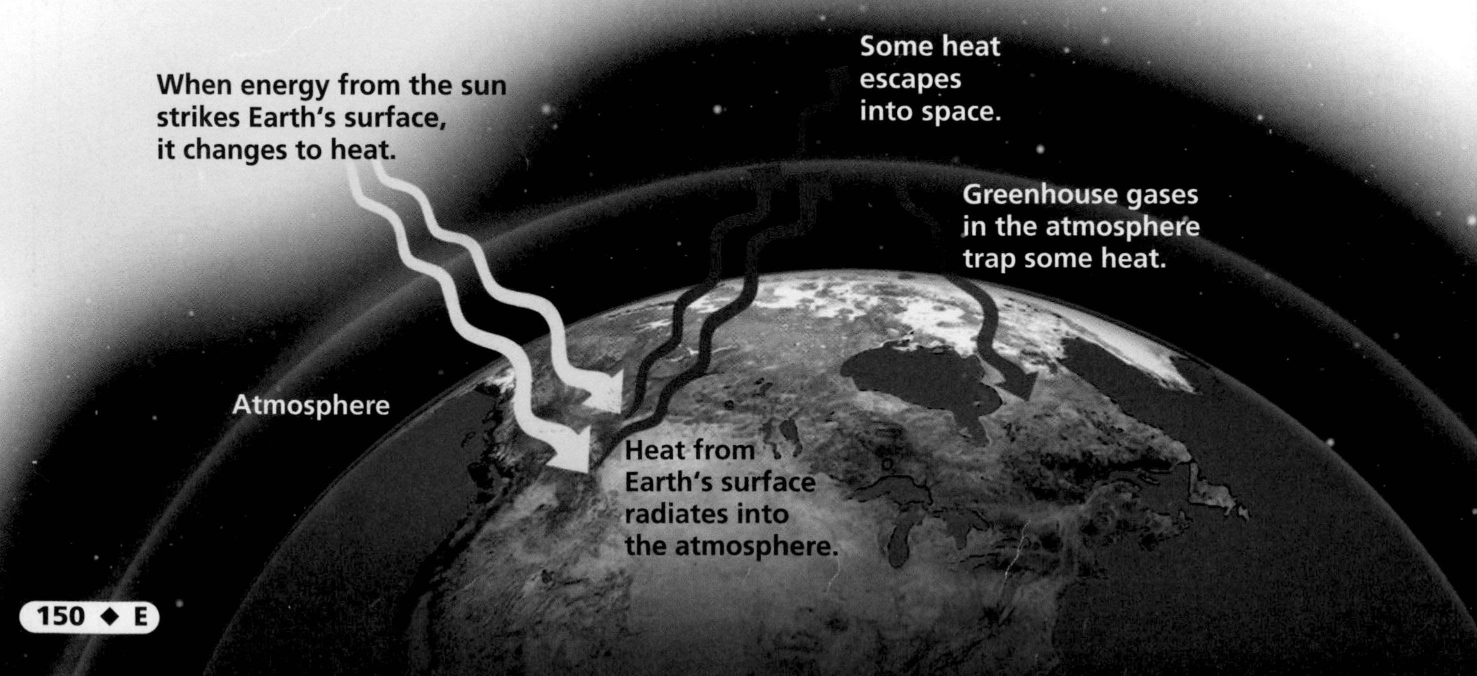

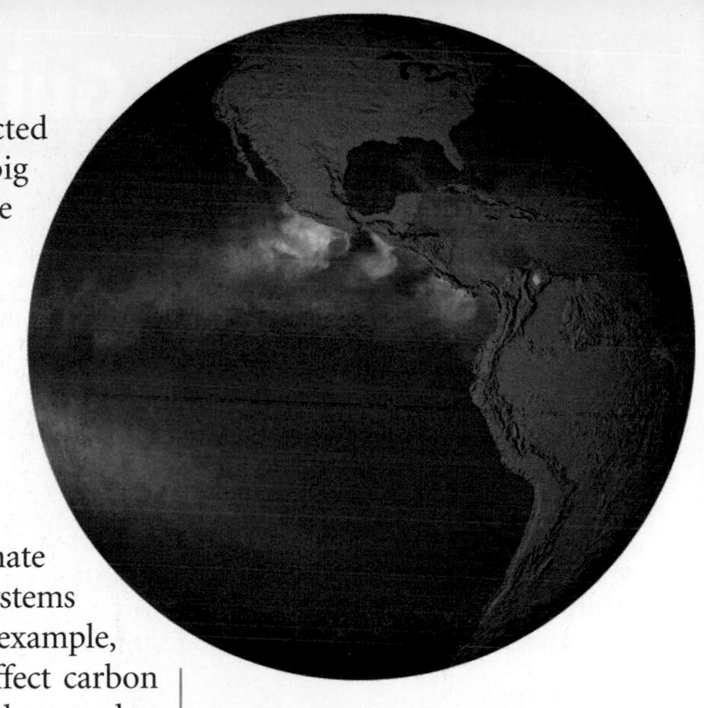

Possible Consequences Although the predicted increase in temperature may not sound like a big change, it could have a huge impact. Parts of the Antarctic ice cap would melt, raising the level of the oceans and causing increased flooding. The temperature change would affect climate patterns all over the world. This change would, in turn, affect where crops could be grown. There might also be more hurricanes and other severe storms.

The Difficulty of Predicting Climate Change It is difficult to predict how Earth's climate will be affected by changes in the atmosphere. The systems that determine climate are very complex. For example, Earth's oceans, forests, clouds, and volcanoes all affect carbon dioxide levels in the atmosphere. It is difficult to know what impact each of these factors might have on climate change.

Scientists have studied climate systems for less than a century, a very short time to understand processes that can take thousands of years. Most scientists base their global climate predictions on computer models. But only time will tell if their long-range predictions have been accurate.

FIGURE 24
Predicting Climate Change
This computer-generated image of Earth shows ocean temperatures near North and South America. The lightest colors indicate the warmest temperatures. The darkest colors indicate the coolest temperatures. Images like this can help scientists predict climate change.

What might be three consequences of global warming?

Section 5 Assessment

Target Reading Skill Outlining Use the information in your outline about global atmospheric changes to help you answer the questions below.

Reviewing Key Concepts

1. a. **Reviewing** How have human activities affected the ozone layer?
   b. **Relating Cause and Effect** What part of the ozone cycle do CFCs interrupt? What effect does this have?
   c. **Predicting** Exposure to ultraviolet radiation can cause skin cancer. How would you expect the thinning of the ozone layer to affect skin cancer rates? Explain.
2. a. **Identifying** What human activities have led to increased levels of carbon dioxide in the atmosphere?
   b. **Explaining** Explain how increased carbon dioxide levels could be linked to global climate changes.
   c. **Problem Solving** What are some steps people could take to reduce the amount of carbon dioxide that enters the atmosphere?

Math Practice

3. **Calculating a Concentration** Draw a picture to show what is meant by each of the following concentrations. Then express each concentration in three different ways.
   a. 4 parts per 10
   b. 19 parts per 100
   c. 7 to 10
   d. 27 : 100

Chapter 4 Study Guide

The BIG Idea

Human Impact on the Environment Human activities can change the land, produce solid waste, and pollute air and water. But methods exist to restore damaged land, solve the solid waste problem, and reduce pollution.

1 Conserving Land and Soil

Key Concepts

- Three uses that change the land are agriculture, mining, and development.
- Fertile soil is made up of several layers, including litter, topsoil, and subsoil.
- Poor soil management can cause erosion, nutrient depletion, and desertification. Damaged soil can sometimes be restored.

Key Terms

• development • litter • topsoil • subsoil
• bedrock • erosion • nutrient depletion
• fertilizer • desertification • drought
• land reclamation

2 Waste Disposal and Recycling

Key Concepts

- Three methods of handling solid waste are burning, burying, and recycling. Each method has advantages and disadvantages.
- One way to help solve the solid waste problem is to practice the "three R's"—reduce, reuse, and recycle.
- Hazardous wastes that are not disposed of in carefully designed landfills may be incinerated or broken down by living organisms. Liquid wastes may be stored in deep rock layers.

Key Terms

• municipal solid waste • incineration
• leachate • sanitary landfill • recycling
• biodegradable • composting
• hazardous waste

3 Water Pollution and Solutions

Key Concepts

- Fresh water is scarce because about 97 percent of the water on Earth is salt water.
- Wastes produced by households, agriculture, industry, and mining can end up in water.
- Keeping water clean requires proper sewage treatment, the reduction of pollutants, and the effective cleanup of oil and gasoline spills.

Key Terms

• groundwater • pollutant • sewage
• pesticide • sediment

4 Air Pollution and Solutions

Key Concepts

- The major source of smog is emissions from vehicles. Acid rain is caused by emissions from some power plants and factories.
- Some indoor air pollutants only affect people who are sensitive to them. Other indoor air pollutants can affect anyone.
- The key to reducing air pollution is to control emissions.

Key Terms

• emissions • photochemical smog • ozone
• temperature inversion • acid rain • radon

5 Global Changes in the Atmosphere

Key Concepts

- A major cause of the ozone hole is a group of gases called CFCs, or chlorofluorocarbons.
- Human activities that increase carbon dioxide levels may add to the greenhouse effect.

Key Terms

• ozone layer • chlorofluorocarbon
• greenhouse effect • global warming

Review and Assessment

For: Self-Assessment
Visit: PHSchool.com
Web Code: cea-5040

Organizing Information

Concept Mapping Copy the concept map about air pollution onto a separate sheet of paper. Then complete it and add a title. (For more on Concept Mapping, see the Skills Handbook.)

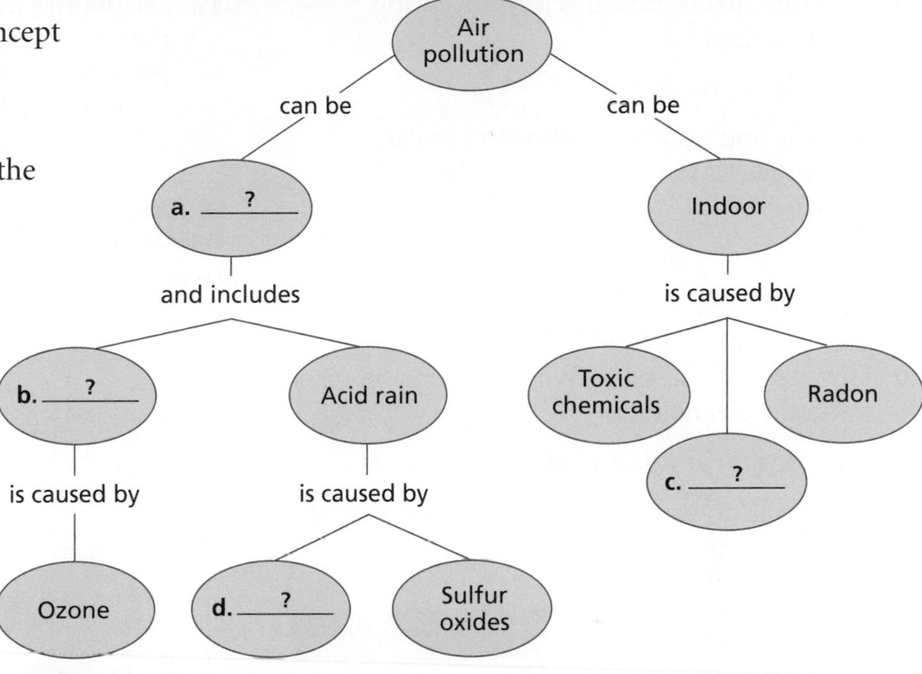

Reviewing Key Terms

Choose the letter of the best answer.

1. The advance of desert-like conditions into areas that previously were fertile is called
   a. desertification.
   b. crop rotation.
   c. nutrient depletion.
   d. land reclamation.
2. Which of the following is a biodegradable waste?
   a. a glass jar **b.** a metal can
   c. an apple core **d.** a plastic bag
3. The water and waste materials washed down toilets and sinks are called
   a. pesticides.
   b. sewage.
   c. industrial chemicals.
   d. fertilizers.
4. Pollutants that are released into the air are called
   a. emissions.
   b. leachate.
   c. sewage.
   d. sediment.
5. Which gas is thought to be one of the causes of global warming?
   a. radon
   b. ozone
   c. carbon dioxide
   d. carbon monoxide

Writing in Science

Research Report Suppose that you are an ecologist studying animals that live in a body of water near a big city. Write a report explaining how specific human activities might affect the body of water and the animals that rely on it.

Land, Water, and Air Resources
Video Preview
Video Field Trip
▶ Video Assessment

Review and Assessment

Checking Concepts

6. Describe two techniques for preventing nutrient depletion.
7. What is a drought?
8. What is one way that communities can encourage residents to produce less solid waste?
9. Explain how a person might be exposed to a hazardous substance that was buried underground many years ago.
10. How can a small oil spill in the ocean be naturally cleaned up?
11. How does acid rain form?
12. What role do water vapor and carbon dioxide play in the greenhouse effect?

Thinking Critically

13. **Problem Solving** In strip mining, a layer of soil is removed to expose a resource, such as coal, underneath. What methods could be used to restore this damaged land?
14. **Applying Concepts** Why is it unsafe to bury or incinerate radioactive waste?
15. **Making Generalizations** Would you expect the levels of photochemical smog to be worse in cities or in rural areas? Explain.
16. **Interpreting Diagrams** What process is represented in the diagram?

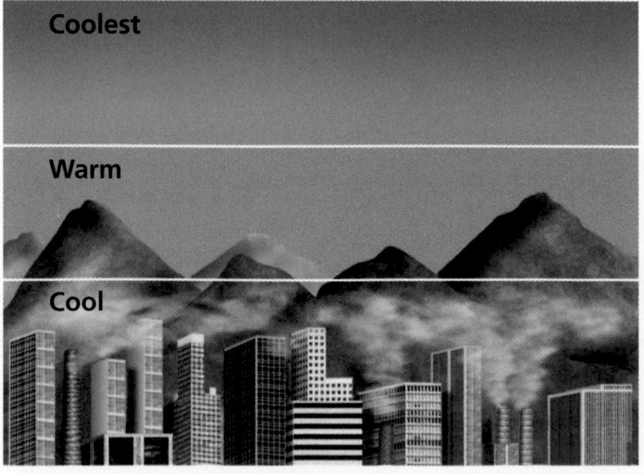

Math Practice

17. **Calculating a Concentration** The concentration of iron in one water sample is 500 parts per million. The iron concentration in a second sample is 300 parts per million. Which sample has a higher iron concentration?

Applying Skills

Use the graph showing carbon dioxide levels to answer Questions 18–21.

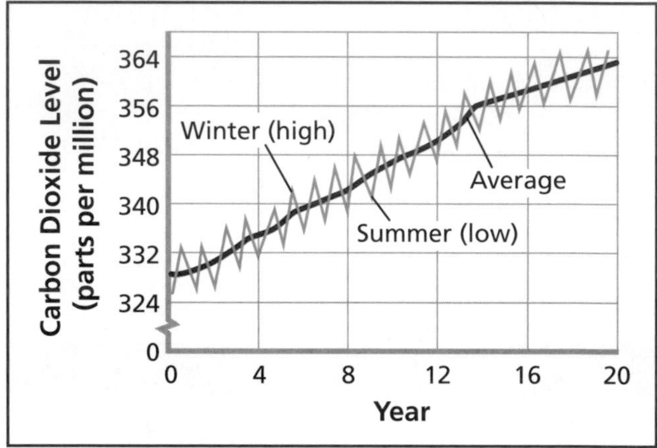

18. **Reading Graphs** What is the best title for this graph?
19. **Interpreting Data** What was the average level of carbon dioxide in the atmosphere at the beginning of the study? What was the average level of carbon dioxide in Year 20 of the study?
20. **Calculating** How much did the average level of carbon dioxide increase during the study?
21. **Developing Hypotheses** In each year of the study, the winter level of carbon dioxide was higher than the summer level. Suggest an explanation for this.

Lab zone Chapter Project

Performance Assessment Share your project with your classmates. Explain the difference between your package and the original package, including the amount and type of materials. Then demonstrate how your package protects the product at least as well as the original package.

Standardized Test Prep

Test-Taking Tip

Watching for Qualifiers *(Most, Least, Best)*

Many multiple-choice questions use qualifiers such as *most, least,* and *best.* For example, you might be asked which two organisms are MOST like each other, or what is the BEST conclusion that can be made on the basis of experimental data. When you answer that kind of question, you need to read the answer choices very carefully. Some of the answers may be partially correct. Look for the best and most-complete answer.

Sample Question

Which of the following is MOST likely to lead to desertification of farmland?

A use of fertilizers **B** irrigation
C overgrazing **D** logging

Answer

The best answer is **C**. Although choice **D** can also lead to desertification, overgrazing is more likely than logging to cause desertification of farmland.

Choose the letter of the best answer.

1. The diagram shows the different layers of soil. In which soil layer would you expect to find many species of organisms as well as rock fragments, nutrients, and decaying matter?

A Layer W
B Layer X
C Layer Y
D Layer Z

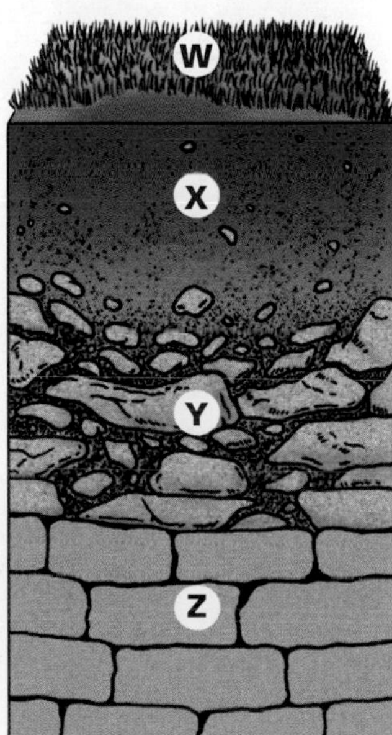

2. Farmer Brown plants corn in all of his fields every year. What is the MOST likely result of his farming methods?

F soil erosion
G nutrient depletion
H desertification
J land reclamation

3. How can sediments affect the water supply?

A They can block sunlight, preventing algae and plants from growing.
B They can cause the growth of bacteria, which use up oxygen in the water.
C They can cause algae to grow, preventing light from reaching other organisms in the water.
D They can change the temperature of the water, causing fish and other organisms to die.

4. Suppose you were to perform an experiment measuring the soil erosion resulting from different amounts of rain. What would the manipulated variable in this experiment be?

F time **G** depth of soil
H amount of rain **J** type of soil

5. The Environmental Protection Agency (EPA) monitors air quality around the country. According to the EPA, exposure to levels of sulfur dioxide in the air greater than 14 parts per million is harmful to public health and the environment. In which of the following ways could you also write this concentration of sulfur dioxide?

A $\frac{14}{10{,}000{,}000}$
B 14 to 1,000,000.
C 14 : 1,100,000.
D $\frac{140}{100{,}000}$

Constructed Response

6. Human activities are the most common causes of water pollution. List three types of human activities. Then explain how each type of activity can pollute water.

Chapter 5 Energy Resources

The BIG Idea
Energy Resources and Technology

What are the advantages and disadvantages of renewable and nonrenewable energy resources?

Chapter Preview

Well-maintained electrical lines help ensure that electrical energy continues to flow. ▶

Energy Resources

▶ Video Preview
Video Field Trip
Video Assessment

Lab zone™ Chapter **Project**

Energy Audit

How much energy does it take to keep your school running? In this chapter's project, you will work in a group to study energy use in your school.

Your Goal To report on one type of energy use in your school and make suggestions for saving energy

To complete this project, you must

- survey the types and amount of energy used in one area of your school
- identify ways to conserve energy in that area
- prepare a written report summarizing your observations and proposing your suggestions
- follow the safety guidelines in Appendix A

Plan It! Select an area of the school to study, such as a classroom, the cafeteria, or the school grounds. You could also consider the school's heating or cooling system or transportation to and from school. Then decide what type of data you will collect. When you begin your study, look for ways to reduce energy use.

Section 1

Fossil Fuels

Reading Preview

Key Concepts

- How do fuels provide energy?
- What are the three major fossil fuels?
- Why are fossil fuels considered nonrenewable resources?

Key Terms

- fuel • energy transformation
- combustion • fossil fuel
- hydrocarbon • petroleum
- refinery • petrochemical

Target Reading Skill

Building Vocabulary Using a word in a sentence helps you think about how best to explain the word. After you read the section, reread the paragraphs that contain definitions of Key Terms. Use all the information you have learned to write a meaningful sentence using each Key Term.

Lab zone Discover Activity

What's in a Piece of Coal?

1. Observe a chunk of coal. Record your observations in as much detail as possible, including its color, texture, and shape.
2. Now use a hand lens to observe the coal more closely.
3. Examine your coal for fossils—imprints of plant or animal remains.

Think It Over

Observing What did you notice when you used the hand lens compared to your first observations? What do you think coal is made of?

How did you travel to school today? Whether you traveled in a car or a bus, walked, or rode your bike, you used some form of energy. The source of that energy was a fuel. A **fuel** is a substance that provides energy—such as heat, light, motion, or electricity—as the result of a chemical change.

Energy Transformation and Fuels

Rub your hands together quickly for several seconds. Did they become warmer? When you moved your hands, they had mechanical energy, the energy of motion. The friction of your hands rubbing together converted the mechanical energy to thermal energy, which you felt as heat. A change from one form of energy to another is called an **energy transformation,** or an energy conversion.

Gasoline is a fossil fuel.

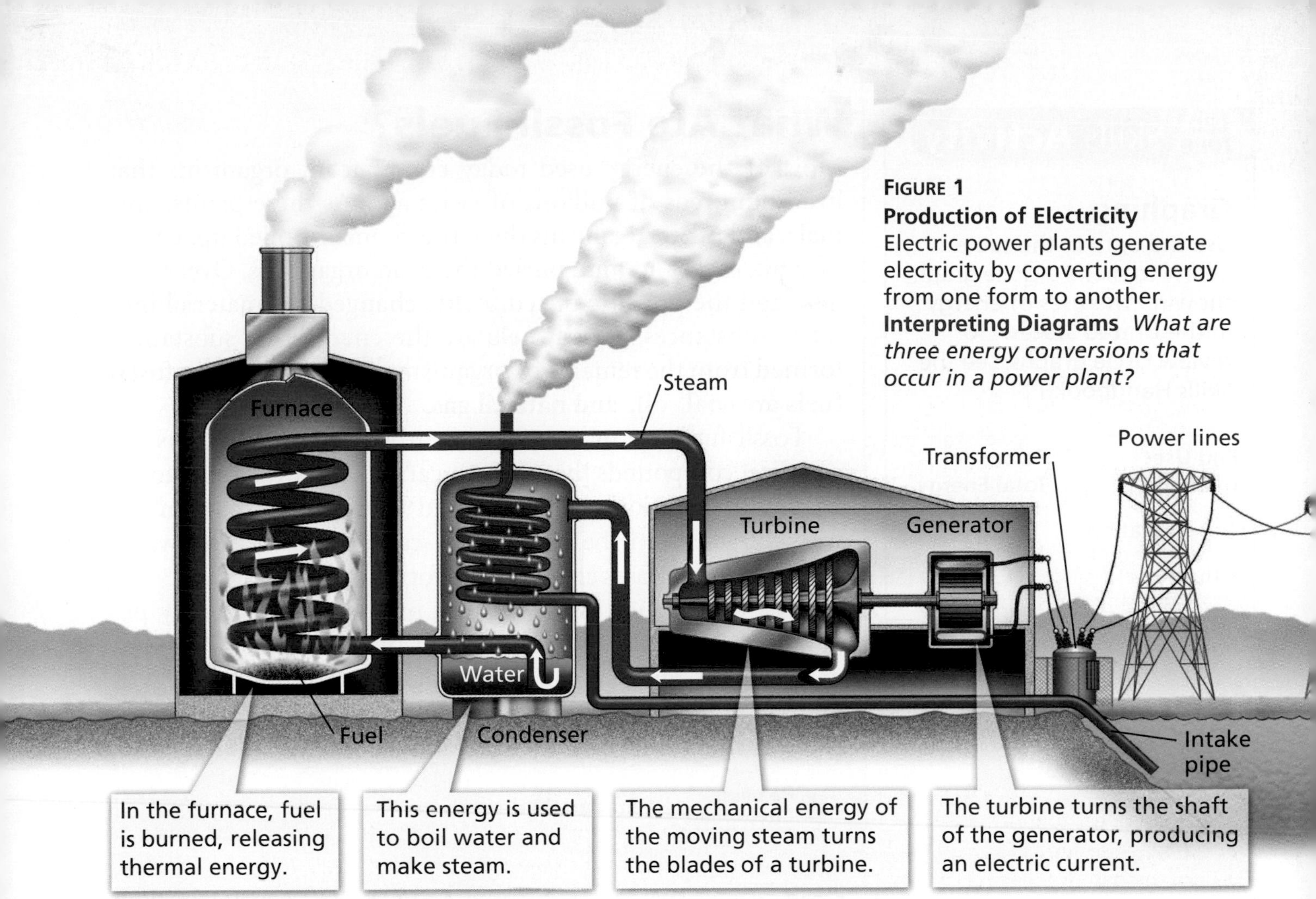

Steam

Furnace

Water

Fuel

Condenser

Turbine

Generator

Transformer

Power lines

Intake pipe

In the furnace, fuel is burned, releasing thermal energy.

This energy is used to boil water and make steam.

The mechanical energy of the moving steam turns the blades of a turbine.

The turbine turns the shaft of the generator, producing an electric current.

FIGURE 1
Production of Electricity
Electric power plants generate electricity by converting energy from one form to another.
Interpreting Diagrams *What are three energy conversions that occur in a power plant?*

Combustion Fuels contain stored chemical energy, which can be released by **combustion,** or burning. **When fuels are burned, the chemical energy that is released can be used to generate another form of energy, such as heat, light, motion, or electricity.** For example, when the gasoline in a car's engine is burned, it undergoes a chemical change. Some of the chemical energy stored in the gasoline is converted into thermal energy. This thermal energy is then converted to mechanical energy that moves the car.

Production of Electricity The chemical energy stored in fuels can be used to generate electricity. In an electric power plant, the thermal energy produced by burning fuel is used to boil water, making steam, as shown in Figure 1. The mechanical energy of the steam then turns a turbine. The turbine is connected to a generator, which consists of powerful magnets surrounded by coils of copper wire. As the magnets turn inside the wire coil, an electric current is produced. This current flows through power lines to homes and industries.

What energy transformations occur in a car's engine?

For: Links on fossil fuels
Visit: www.SciLinks.org
Web Code: scn-0551

Lab zone **Skills Activity**

Graphing

Use the data in the table below to make a circle graph showing the uses of energy in the United States. (To review circle graphs, see the Skills Handbook.)

End Use of Energy	Percent of Total Energy
Transportation	26.5
Industry	38.1
Homes and businesses	35.4

What Are Fossil Fuels?

Most of the energy used today comes from organisms that lived hundreds of millions of years ago. As these plants, animals, and other organisms died, their remains piled up. Layers of sand, rock, and mud buried the dead organisms. Over time, heat and the pressure of sediments changed the material into other substances. **Fossil fuels** are the energy-rich substances formed from the remains of organisms. **The three major fossil fuels are coal, oil, and natural gas.**

Fossil fuels are made of hydrocarbons. **Hydrocarbons** are chemical compounds that contain carbon and hydrogen atoms. During combustion, the carbon and hydrogen atoms combine with oxygen from the air to form carbon dioxide and water. Combustion releases energy in the forms of heat and light.

The combustion of fossil fuels provides more energy per kilogram than does the combustion of other fuels. One kilogram of coal, for example, can provide twice as much energy as one kilogram of wood. Oil and natural gas can provide three times as much energy as an equal mass of wood.

What are hydrocarbons?

Coal Coal is a solid fossil fuel formed from plant remains. Figure 2 shows the process by which coal forms. People have burned coal to produce heat for thousands of years. Wood was more convenient and cheaper than coal for most people until the Industrial Revolution of the 1800s, however. The huge energy needs of growing industries then made it worthwhile to find, mine, and transport coal. Today, coal makes up about 23 percent of the fuel used in the United States. Most of that coal fuels electrical power plants.

Before coal can be used to produce energy, it has to be mined, or removed from the ground. Miners use machines to chop the coal into chunks and lift it to the surface. Coal mining can be a dangerous job. Thousands of miners have been killed or injured in accidents in the mines. Many more suffer from lung diseases. Fortunately, modern safety procedures and better equipment have made coal mining safer.

Coal is the most plentiful fossil fuel in the United States. It is fairly easy to transport and provides a lot of energy when burned. But coal also has some disadvantages. Coal mining can increase erosion. Runoff from coal mines can cause water pollution. Burning most types of coal results in more air pollution than other fossil fuels. And coal mining can be dangerous.

FIGURE 2
Coal Formation
Coal is formed from the remains of trees and other plants that grew in swamps hundreds of millions of years ago. **Relating Diagrams and Photos** *What are two ways that peat and coal differ?*

Decomposing Plant Matter
When swamp plants die, their decomposing remains build up.

Peat
Over time, plant remains pile up and form peat. Peat can be burned as fuel.

Coal
Under increasing pressure from sediments, peat is compacted. Eventually, peat becomes coal. Coal is a more efficient fuel than peat.

FIGURE 3
Oil Production
Crude oil is first pumped out of the ground and then refined. In the refining process, crude oil is heated and separated to make different products.

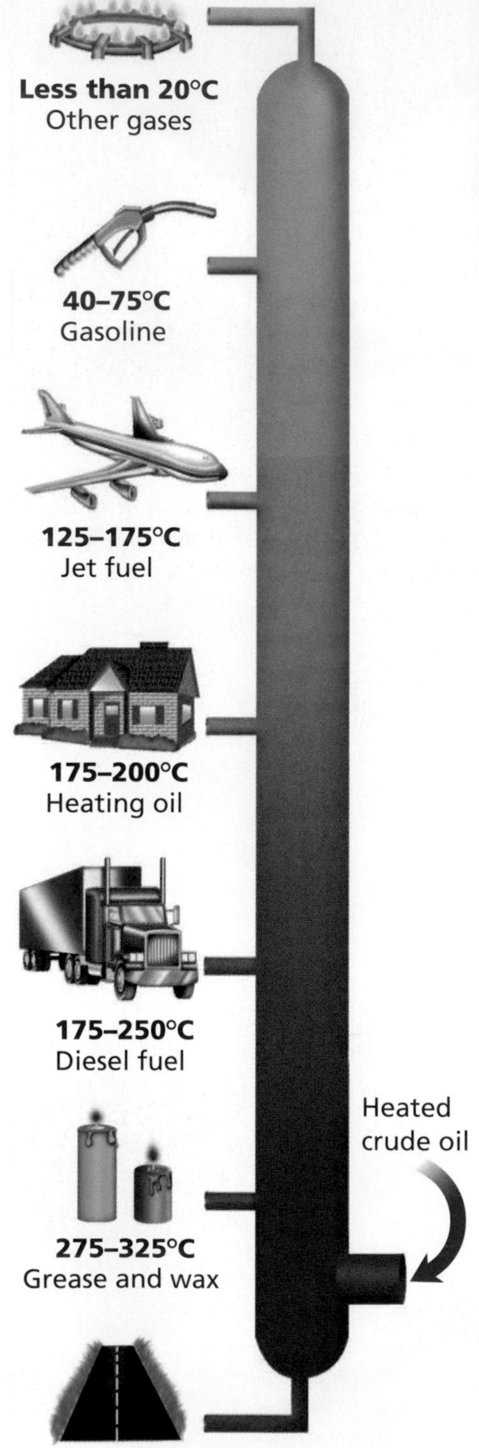

Oil Oil is a thick, black, liquid fossil fuel. It formed from the remains of small animals, algae, and other organisms that lived in oceans and shallow inland seas hundreds of millions of years ago. **Petroleum** is another name for oil, from the Latin words *petra* (rock) and *oleum* (oil). Petroleum accounts for more than one third of the energy produced in the world. Fuel for most cars, airplanes, trains, and ships comes from petroleum. In addition, many homes are heated by oil.

Most oil deposits are located underground in tiny holes in sandstone or limestone. The oil fills the holes somewhat like the way water fills the holes of a sponge. Because oil deposits are usually located deep below the surface, finding oil is difficult. Scientists can use sound waves to test an area for oil. Even using this technique, however, only about one out of every six wells drilled produces a usable amount of oil.

When oil is first pumped out of the ground, it is called crude oil. To be made into useful products, crude oil must undergo a process called refining. A factory in which crude oil is heated and separated into fuels and other products is called a **refinery.** In Figure 3, you can see some of the products made by refining crude oil. Many other products you use every day are also made from crude oil. **Petrochemicals** are compounds that are made from oil. Petrochemicals are used to make plastics, paints, medicines, and cosmetics.

What is a refinery?

Natural Gas Natural gas is a mixture of methane and other gases. Natural gas forms from some of the same organisms as oil. Because it is less dense than oil, natural gas often rises above an oil deposit, forming a pocket of gas in the rock.

Pipelines transport natural gas from its source to the places where it is used. If all the gas pipelines in the United States were connected, they would reach to the moon and back—twice! Natural gas can also be compressed into a liquid and stored in tanks as fuel for trucks and buses.

Natural gas has several advantages. It produces large amounts of energy but lower levels of many air pollutants than coal or oil. It is also easy to transport once the network of pipelines is built. One disadvantage of natural gas is that it is highly flammable. A gas leak can cause a violent explosion and fire.

Gas companies help to prevent dangerous explosions from leaks. If you use natural gas in your home, you probably are familiar with the "gas" smell that alerts you whenever there is unburned gas in the air. You may be surprised to learn that natural gas actually has no odor at all. What causes the strong smell? Gas companies add a chemical with a distinct smell to the gas before it is piped to homes and businesses so that people can detect a gas leak.

FIGURE 4
Natural Gas Pipelines
More than 2,500,000 kilometers of natural gas pipelines run underground in the United States. Here, a technician prepares a new section of pipe.

Math Analyzing Data

Fuels and Electricity

The circle graph shows which energy sources are used to produce electricity in the United States.

1. **Reading Graphs** What does each wedge of the circle represent?
2. **Interpreting Data** Which energy source is used to generate most of the electricity in the United States?
3. **Drawing Conclusions** What percentage of the electricity production in the United States relies on fossil fuels?
4. **Predicting** How might the circle graph differ 50 years from now? Give reasons to support your prediction.

United States Electricity Production by Energy Source

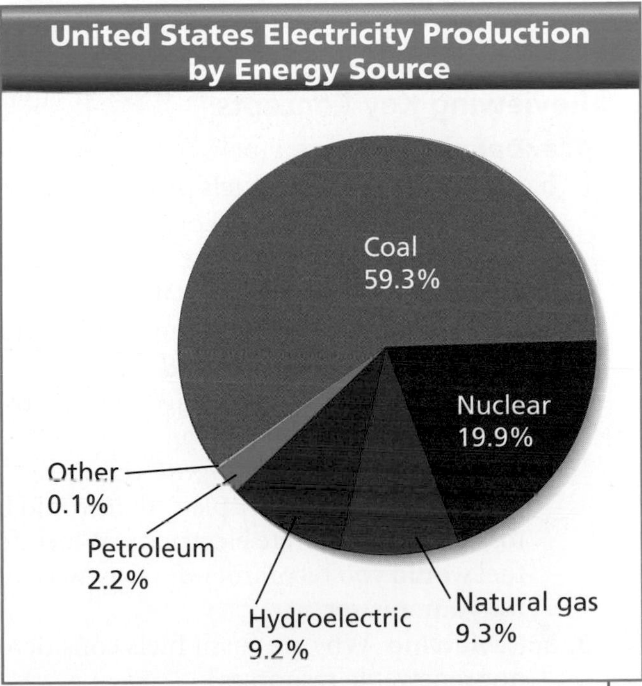

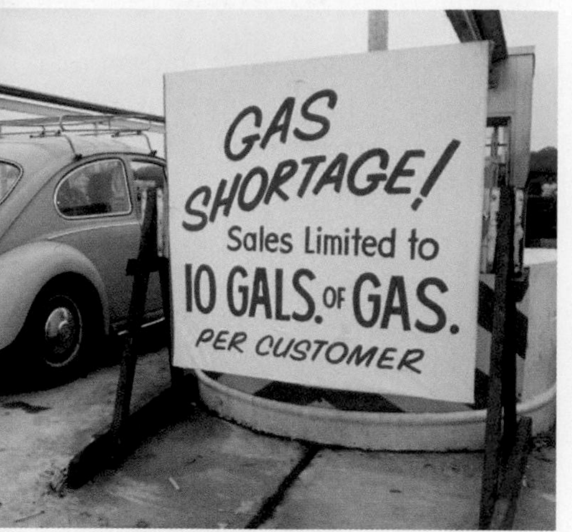

FIGURE 5
Supply and Demand
In the 1970s, a group of oil-exporting nations reduced their oil exports to the United States. Gasoline shortages resulted.

Fuel Supply and Demand

The many advantages of using fossil fuels as an energy source have made them essential to modern life. **But since fossil fuels take hundreds of millions of years to form, they are considered nonrenewable resources.** For example, Earth's known oil reserves took 500 million years to form. One fourth of this oil has already been used. If fossil fuels continue to be used more rapidly than they are formed, the reserves will eventually be used up.

Many nations that consume large amounts of fossil fuels have very small reserves. They have to buy oil, natural gas, and coal from nations with large supplies. The United States, for example, uses about one third of all the oil produced in the world. But only 3 percent of the world's oil supply is located in this country. The difference must be purchased from countries with large oil supplies. The uneven distribution of fossil fuel reserves has often been a cause of political problems in the world.

Why are some nations dependent on others for fossil fuels?

Section 1 Assessment

Target Reading Skill Building Vocabulary Use your sentences to help you answer the questions below.

Reviewing Key Concepts

1. a. **Defining** What is a fuel?
   b. **Explaining** How do fuels provide energy?
   c. **Sequencing** Describe in order the energy transformations that occur in the production of electricity at a power plant.
2. a. **Listing** What are the three main fossil fuels?
   b. **Comparing and Contrasting** List an advantage and a disadvantage of each fossil fuel discussed in this section.
   c. **Making Judgments** Suppose you were designing a new power plant that would burn fossil fuel to generate electricity. Which fossil fuel would you recommend? Give two reasons for your answer.
3. a. **Reviewing** Why are fossil fuels considered nonrenewable resources?
   b. **Problem Solving** List three things you can do to reduce your dependence on fossil fuels.

Lab zone At-Home Activity

Heating Fuel Pros and Cons Talk to an adult family member to find out what type of fuel heats or cools your home. Then, with the family member, list some advantages and disadvantages of that type of fuel. Share what you learned with your classmates. What fuel source is used by the majority of students in your class?

Section 2

• Tech & Design •

Renewable Sources of Energy

Reading Preview

Key Concepts

- What forms of energy does the sun provide?
- What are some renewable sources of energy?

Key Terms

- solar energy
- hydroelectric power
- biomass fuel
- gasohol
- geothermal energy

Target Reading Skill

Previewing Visuals Before you read, preview Figure 7. Then write two questions that you have about the diagram in a graphic organizer like the one below. As you read, answer your questions.

Solar House

Q. How does the house capture solar energy?
A.
Q.

Lab zone Discover Activity

Can You Capture Solar Energy?

1. Pour 250 milliliters of water into each of two resealable, clear plastic bags.
2. Record the water temperature in each bag. Seal the bags.
3. Put one bag in a dark or shady place. Put the other bag in a place where it will receive direct sunlight.
4. Predict what the temperature of the water in each bag will be after 30 minutes.
5. Record the temperatures after 30 minutes.

Think It Over

Developing Hypotheses How did the water temperature in each bag change? What could account for these results?

You've just arrived at the campsite for your family vacation. The sun streaming through the trees warms your face. A breeze stirs, carrying with it the smell of a campfire. Maybe you'll start your day with a dip in the warm water of a nearby hot spring.

You might be surprised to learn that even in these woods, you are surrounded by energy resources. The sun warms the air, the wind blows, and heat from inside Earth warms the waters of the spring. These sources of energy are all renewable—they are constantly being supplied. Scientists are trying to find ways to put these renewable energy resources to work to meet people's energy needs.

Campers surrounded by renewable resources ▶

Harnessing the Sun's Energy

The warmth you feel on a sunny day is **solar energy,** or energy from the sun. **The sun constantly gives off energy in the forms of light and heat.** Solar energy is the source, directly or indirectly, of most other renewable energy resources. In one day, Earth receives enough solar energy to meet the energy needs of the entire world for 40 years. Solar energy does not cause pollution, and it will not run out for billions of years.

So why hasn't solar energy replaced energy from fossil fuels? One reason is that solar energy is only available when the sun is shining. Another problem is that the energy Earth receives from the sun is very spread out. To obtain a useful amount of power, it is necessary to collect solar energy from a large area.

FIGURE 6
Solar Collector
This mirror collects energy from the sun and powers an electric plant in New South Wales, Australia. **Inferring** *Why is the Australian desert a practical location for a solar power plant?*

Solar Power Plants One way to capture the sun's energy involves using giant mirrors. In a solar power plant, rows of mirrors focus the sun's rays to heat a tank of water. The water boils, creating steam, which can then be used to generate electricity.

Solar Cells Solar energy can be converted directly into electricity in a solar cell. A solar cell has a negative and a positive terminal, like a battery. When light hits the cell, an electric current is produced. Solar cells power some calculators, lights, and other small devices. However, it would take more than 5,000 solar cells the size of your palm to produce enough electricity for a typical American home.

Passive Solar Heating Solar energy can be used to heat buildings with passive solar systems. A passive solar system converts sunlight into thermal energy, which is then distributed without using pumps or fans. Passive solar heating is what occurs in a parked car on a sunny day. Solar energy passes through the car's windows and heats the seats and other car parts. These parts transfer heat to the air, and the inside of the car warms. The same principle can be used to heat a home.

Active Solar Heating An active solar system captures the sun's energy, and then uses pumps and fans to distribute the heat. First, light strikes the dark metal surface of a solar collector. There, it is converted to thermal energy. Water is pumped through pipes in the solar collector to absorb the thermal energy. The heated water then flows to a storage tank. Finally, pumps and fans distribute the heat throughout the building.

How do solar cells work?

FIGURE 7
Solar House

A solar house uses passive and active heating systems to convert solar energy into heat and electricity.

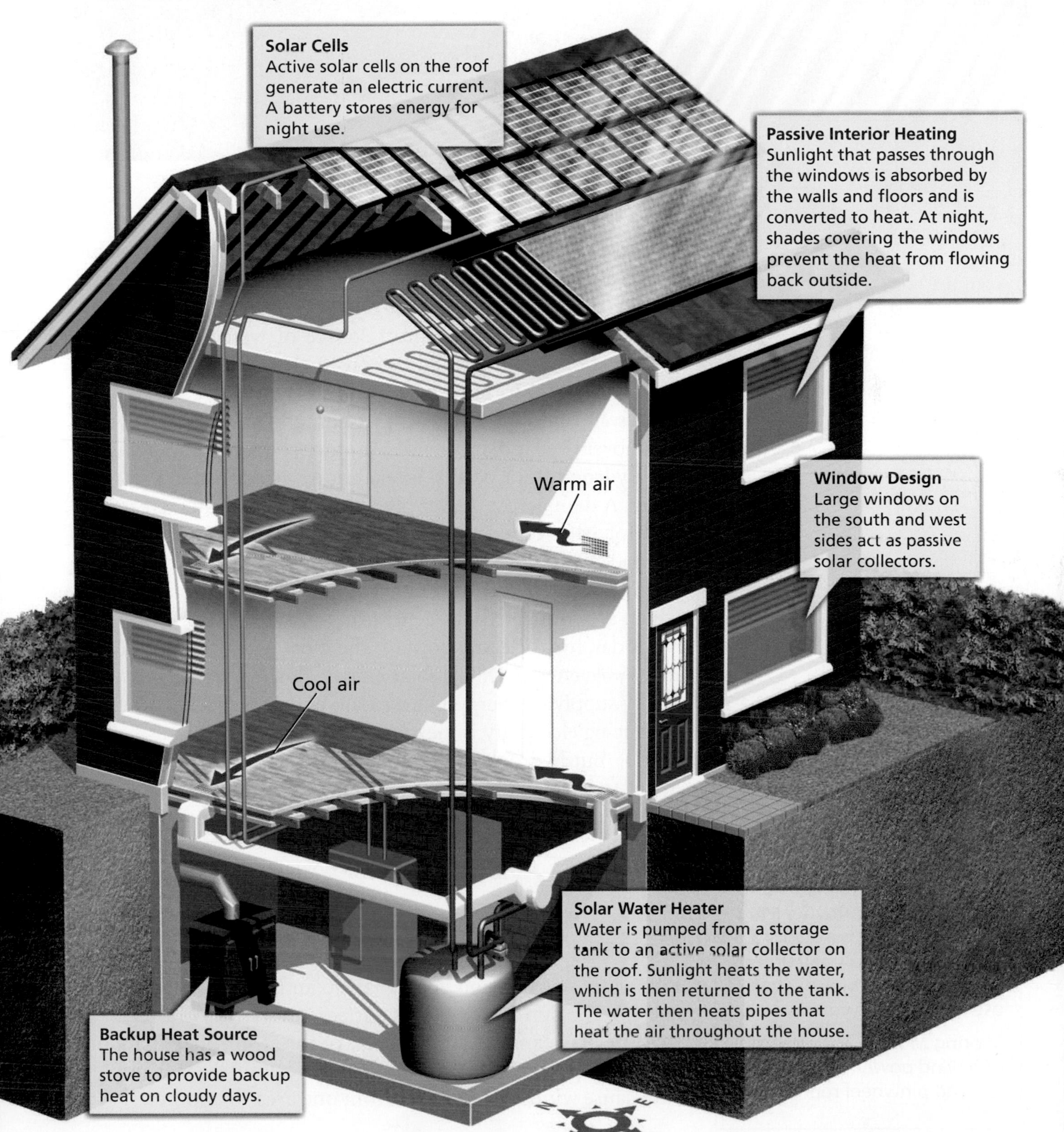

FIGURE 8
Water and Wind Power
Both this dam in Arizona and this wind farm in California use renewable sources of energy to generate power.

Hydroelectric Power

The sun is one source of renewable energy. **Other renewable sources of energy include water, the wind, biomass fuels, geothermal energy, and hydrogen.**

Solar energy is the indirect source of water power. Recall that in the water cycle, energy from the sun heats water on Earth's surface, forming water vapor. The water vapor condenses and falls back to Earth as rain and snow. As the water flows over the land, it provides another source of energy.

Hydroelectric power is electricity produced by flowing water. A dam across a river blocks the flow of water, creating a body of water called a reservoir. When a dam's control gates are opened, water flows through tunnels at the bottom of the dam. As the water moves through the tunnels, it turns turbines, which are connected to a generator.

Today, hydroelectric power is the most widely used source of renewable energy. Unlike solar energy, flowing water provides a steady supply of energy. Once a dam and power plant are built, producing electricity is inexpensive and does not create air pollution. But hydroelectric power has limitations. In the United States, most suitable rivers have already been dammed. And dams can have negative effects on the environment.

What is hydroelectric power?

Capturing the Wind

Like water power, wind energy is also an indirect form of solar energy. The sun heats Earth's surface unevenly. As a result of this uneven heating, different areas of the atmosphere have different temperatures and air pressures. The differences in pressure cause winds as air moves from one area to another.

Lab zone Try This Activity

Blowing in the Wind

You can make a model that shows how wind can do the work necessary to produce energy. Using a pinwheel and other materials, construct a device that lifts a small object when the wind blows. Then use a fan to test your device.

Making Models What parts of a wind power plant do the fan and pinwheel represent?

Wind can be used to turn a turbine and generate electricity. Wind farms consist of many windmills. Together, the windmills generate large amounts of power.

Wind is the fastest-growing energy source in the world. Wind energy does not cause pollution. In places where fuels are difficult to transport, wind energy is the major source of power.

But wind energy has drawbacks. Few places have winds that blow steadily enough to provide much energy. Wind energy generators are noisy and can be destroyed by very strong winds. Still, as fossil fuels become more scarce, wind energy will become more important.

FIGURE 9
Biomass Fuels
Biomass fuels are fuels that are made from living things.
Comparing and Contrasting *How are biomass fuels similar to energy sources such as wind and water? How are they different?*

Biomass Fuels

Wood was probably the first fuel ever used for heat and light. Wood belongs to a group of fuels called **biomass fuels,** which are made from living things. Other biomass fuels include leaves, food wastes, and even manure. As fossil fuel supplies shrink, people are taking a closer look at biomass fuels. For example, when oil prices rose in the early 1970s, Hawaiian sugar cane farmers began burning sugar cane wastes to generate electricity. At one point, these wastes provided almost one fourth of the electricity used on the island of Kauai.

▲ A woman uses a wood-fired oven in Nepal.

Aside from being burned as fuel, biomass materials can also be converted into other fuels. For example, corn, sugar cane, and other crops can be used to make alcohol. Adding the alcohol to gasoline forms a mixture called **gasohol.** Gasohol can be used as fuel for cars. Bacteria can produce methane gas when they decompose biomass materials in landfills. That methane can be used to heat buildings. And some crops, such as soybeans, can produce oil that can be used as fuel, which is called biodiesel fuel.

▲ This car runs on vegetable oil.

Biomass fuels are renewable resources. But it takes time for new trees to replace those that have been cut down. And producing alcohol and methane in large quantities is expensive. As a result, biomass fuels are not widely used today in the United States. But as fossil fuels become scarcer, biomass fuels may play a larger role in meeting energy needs.

Reading Checkpoint **What is gasohol?**

For: Links on renewable energy
Visit: www.SciLinks.org
Web Code: scn-0552

Tapping Earth's Energy

Below Earth's surface are pockets of very hot liquid rock called magma. In some places, magma is very close to the surface. The intense heat from Earth's interior that warms the magma is called **geothermal energy.**

In certain regions, such as Iceland and New Zealand, magma heats underground water to the boiling point. In these places, the hot water and steam can be valuable sources of energy. For example, in Reykjavík, Iceland, 90 percent of homes are heated by water warmed underground in this way. Geothermal energy can also be used to generate electricity, as shown in Figure 10.

Geothermal energy is an unlimited source of cheap energy. But it does have disadvantages. There are only a few places where magma comes close to Earth's surface. Elsewhere, very deep wells would be needed to tap this energy. Drilling deep wells is very expensive. Even so, geothermal energy is likely to play a part in meeting energy needs in the future.

How can geothermal energy be used to generate electricity?

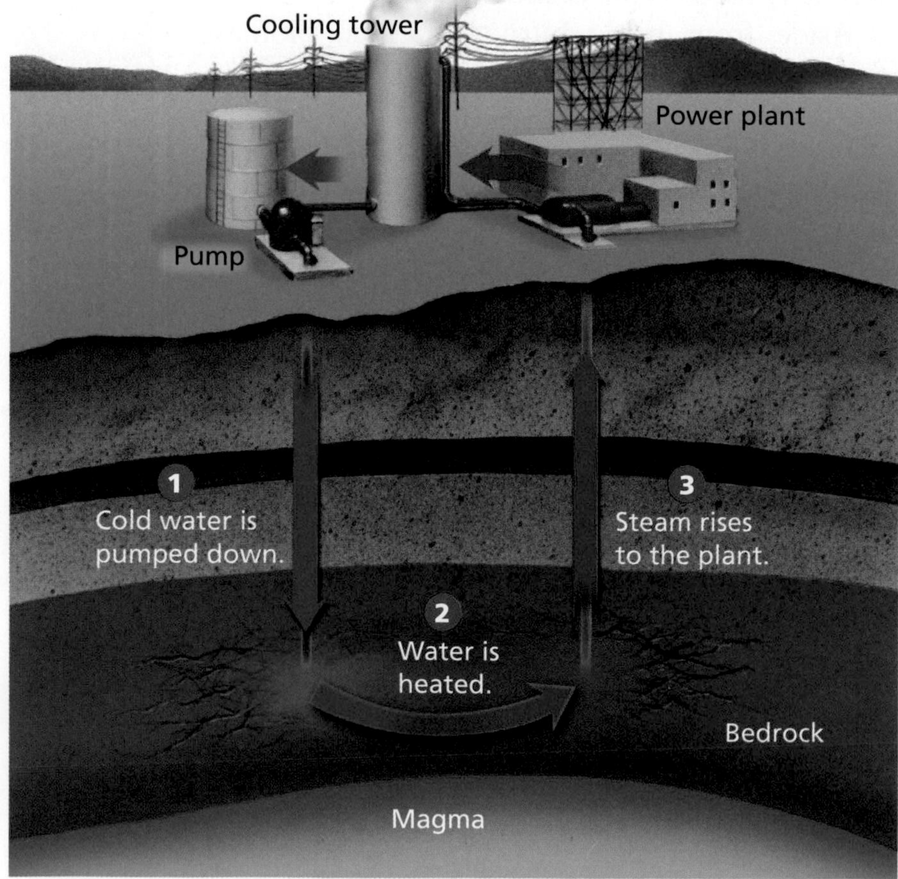

FIGURE 10
Geothermal Energy
A geothermal power plant uses heat from Earth's interior as an energy source. Cold water is piped deep into the ground, where it is heated by magma. The resulting steam can be used for heat or to generate electricity.
Making Generalizations *What is one advantage and one disadvantage of geothermal energy?*

The Promise of Hydrogen Power

Now that you have read about so many energy sources, consider a fuel with this description: It burns cleanly. It creates no smog or acid rain. It exists on Earth in large supply.

This ideal-sounding fuel is real—it's hydrogen. Unfortunately, almost all the hydrogen on Earth is combined with oxygen in water. Pure hydrogen can be obtained by passing an electric current through water. But it takes more energy to obtain the hydrogen than is produced by burning it.

Still, scientists find hydrogen power promising. At present, hydroelectric plants decrease their activity when the demand for electricity is low. Instead, they could run at full capacity all the time, using the excess electricity to produce hydrogen. Similarly, solar power plants often generate more electricity than is needed during the day. This extra electricity could be used to produce hydrogen. Scientists are also searching for other ways to produce hydrogen cheaply from water.

Car manufacturers are now developing cars that run on hydrogen fuel cells. These would produce water as emissions. That water might then be used again as fuel. You can see that if scientists can find a way to produce hydrogen cheaply, it could someday be an important source of energy.

Reading Checkpoint In what common substance is most hydrogen on Earth found?

FIGURE 11
Hydrogen Power
The object fascinating these astronauts is a bubble of water—the harmless byproduct of the hydrogen fuel cells used on the space shuttle.

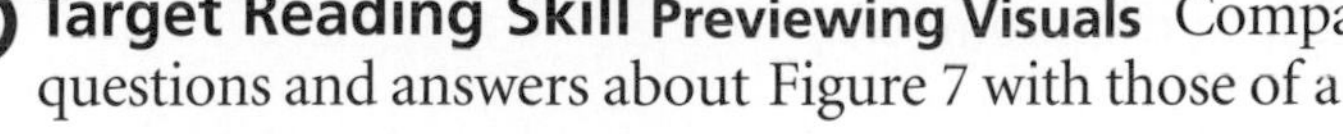

Section 2 Assessment

Target Reading Skill Previewing Visuals Compare your questions and answers about Figure 7 with those of a partner.

Reviewing Key Concepts

1. a. **Identifying** What two forms of energy does the sun supply?
   b. **Explaining** What are two reasons that solar energy has not replaced energy from fossil fuels?
   c. **Applying Concepts** A friend of yours argues that shopping malls should use solar energy to conserve fossil fuels. How would you respond?
2. a. **Listing** List five renewable energy sources other than solar energy.
   b. **Classifying** Which of the renewable energy sources that you listed are actually indirect forms of solar energy? Explain.
   c. **Predicting** Which source of renewable energy do you think is most likely to be used in your community in 50 years? Give reasons to support your answer.

Writing in Science

Advertisement Write an advertisement for one of the renewable energy sources discussed in this section. Be sure to mention how its advantages make it superior to the other energy sources. Also mention how scientists might be able to overcome its disadvantages.

Lab zone

Technology Lab

• Tech & Design •

Design and Build a Solar Cooker

Problem

What is the best shape for a solar cooker?

Skills Focus

designing a solution, evaluating the design

Materials

- scissors
- frozen vegetables
- 3 sheets of aluminum foil
- 3 sheets of oaktag paper
- wooden or plastic stirrers
- glue
- 3 thermometers
- tape
- clock or watch
- optional materials provided by your teacher

Procedure  

PART 1 Research and Investigate

1. Glue a sheet of aluminum foil, shiny side up, to each sheet of oaktag paper. Before the glue dries, gently smooth out any wrinkles in the foil.
2. Bend one sheet into a U shape. Leave another sheet flat. Bend another sheet into a shape of your own choosing.
3. Predict which shape will produce the largest temperature increase when placed in the sun. Write down your prediction and explain your reasons.
4. Place the aluminum sheets in direct sunlight. Use wood blocks or books to hold the sheets in position, if necessary.
5. Record the starting temperature on each thermometer.
6. Place the thermometer bulbs in the center of the aluminum shapes. After 15 minutes, record the final temperature on each thermometer.

PART 2 Design and Build

7. Using what you learned in Part 1, design a solar cooker that can cook frozen vegetables. Your solar cooker should
   - be no larger than 50 cm on any side
   - cook the vegetables in less than 10 minutes
   - be made of materials approved by your teacher
8. Prepare a written description of your plan that includes a sketch of your cooker. Include a list of materials and an operational definition of a "well-cooked" vegetable. Obtain your teacher's approval for your design. Then build your solar cooker.

PART 3 Evaluate and Redesign

9. Test your solar cooker by spearing some frozen vegetables on the stirrers. Time how long it takes to cook the vegetables. Make note of any problems with your solar cooker design.
10. Based on your test, decide how you could improve the design of your cooker. Then make any desired changes to your cooker and test how the improved cooker functions.

Analyze and Conclude

1. **Identifying a Need** In what situations might it be important to have an efficient cooker that does not use fuel?
2. **Designing a Solution** How did you incorporate what you learned in Part 1 into your design in Part 2? For example, which shape did you use in your cooker design?
3. **Evaluating the Design** When you tested your solar cooker, what problems did you encounter?
4. **Redesigning** In what ways did you change your design for your second test? How did the redesign improve the performance of your cooker?
5. **Working With Design Constraints** Why might it be important for solar cookers to use inexpensive, readily available materials?
6. **Evaluating the Impact on Society** How can solar-powered devices help meet the world's future energy needs? What limitation do solar-powered devices have?

Communicate

Design an advertisement for your solar cooker that will appear in a camping magazine. Make sure your ad describes the benefits of solar cookers in general, and of your design in particular.

Section 3

Nuclear Energy

Reading Preview

Key Concepts

- What happens during a nuclear fission reaction?
- How does a nuclear power plant produce electricity?
- How does a nuclear fusion reaction occur?

Key Terms

- nucleus
- nuclear fission
- reactor vessel
- fuel rod
- control rod
- meltdown
- nuclear fusion

Target Reading Skill

Comparing and Contrasting

As you read, compare fission and fusion reactions in a Venn diagram like the one below. Write the similarities in the space where the circles overlap and the differences on the left and right sides.

Nuclear Fission **Nuclear Fusion**

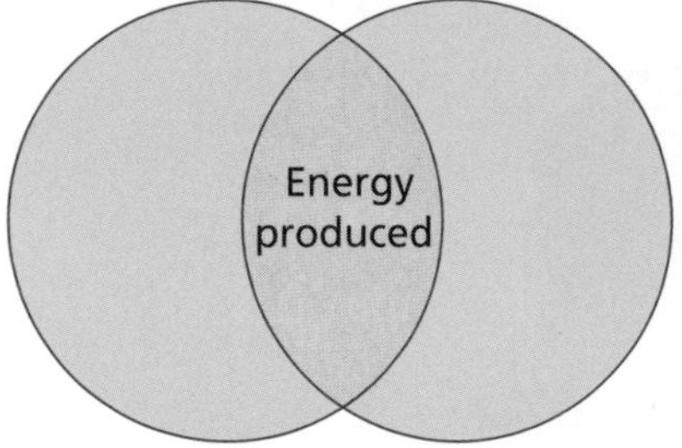

Lab zone Discover **Activity**

Why Do They Fall?

1. Line up 15 dominoes to form a triangle.
2. Knock over the first domino so that it falls against the second row of dominoes. Observe the results.
3. Set up the dominoes again, but then remove the dominoes in the third row from the lineup.
4. Knock over the first domino again. Observe what happens.

Think It Over

Inferring Suppose each domino produced a large amount of energy when it fell over. Why might it be helpful to remove the dominoes as you did in Step 3?

Wouldn't it be great if people could use the same method as the sun to produce energy? In a way, they can! The kind of reactions that power the sun involve the central cores of atoms. The central core of an atom that contains the protons and neutrons is called the **nucleus** (plural *nuclei*). Reactions that involve nuclei, called nuclear reactions, result in tremendous amounts of energy. Two types of nuclear reactions are fission and fusion.

Nuclear Fission

Nuclear reactions convert matter into energy. As part of his theory of relativity, Albert Einstein developed a formula that described the relationship between energy and matter. You have probably seen this famous equation: $E = mc^2$. In the equation, the E represents energy and the m represents mass. The c, which represents the speed of light, is a very large number. This equation states that when matter is changed into energy, an enormous amount of energy is released.

▲ **Albert Einstein 1879–1955**

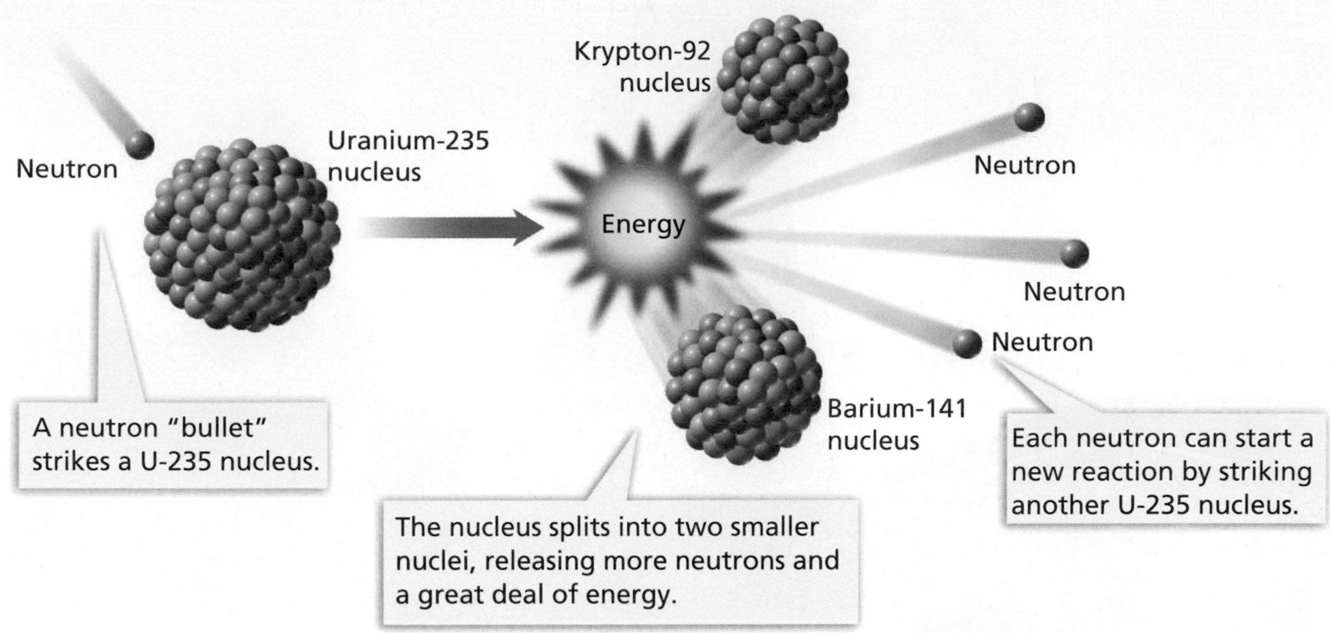

FIGURE 12
Nuclear Fission
A great deal of energy is released in a nuclear fission reaction.
Interpreting Diagrams *How does a nuclear fission reaction begin?*

Fission Reactions **Nuclear fission** is the splitting of an atom's nucleus into two smaller nuclei. The fuel for the reaction is a large atom that has an unstable nucleus, such as uranium-235 (U-235). A neutron is shot at the U-235 atom at high speed. **When the neutron hits the U-235 nucleus, the nucleus splits apart into two smaller nuclei and two or more neutrons.** The total mass of all these particles is a bit less than the mass of the original nucleus. The small amount of mass that makes up the difference has been converted into energy—a lot of energy, as described by Einstein's equation.

Meanwhile, the fission reaction has produced three more neutrons. If any of these neutrons strikes another nucleus, the fission reaction is repeated. More neutrons and more energy are released. If there are enough nuclei nearby, the process repeats in a chain reaction, just like a row of dominoes falling. In a nuclear chain reaction, the amount of energy released increases rapidly with each step in the chain.

Energy From Fission What happens to all the energy released by these fission reactions? If a nuclear chain reaction is not controlled, the released energy causes a huge explosion. The explosion of an atomic bomb is an uncontrolled nuclear fission reaction. A few kilograms of matter explode with more force than several thousand tons of dynamite. However, if the chain reaction is controlled, the energy is released as heat, which can be used to generate electricity.

What happens if a nuclear chain reaction is not controlled?

Lab zone Skills Activity

Calculating

A pellet of U-235 produces as much energy as 615 liters of fuel oil. An average home uses 5,000 liters of oil a year. How many U-235 pellets would be needed to supply the same amount of energy?

FIGURE 13
Nuclear Power
Nuclear power plants generate much of the world's electricity. The inset shows autunite, one of the ores of uranium. The uranium fuel for nuclear power plants is refined from uranium ores.

Nuclear Power Plants

Controlled nuclear fission reactions take place inside nuclear power plants. Nuclear power plants generate much of the world's electricity—about 20 percent in the United States and more than 70 percent in France. **In a nuclear power plant, the heat released from fission reactions is used to change water into steam. The steam then turns the blades of a turbine to generate electricity.** Look at the diagram of a nuclear power plant in Figure 14. In addition to the generator, it has two main parts: the reactor vessel and the heat exchanger.

Reactor Vessel The **reactor vessel** is the part of the nuclear reactor where nuclear fission occurs. The reactor contains rods of U-235, called **fuel rods.** When several fuel rods are placed close together, a series of fission reactions occurs.

If the reactor vessel gets too hot, control rods are used to slow down the chain reactions. **Control rods,** made of the metal cadmium, are inserted between the fuel rods. The cadmium absorbs neutrons released during fission and slows the speed of the chain reactions. The cadmium control rods can then be removed to speed up the chain reactions again.

Heat Exchanger Heat is removed from the reactor vessel by water or another fluid that is pumped through the reactor. This fluid passes through a heat exchanger. There, the fluid boils water to produce steam, which runs the electrical generator. The steam is condensed again and pumped back to the heat exchanger.

What is the purpose of a control rod?

The Risks of Nuclear Power At first, people thought that nuclear fission would provide an almost unlimited source of clean, safe energy. But accidents at nuclear power plants have led to safety concerns. In 1986, the reactor vessel in a nuclear power plant in Chernobyl, Ukraine, overheated. The fuel rods generated so much heat that they started to melt, a condition called a **meltdown.** The excess heat caused a series of explosions, which injured or killed dozens of people. In addition, radioactive materials escaped into the environment.

Accidents can be avoided by careful planning and improved safety features. A more difficult problem is the disposal of the radioactive wastes. Radioactive wastes remain dangerous for many thousands of years. Scientists must find a way to store these wastes safely for a long period of time.

Go Online
active art
For: Nuclear Power Plant activity
Visit: PHSchool.com
Web Code: cep-5053

FIGURE 14
Nuclear Power Plant
Nuclear fission provides the energy to generate electricity in a nuclear power plant. **Interpreting Diagrams** *In what part of the power plant does nuclear fission occur?*

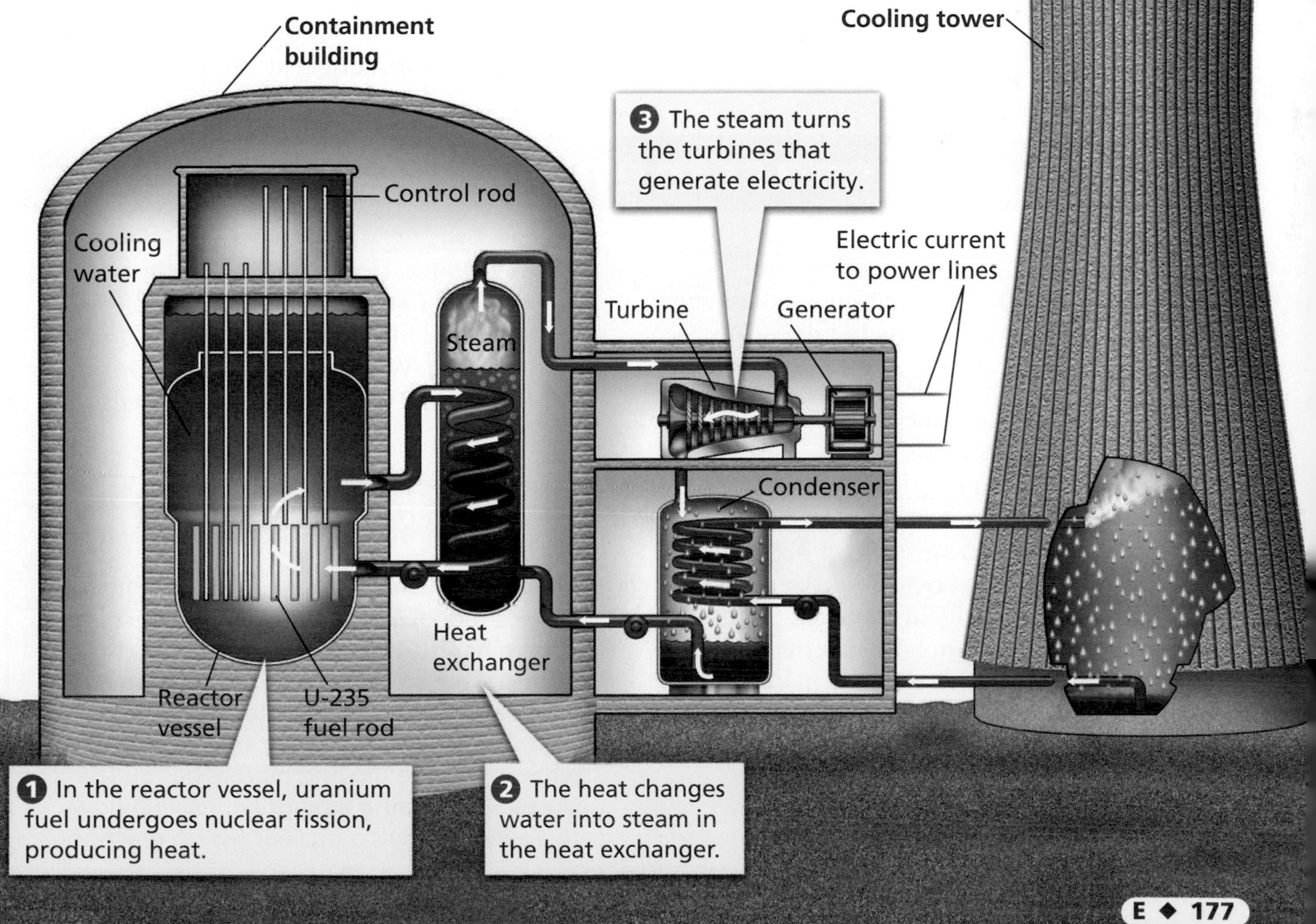

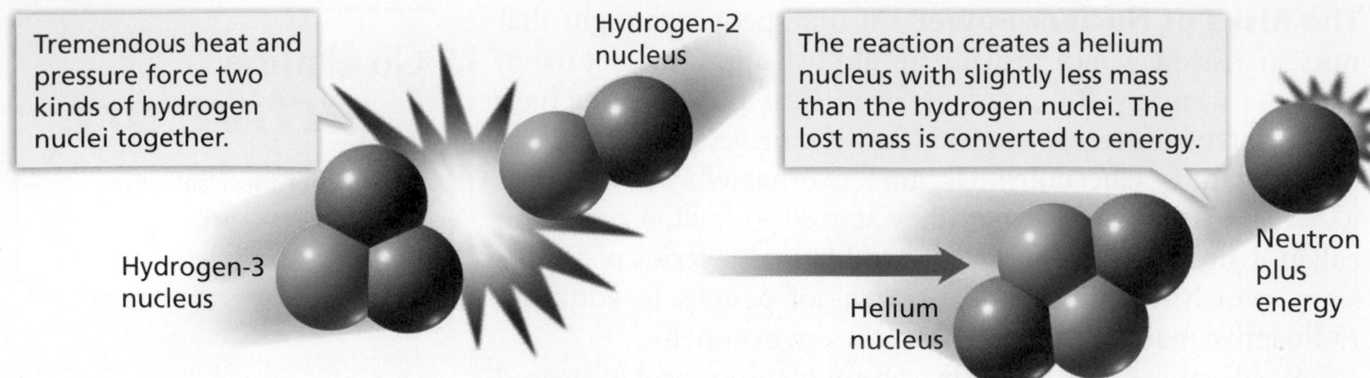

FIGURE 15
Nuclear Fusion
In nuclear fusion, two hydrogen nuclei are forced together, forming a helium nucleus, a neutron, and energy.
Interpreting Diagrams *What is released during a fusion reaction?*

The Quest to Control Fusion

Nuclear fusion is the combining of two atomic nuclei to produce a single larger nucleus. **In nuclear fusion, two hydrogen nuclei combine to create a helium nucleus, which has slightly less mass than the two hydrogen nuclei. The lost mass is converted to energy.**

Nuclear fusion could produce much more energy per unit of atomic mass than nuclear fission. The fuel for a fusion reactor is readily available—water contains one kind of hydrogen needed for fusion. Nuclear fusion should also produce less radioactive waste than nuclear fission. Unfortunately, the pressure and temperature required for a reaction make the construction of a fusion reactor impractical at this time.

Section 3 Assessment

Target Reading Skill Comparing and Contrasting Use the information in your Venn diagram to answer Questions 1 and 3 below.

Reviewing Key Concepts

1. a. **Defining** What is nuclear fission?
   b. **Sequencing** Describe the steps that occur in a nuclear fission reaction.
   c. **Classifying** Is nuclear fission a renewable or nonrenewable energy source? Explain.
2. a. **Identifying** What type of nuclear reaction produces electricity in a nuclear power plant?
   b. **Explaining** Explain how electricity is produced in a nuclear power plant.
   c. **Predicting** What might happen in a nuclear power plant if too many control rods were removed?
3. a. **Reviewing** Define nuclear fusion.
   b. **Relating Cause and Effect** How is energy produced during a nuclear fusion reaction?
   c. **Inferring** What is preventing fusion energy from filling our current energy needs?

Lab zone At-Home **Activity**

Shoot the Nucleus With a family member, make a model of a nuclear fission reaction. Place a handful of marbles on the floor in a tight cluster, so that they touch one another. Step back about a half meter from the marbles. Shoot a marble at the cluster. Note what effect the moving marble has on the cluster. Then using a diagram, explain how this event models a nuclear fission reaction.

Section 4

Energy Conservation

Reading Preview

Key Concept

- What are two ways to preserve our current energy sources?

Key Terms

- efficiency
- insulation
- energy conservation

Target Reading Skill

Using Prior Knowledge Before you read, write what you know about energy efficiency and conservation in a graphic organizer like the one below. As you read, write what you learn.

What You Know
1. I turn off lights to conserve energy. 2.

What You Learned
1. 2.

Lab zone Discover **Activity**

Which Bulb Is More Efficient?

1. Record the light output (listed in lumens) from the packages of a 60-watt incandescent light bulb and a 15-watt compact fluorescent bulb.
2. Place the fluorescent bulb in a lamp socket. **CAUTION:** *Make sure the lamp is unplugged.*
3. Plug in the lamp and turn it on. Hold the end of a thermometer about 8 centimeters from the bulb.
4. Record the temperature after five minutes.
5. Turn off and unplug the lamp. When the bulb is cool, remove it. Repeat Steps 2, 3, and 4 with the incandescent light bulb.

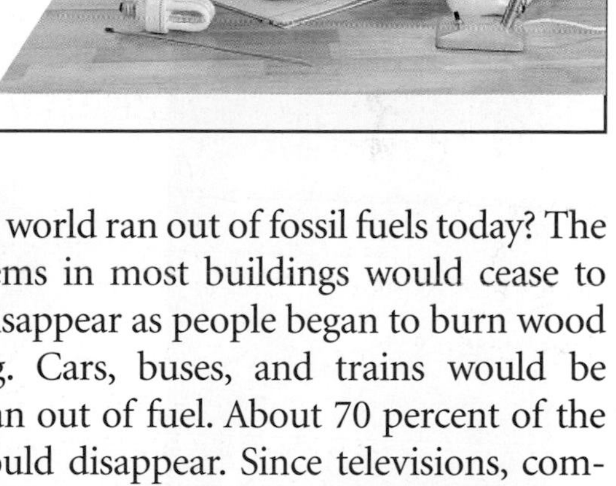

Think It Over

Inferring The 60-watt bulb uses four times as much energy as the 15-watt bulb. Does it also provide four times as much light output? If not, how can you account for the difference?

What would happen if the world ran out of fossil fuels today? The heating and cooling systems in most buildings would cease to function. Forests would disappear as people began to burn wood for heating and cooking. Cars, buses, and trains would be stranded wherever they ran out of fuel. About 70 percent of the world's electric power would disappear. Since televisions, computers, and telephones depend on electricity, communication would be greatly reduced. Lights, microwave ovens, and most other home appliances would no longer work.

Although fossil fuels won't run out immediately, they also won't last forever. Most people think that it makes sense to use fuels more wisely now to avoid fuel shortages in the future. **One way to preserve our current energy resources is to increase the efficiency of our energy use. Another way is to conserve energy whenever possible.**

Energy Efficiency

One way to make energy resources last longer is to use fuels more efficiently. **Efficiency** is the percentage of energy that is actually used to perform work. The rest of the energy is "lost" to the surroundings, usually as heat. People have developed many ways to increase energy efficiency.

Heating and Cooling One method of increasing the efficiency of heating and cooling systems is insulation. **Insulation** is a layer of material that traps air to help block the transfer of heat between the air inside and outside a building. You have probably seen insulation made of fiberglass, which looks like pink cotton candy. A layer of fiberglass 15 centimeters thick insulates a room as well as a brick wall 2 meters thick!

Trapped air can act as insulation in windows, too. Many windows consist of two panes of glass with space between them. The air between the panes of glass acts as insulation.

• Tech & Design in History •

Energy-Efficient Products

Scientists and engineers have developed many technologies that improve energy efficiency and reduce energy use.

1932 Fiberglass Insulation
Long strands of glass fibers trap air and keep buildings from losing heat. Less fuel is used for heating.

1936 Fluorescent Lighting
Fluorescent bulbs were introduced to the public at the hundredth anniversary celebration of the United States Patent Office. Because these bulbs use less energy than incandescent bulbs, most offices and schools use fluorescent lights today.

1958 Solar Cells
More than 150 years ago, scientists discovered that silicon can convert light into electricity. The first useful application of solar cells was to power the radio on a satellite. Now solar cells are even used on experimental cars like the one above.

1930 1940 1950 1960

Lighting Much of the electricity used for home lighting is wasted. For example, less than 10 percent of the electricity that an incandescent light bulb uses is converted into light. The rest is given off as heat. In contrast, compact fluorescent bulbs use about one fourth as much energy to provide the same amount of light.

Transportation Engineers have improved the energy efficiency of cars by designing better engines and tires. Another way to save energy is to reduce the number of cars on the road. In many communities, public transit systems provide an alternative to driving. Other cities encourage carpooling. Many cities now set aside lanes for cars containing two or more people.

What are two examples of insulation?

Writing in Science

Research and Write Design an advertisement for one of the energy-saving inventions described in this timeline. The advertisement may be a print, radio, or television ad. Be sure that your advertisement clearly explains the benefits of the invention.

1967 Microwave Ovens

The first countertop microwave oven for the home was introduced. Microwaves cook food by heating the water the food contains. Unlike a conventional oven, a microwave oven heats only the food. And preheating is unnecessary, saving even more energy.

1981 High-Efficiency Window Coatings

Materials that reflect sunlight were first used to coat windows in the early 1980s. This coating reduces the air conditioning needed to keep the inside of the building cool.

1997 Hydrogen-Powered Vehicles

Hydrogen fuel cells produce no polluting emissions. In 1997, two major automakers unveiled experimental hydrogen-powered cars. The first mass-produced hydrogen-powered cars are expected around 2010.

1970 1980 1990 2000

FIGURE 16
Energy Conservation
There are many ways you can conserve energy.

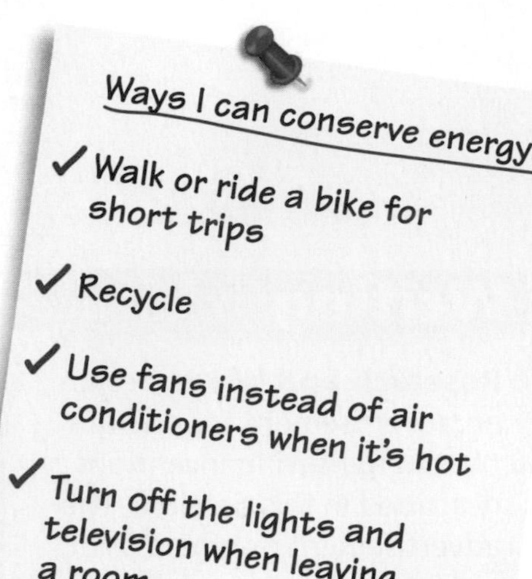

Energy Conservation

Another approach to making energy resources last longer is conservation. **Energy conservation** means reducing energy use.

You can reduce your personal energy use by changing your behavior in some simple ways. For example, if you walk to the store instead of getting a ride, you are conserving the gasoline it would take to drive to the store. You can also follow some of the suggestions in Figure 16.

While these suggestions seem like small things, multiplied by millions of people they add up to a lot of energy saved for the future.

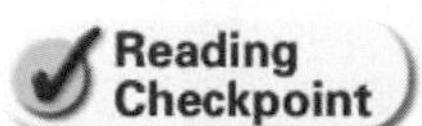

What are two ways you can reduce your personal energy use?

Section 4 Assessment

Target Reading Skill Using Prior Knowledge Review your graphic organizer and revise it based on what you just learned in the section.

Reviewing Key Concepts

1. a. **Identifying** What are the two keys to preserving our current energy resources?
   b. **Applying Concepts** How does insulating buildings help to preserve energy resources? How does carpooling preserve resources?
   c. **Predicting** One office building contains only incandescent lights. The building next door contains only fluorescent lights. Predict which building has higher energy bills. Explain your answer.

Writing in Science

Energy Savings Brochure
Conduct an energy audit of your home. Look for places where energy is being lost, such as cracks around doors. Also look for ways to reduce energy use, such as running the dishwasher only when it is full. Then create a short, illustrated brochure of energy-saving suggestions. Keep the brochure where everyone can see it.

Lab zone Consumer Lab

Keeping Comfortable

Problem

How well do different materials prevent heat transfer?

Skills Focus

measuring, controlling variables

Materials 

- watch or clock
- beakers
- ice water
- hot water
- thermometers or temperature probes
- containers and lids made of paper, glass, plastic, plastic foam, and metal

Procedure   

1. Use a pencil to poke a hole in the lid of a paper cup. Fill the cup halfway with cold water.
2. Put the lid on the cup. Insert a thermometer into the water through the hole. (If you are using a temperature probe, see your teacher for instructions.) When the temperature stops dropping, place the cup in a beaker. Add hot water to the beaker until the water level is about 1 cm below the lid.
3. Record the water temperature once every minute until it has increased by 5°C. Use the time it takes for the temperature to increase 5°C as a measure of the effectiveness of the paper cup in preventing heat transfer.
4. Choose three other containers and their matching lids to test. Design an experiment to compare how well those materials prevent heat transfer. You can use a similar procedure to the one you used in Steps 1–3.

Analyze and Conclude

1. **Measuring** In Step 2, what was the starting temperature of the cold water? How long did it take for the temperature to increase by 5°C? In which direction did the heat flow? Explain.
2. **Making Models** If the materials in Steps 1–3 represented your home in very hot weather, which material would represent the rooms in your home? The outdoor weather? The building walls?
3. **Controlling Variables** In the experiment you conducted in Step 4, what were the manipulated and responding variables? What variables were kept constant?
4. **Drawing Conclusions** Which material was most effective at preventing the transfer of heat? Which was the least effective? Explain how your data support your conclusion.
5. **Communicating** Write a paragraph explaining why the results of your experiment could be useful to people building energy-efficient structures.

Design an Experiment

Design an experiment to compare how well the materials you tested would work if the hot water were inside the cup and the cold water were outside. *Obtain your teacher's permission before carrying out your investigation.*

For: Data sharing
Visit: PHSchool.com
Web Code: ced-5054

Technology and Society

• Tech & Design •

The Hybrid Car

How do you get from here to there? Like most people, you probably rely on cars or buses. Engines that burn fossil fuels power most of these vehicles. To conserve fossil fuels, as well as to reduce air pollution, some car companies have begun to produce hybrid vehicles.

How Are Hybrid Cars Different?

The power source for most cars is a gasoline engine that powers the transmission. Unlike conventional cars, hybrid cars can use both a gasoline engine and an electric motor to turn the transmission. The generated power can be used by the transmission to turn the wheels. Or power can be converted into electricity for later use by the electric motor. Any extra electricity is stored in the car's battery. The gasoline engine in a hybrid car is smaller, more efficient, and less polluting than the engine in a conventional car.

Gasoline Engine The engine burns fuel to provide energy to the car.

Electric Motor and Generator In this model, the electric motor draws energy from the car's battery to help the car speed up. As the car slows down, the generator produces electricity to recharge the car's battery.

Transmission This device transmits power from the engine to the axle that turns the wheels.

Start The car uses power from its battery to start the gasoline engine.

Accelerate When the car accelerates, the electric motor and the gasoline engine work together to power the car.

Brake When the car brakes, the motor acts like a generator and stores electrical energy in the battery.

Are Hybrid Cars the Way to Go?

Hybrid cars consume less gas per mile and emit fewer pollutants than cars that run on gasoline alone. In spite of the benefits, there are some drawbacks to hybrid cars. In general, hybrid cars have less power for climbing steep hills and less acceleration than cars with larger engines. In addition, the large batteries could be an environmental hazard if they end up in a landfill. Drivers must make trade-offs in buying any car.

Mileage per Tank of Gas

Miles Traveled per Tank of Gas (13.2 gallons)
0
100
200
300
400
500
600
700
Conventional
Hybrid
Type of Car

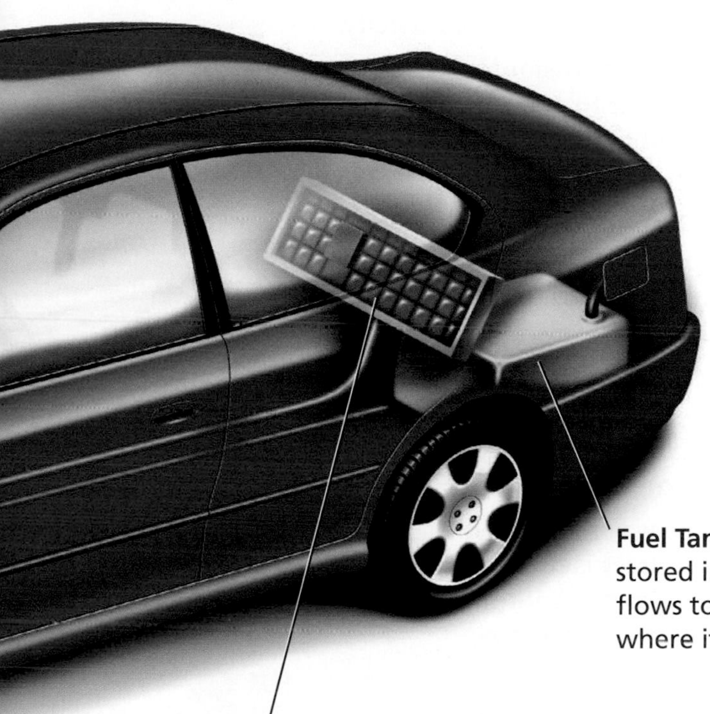

Fuel Tank Gasoline stored in the fuel tank flows to the engine where it's burned.

Battery The car's electric motor uses energy stored in the battery.

Stop
When the car stops or idles, the gasoline engine stops. It restarts when the driver steps on the gas pedal.

Weigh the Impact

1. Identify the Need
Why are some car companies developing hybrid cars?

2. Research
Research hybrid cars currently on the market. Use your findings to list the advantages and disadvantages of hybrid-car technology.

3. Write
Should your family's next car be a conventional or hybrid model? Use the information here and your research findings to write several paragraphs supporting your opinion.

For: More on hybrid cars
Visit: PHSchool.com
Web Code: ceh-5050

Chapter 5 Study Guide

The BIG Idea **Energy Resources and Technology** Renewable and nonrenewable energy resources differ in cost and availability. These resources also differ in the environmental effects of producing and using them.

1 Fossil Fuels

Key Concepts

- When fuels are burned, the chemical energy that is released can be used to generate another form of energy, such as heat, light, motion, or electricity.
- The three major fossil fuels are coal, oil, and natural gas.
- Since fossil fuels take hundreds of millions of years to form, they are considered nonrenewable resources.

Key Terms

fuel
energy transformation
combustion
fossil fuel
hydrocarbon
petroleum
refinery
petrochemical

2 Renewable Sources of Energy

Key Concepts

- The sun constantly gives off energy in the forms of light and heat.
- In addition to solar energy, renewable sources of energy include water, the wind, biomass fuels, geothermal energy, and hydrogen.

Key Terms

solar energy
hydroelectric power
biomass fuel
gasohol
geothermal energy

3 Nuclear Energy

Key Concepts

- During nuclear fission, when a neutron hits a U-235 nucleus, the nucleus splits apart into two smaller nuclei and two or more neutrons.
- In a nuclear power plant, the heat released from fission reactions is used to change water into steam. The steam then turns the blades of a turbine to generate electricity.
- In nuclear fusion, two hydrogen nuclei combine to create a helium nucleus, which has slightly less mass than the two hydrogen nuclei. The lost mass is converted to energy.

Key Terms

nucleus
nuclear fission
reactor vessel
fuel rod
control rod
meltdown
nuclear fusion

4 Energy Conservation

Key Concept

- One way to preserve our current energy resources is to increase the efficiency of our energy use. Another way is to conserve energy whenever possible.

Key Terms

efficiency
insulation
energy conservation

Review and Assessment

Go Online PHSchool.com
For: Self-Assessment
Visit: PHSchool.com
Web Code: cea-5050

Organizing Information

Comparing and Contrasting Copy the graphic organizer about sources of energy onto a separate sheet of paper. Then complete it and add a title. (For more on Comparing and Contrasting, see the Skills Handbook.)

Energy Type	Advantage	Disadvantage
Coal	Easy to transport	a. ?
Oil	b. ?	Nonrenewable
Solar	c. ?	d. ?
Wind	e. ?	f. ?
Hydroelectric	No pollution	g. ?
Geothermal	h. ?	i. ?
Nuclear	j. ?	Radioactive waste

Reviewing Key Terms

Choose the letter of the best answer.

1. Which of the following is *not* a fossil fuel?
   a. coal
   b. wood
   c. oil
   d. natural gas
2. Wind and water energy are both indirect forms of
   a. nuclear energy.
   b. electrical energy.
   c. solar energy.
   d. geothermal energy.
3. Which of the following is *not* a biomass fuel?
   a. methane
   b. gasohol
   c. hydrogen
   d. sugar cane wastes
4. The particle used to start a nuclear fission reaction is a(n)
   a. neutron.
   b. electron.
   c. proton.
   d. atom.
5. A part of a nuclear power plant that undergoes a fission reaction is called a
   a. turbine.
   b. control rod.
   c. heat exchanger.
   d. fuel rod.

If the statement is true, write *true.* If it is false, change the underlined word or words to make the statement true.

6. The process of burning a fuel for energy is called <u>combustion</u>.
7. Most of the energy used today comes from <u>fossil fuels</u>.
8. Products made from petroleum are called <u>hydrocarbons</u>.
9. Geothermal energy is an example of a <u>nonrenewable</u> energy source.
10. <u>Insulation</u> means reducing energy use.

Writing in Science

Letter In a letter to a friend, predict how solar energy will change your life over the next 20 years. Include specific details in your description.

Energy Resources
Video Preview
Video Field Trip
▶ Video Assessment

Review and Assessment

Checking Concepts

11. Describe how coal forms.

12. What is natural gas? How is natural gas transported to where it is needed?

13. Describe three features of a solar home. (Your answer may include passive and active solar systems.)

14. Explain why solar energy is the indirect source of hydroelectric power.

15. Explain how wind can be used to generate electricity.

16. How is a nuclear fission reaction controlled in a nuclear reactor?

17. Define energy efficiency. Give three examples of inventions that increase energy efficiency.

Thinking Critically

18. Comparing and Contrasting Discuss how the three major fossil fuels are alike and how they are different.

19. Predicting Do you think you will ever live in a solar house? Support your prediction with details about the climate in your area.

20. Classifying State whether each of the following energy sources is renewable or nonrenewable: coal, solar power, natural gas, hydrogen. Give a reason for each answer.

21. Making Judgments Write a short paragraph explaining why you agree or disagree with the following statement: "The United States should build more nuclear power plants to prepare for the future shortage of fossil fuels."

22. Relating Cause and Effect In the nuclear reaction shown below, a neutron is about to strike a U-235 nucleus. What will happen next?

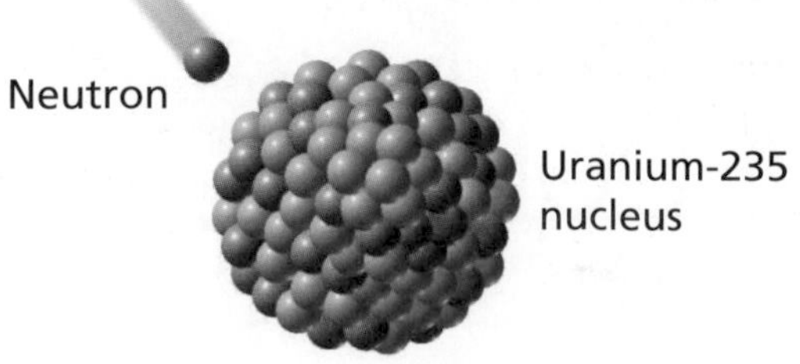

Applying Skills

Use the information in the table to answer Questions 23–27.

The table below shows the world's energy production in 1973 and today.

Energy Source	Units Produced 1973	Units Produced Today
Oil	2,861	3,574
Natural gas	1,226	2,586
Coal	2,238	3,833
Nuclear	203	2,592
Hydroelectric	1,300	2,705
Total	7,828	15,290

23. Interpreting Data How did the total energy production change from 1973 to today?

24. Calculating What percentage of the total world energy production did nuclear power provide in 1973? What percentage does it provide today?

25. Classifying Classify the different energy sources according to whether they are renewable or nonrenewable.

26. Inferring How has the importance of hydroelectric power changed from 1973 to the present?

27. Predicting How do you think the world's energy production will change over the next 40 years? Explain.

Lab zone Chapter Project

Performance Assessment Share your energy-audit report with another group. The group should review the report for clarity, organization, and detail. Make revisions based on feedback from the other group. As a class, discuss each group's findings. Then prepare a class proposal with the best suggestions for conserving energy in your school.

Standardized Test Prep

Test-Taking Tip

Eliminating Incorrect Answers

When answering a multiple-choice question, you can often eliminate some answer choices because they are clearly incorrect. By doing this, you increase your odds of selecting the correct answer.

Sample Question

Geothermal energy is not a widely used source of energy because

A dams can have negative effects on the environment.
B methane gas is produced as a waste product.
C it is difficult to store.
D magma only comes close to Earth's surface in a few locations.

Answer

The correct answer is **D**. You can eliminate **A** because dams are used to produce hydroelectric power. You can also eliminate **B** because methane gas is produced when bacteria decompose biomass materials. Of the two remaining choices, **D** is correct because geothermal energy uses magma from Earth's interior as an energy source.

Choose the letter of the best answer.

1. The interior of your car heats up on a sunny day because of
   A passive solar heating.
   B solar cells.
   C active solar heating.
   D indirect solar heating.

2. The main function of a dam in producing electricity is to
   F form a reservoir for recreation.
   G prevent flooding after a heavy rain.
   H provide a source of fast-moving water.
   J provide a source of wind.

Use the graph to answer Questions 3–4.

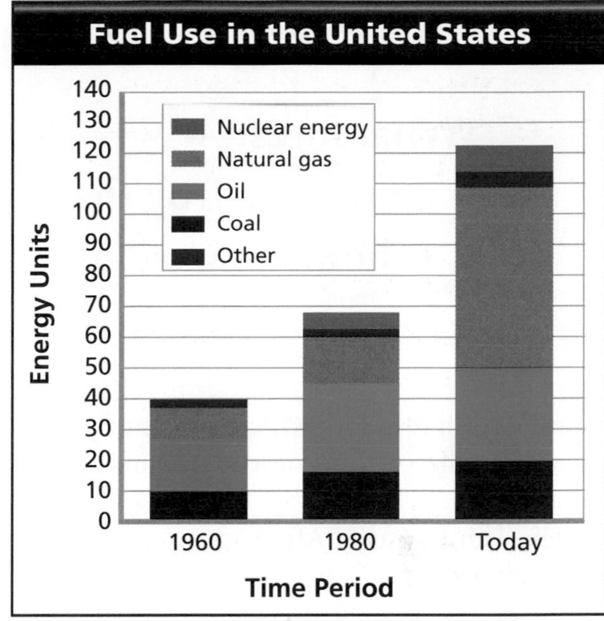

3. According to the graph, most of the fuel sources used in the United States today are
   A renewable fuels. **B** nuclear fuels.
   C fossil fuels. **D** solar energy.

4. Which statement about fuel use in the United States is best supported by the graph?
   F Natural gas has become the most widely used fuel source.
   G Nuclear energy is not used today.
   H Coal is becoming the main source of fuel.
   J The amount of oil being used today has greatly decreased since 1980.

5. Which of the following is the first step in producing electricity in a nuclear reactor?
   A Steam turns the blades of a turbine.
   B Water boils to produce steam.
   C U-235 atoms are split by nuclear fission.
   D Heat is released.

Constructed Response

6. Explain what is meant by this statement: Electricity is *not* itself a source of energy. Then choose one energy source and explain how it can be used to produce electricity.

African Rain Forests

What forest—

- **contains a frog that's 30 cm long?**
- **is home to gorillas, pottos, and pygmy hippos?**
- **is preserving diversity?**

It's an African rain forest. Thousands of plants and animals live here, from colorful orchids to fruit bats to elephants.

The rain forests of Africa grow near the equator. About 70 percent of the rain forests are in central Africa, in the vast basin of the great Congo River. Some parts of the central African rain forest are so dense and hard to reach that explorers have never visited them. East Africa, which is drier, has only scattered areas of rain forest.

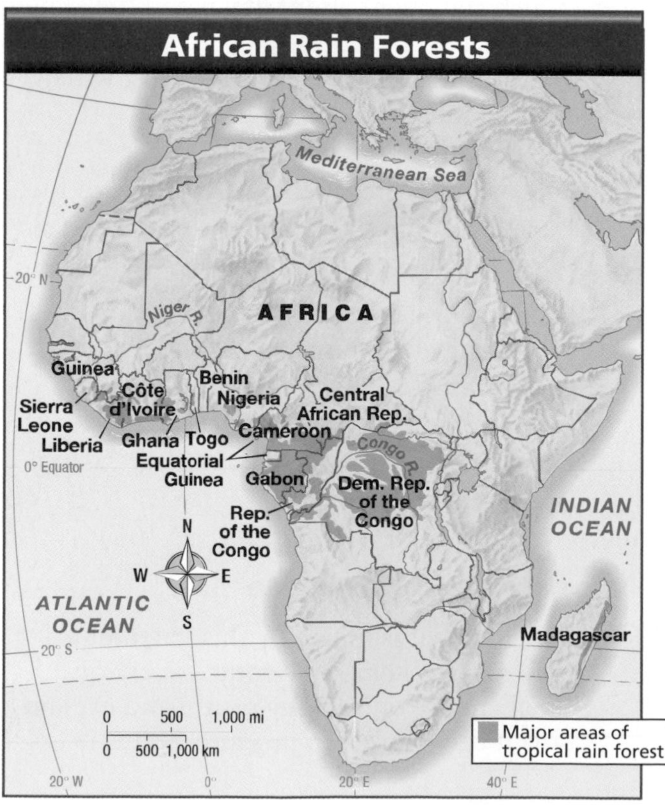

Golden Potto
This golden potto eats insects and fruits in the African rain forest.

Rain Forest Layers

The rain forest is really many forests in one—like different levels in an apartment building. Each layer varies in climate and is home to different plants and animals. The four layers are the emergent layer, the canopy, the understory, and the forest floor.

Over time, plants and animals have developed unusual adaptations to life at different layers of the rain forest. Some monkeys living in the canopy have long, muscular legs so they can run and leap through branches. Others have strong teeth and jaws that allow them to crunch fruits, nuts, and seeds. Some monkeys that live mainly on the forest floor have shorter tails but longer front legs.

Emergent Layer 40–70 Meters
This layer is formed by a few taller trees that poke through the canopy. The emergent layer captures the most rain, sunlight, heat, and wind. Colobus monkeys and vast numbers of birds live at this level.

Black and White Colobus Monkey

Canopy 10–40 Meters
The canopy is the dense "roof" of the rain forest. The crowns of trees capture sunlight to use in photosynthesis. Rain and sunlight filter through thick vegetation. Epiphytic orchids grow to the top of the canopy.

Epiphytic Orchid

Paradise Flycatcher

Understory 0–10 Meters
The understory has trees and plants that need little light. Pythons lurk in the vegetation. Some small animals such as squirrels glide from branch to branch.

Forest Floor 0 Meters
The forest floor is dark and humid. Pygmy hippos forage for food on the forest floor. Pygmy hippos are just one tenth the size of common hippos.

Pygmy Hippo

Science Activity

Design a rain forest animal that is adapted to life at a certain level of the rain forest. Consider how your animal lives, how it travels, and what food it eats. Outline its characteristics and explain how each adaptation helps the animal survive. Draw a sketch of your design.

Reaching for Sunlight

Most rain forest trees are evergreens with broad leathery leaves. Some, like the African yellowwood, are conifers. Because the forest is so dense, trees must grow tall and straight to reach sunlight at the top of the canopy.

Along rivers, the floor and understory of the rain forest are a tangle of thick vegetation. But deep in the rain forest the floor is surprisingly bare. The canopy trees prevent sunlight from reaching plants below. Water drips from the leaves of the canopy high overhead. Young trees have the best chance to grow when older trees fall and open up sunny clearings.

West Africa's tropical forests contain many valuable trees. African mahogany and teak are used to make furniture, tools, and boats. Oil from the oil palm is used in soaps, candles, and some foods. Trees, such as ebony, that can tolerate shade grow slowly and develop dark, hard, long-lasting wood.

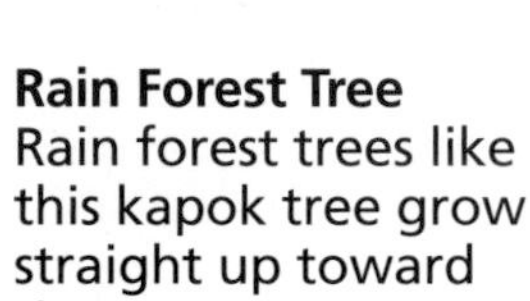

Rain Forest Tree
Rain forest trees like this kapok tree grow straight up toward the sun.

Trees of the Rain Forest

Tree	Maximum Height
African oil palm	18 m
African yellowwood	20 m
Cape fig	7 m
Ebony	30 m
Kapok	70 m
Raffia palm	12 m
Teak	46 m

30 m
20 m
10 m
0 m

Math Activity

The table on this page gives the height of some of the trees in the rain forest. Use the information in the table to make a bar graph. Label the horizontal axis with the tree names. Use the vertical axis to show the heights of the trees.

- Which tree has the greatest maximum height? The least maximum height?
- What is the difference between the maximum heights of the tallest and the shortest trees?
- What is the average maximum height of all the trees shown in the graph?

Bark Cloth
Traditional Mbuti clothing is made of bark cloth.

Ituri Forest People

The native peoples of the African rain forest live as they have for thousands of years—by hunting and gathering. The forest supplies them with everything they need—food, water, firewood, building materials, and medicines.

One group of rain forest dwellers is the Mbuti people. The Mbuti live in the Ituri forest of the Democratic Republic of the Congo. Many of the Mbuti are quite small. The men hunt game, such as gazelle and antelope. The women gather wild fruits, nuts, and greens. Their traditional Mbuti clothing is made of tree bark and is wrapped around the waist. The bark is beaten to make it soft. Then it's decorated with geometric designs.

Most Mbuti live as nomads, with no settled home. Every few months they set up new hunting grounds. They build temporary dome-shaped huts of branches and leaves. Hunting groups of about 10 to 25 families live together.

Modern Africa has brought changes to the forest people, especially for those who live near the edges of the rain forest. For a few months of the year, some Mbuti work as laborers for farmers who live in villages at the edge of the forest. When their work is finished, the Mbuti return to the Ituri forest. Most forest people prefer not to cultivate their own land. Since the farmers don't hunt, they trade their goods for meat. In exchange for meat, the Mbuti receive goods such as iron tools, cooking pots, clothes, bananas, and other farm produce.

The Mbuti
The Mbuti hunt and fish along the Congo River.

Social Studies Activity

List the goods that forest people and farmers might have to trade. Assume that no modern conveniences, such as tractors and stoves, are available. In writing, explain how goods might be exchanged. Assign a value to the farmers' goods and the Mbuti goods, depending upon each group's needs. How would the trading process change if money were exchanged?

Climbing the Canopy

Much of the rain forest is still a mystery because it's so difficult for scientists to study the canopy. Native forest people sometimes climb these tall trees using strong, thick vines called lianas as support. But rain forest scientists have had to find different methods. Naturalist Gerald Durrell, working in the African rain forest, was lucky enough to find another way to observe the canopy. He describes it here.

Gerald Durrell
British conservationist Gerald Durrell wrote about his adventures with wildlife around the world. In this photo, Durrell holds an anteater.

While the canopy is one of the most richly inhabited regions of the forest it is also the one that causes the naturalist the greatest frustration. There he is, down in the gloom among the giant tree trunks, hearing the noises of animal life high above him and having half-eaten fruit, flowers, or seeds rained on him by legions of animals high in their sunlit domain—all of which he cannot see. Under these circumstances the naturalist develops a very bad temper and a permanent crick in the neck.

However, there was one occasion when I managed to transport myself into the forest canopy, and it was a magical experience. It happened in West Africa when I was camped on the thickly forested lower slopes of a mountain called N'da Ali. Walking through the forest one day I found I was walking along the edge of a great step cut out of the mountain. The cliff face, covered with creepers, dropped away for about 50 yards, so that although I was walking through forest, just next to me and slightly below was the canopy of the forest growing up from the base of the cliff. This cliff was over half a mile in length and provided me with a natural balcony from which I could observe the treetop life simply by lying on the cliff edge, concealed in the low undergrowth.

Over a period of about a week I spent hours up there and a whole pageant of wildlife passed by. The numbers of birds were incredible, ranging from minute glittering sunbirds in rainbow coloring, zooming like helicopters from blossom to blossom as they fed on the nectar, to the flocks of huge black hornbills with their monstrous yellow beaks who flew in such an ungainly manner and made such a noise over their choice of forest fruits.

From early morning to evening when it grew too dark to see, I watched this parade of creatures. Troops of monkeys swept past, followed by attendant flocks of birds who fed eagerly on the insects that the monkeys disturbed during their noisy crashing through the trees. Squirrels chased each other, or hotly pursued lizards, or simply lay spread-eagled on branches high up in the trees, enjoying the sun.

African Eagle

Language Arts Activity

Besides being an experienced naturalist and writer, Gerald Durrell was also a careful observer. In this selection, he describes in detail the "magical experience" of being in the canopy. Reread Durrell's description. Now work with a partner to write and design a pamphlet that will persuade visitors to come to an African rain forest. For your pamphlet, write strong, lively descriptions of what you might see, hear, and experience. Be persuasive.

Tie It Together

Celebrate Diversity

Rain forests have the greatest biodiversity—variety of plant and animal life—of any ecosystem on Earth. Many species have yet to be discovered! Plan a display for your school to celebrate biodiversity in the rain forests. Include drawings, photos, and detailed captions.

- On a large map, locate and label Earth's tropical rain forests. Divide into groups to choose one rain forest region to research, such as Africa, Brazil, Costa Rica, Hawaii, or Borneo.
- With your group, study several animal and plant species in your chosen rain forest. You might choose monkeys, butterflies, birds, orchids, or medicinal plants.
- For each species, describe its appearance, where it occurs in the rain forest, its role in the ecosystem, and how it is useful to humans.

Grass Frog

Comet Moth

Mandrill

Think Like a Scientist

Scientists have a particular way of looking at the world, or scientific habits of mind. Whenever you ask a question and explore possible answers, you use many of the same skills that scientists do. Some of these skills are described on this page.

Observing

When you use one or more of your five senses to gather information about the world, you are **observing.** Hearing a dog bark, counting twelve green seeds, and smelling smoke are all observations. To increase the power of their senses, scientists sometimes use microscopes, telescopes, or other instruments that help them make more detailed observations.

An observation must be an accurate report of what your senses detect. It is important to keep careful records of your observations in science class by writing or drawing in a notebook. The information collected through observations is called evidence, or data.

Inferring

When you interpret an observation, you are **inferring,** or making an inference. For example, if you hear your dog barking, you may infer that someone is at your front door. To make this inference, you combine the evidence—the barking dog—and your experience or knowledge—you know that your dog barks when strangers approach—to reach a logical conclusion.

Notice that an inference is not a fact; it is only one of many possible interpretations for an observation. For example, your dog may be barking because it wants to go for a walk. An inference may turn out to be incorrect even if it is based on accurate observations and logical reasoning. The only way to find out if an inference is correct is to investigate further.

Predicting

When you listen to the weather forecast, you hear many predictions about the next day's weather—what the temperature will be, whether it will rain, and how windy it will be. Weather forecasters use observations and knowledge of weather patterns to predict the weather. The skill of **predicting** involves making an inference about a future event based on current evidence or past experience.

Because a prediction is an inference, it may prove to be false. In science class, you can test some of your predictions by doing experiments. For example, suppose you predict that larger paper airplanes can fly farther than smaller airplanes. How could you test your prediction?

Activity

Use the photograph to answer the questions below.

Observing Look closely at the photograph. List at least three observations.

Inferring Use your observations to make an inference about what has happened. What experience or knowledge did you use to make the inference?

Predicting Predict what will happen next. On what evidence or experience do you base your prediction?

Classifying

Could you imagine searching for a book in the library if the books were shelved in no particular order? Your trip to the library would be an all-day event! Luckily, librarians group together books on similar topics or by the same author. Grouping together items that are alike in some way is called **classifying.** You can classify items in many ways: by size, by shape, by use, and by other important characteristics.

Like librarians, scientists use the skill of classifying to organize information and objects. When things are sorted into groups, the relationships among them become easier to understand.

Activity

Classify the objects in the photograph into two groups based on any characteristic you choose. Then use another characteristic to classify the objects into three groups.

Activity

This student is using a model to demonstrate what causes day and night on Earth. What do the flashlight and the tennis ball in the model represent?

Making Models

Have you ever drawn a picture to help someone understand what you were saying? Such a drawing is one type of model. A model is a picture, diagram, computer image, or other representation of a complex object or process. **Making models** helps people understand things that they cannot observe directly.

Scientists often use models to represent things that are either very large or very small, such as the planets in the solar system, or the parts of a cell. Such models are physical models—drawings or three-dimensional structures that look like the real thing. Other models are mental models—mathematical equations or words that describe how something works.

Communicating

Whenever you talk on the phone, write a report, or listen to your teacher at school, you are communicating. **Communicating** is the process of sharing ideas and information with other people. Communicating effectively requires many skills, including writing, reading, speaking, listening, and making models.

Scientists communicate to share results, information, and opinions. Scientists often communicate about their work in journals, over the telephone, in letters, and on the Internet. They also attend scientific meetings where they share their ideas with one another in person.

Activity

On a sheet of paper, write out clear, detailed directions for tying your shoe. Then exchange directions with a partner. Follow your partner's directions exactly. How successful were you at tying your shoe? How could your partner have communicated more clearly?

Making Measurements

By measuring, scientists can express their observations more precisely and communicate more information about what they observe.

Measuring in SI

The standard system of measurement used by scientists around the world is known as the International System of Units, which is abbreviated as SI (**Système International d'Unités,** in French). SI units are easy to use because they are based on powers of 10. Each unit is ten times larger than the next smallest unit and one tenth the size of the next largest unit. The table lists the prefixes used to name the most common SI units.

Common SI Prefixes		
Prefix	**Symbol**	**Meaning**
kilo-	k	1,000
hecto-	h	100
deka-	da	10
deci-	d	0.1 (one tenth)
centi-	c	0.01 (one hundredth)
milli-	m	0.001 (one thousandth)

Length To measure length, or the distance between two points, the unit of measure is the **meter (m).** The distance from the floor to a doorknob is approximately one meter. Long distances, such as the distance between two cities, are measured in kilometers (km). Small lengths are measured in centimeters (cm) or millimeters (mm). Scientists use metric rulers and meter sticks to measure length.

Common Conversions		
1 km	=	1,000 m
1 m	=	100 cm
1 m	=	1,000 mm
1 cm	=	10 mm

Activity

The larger lines on the metric ruler in the picture show centimeter divisions, while the smaller, unnumbered lines show millimeter divisions. How many centimeters long is the shell? How many millimeters long is it?

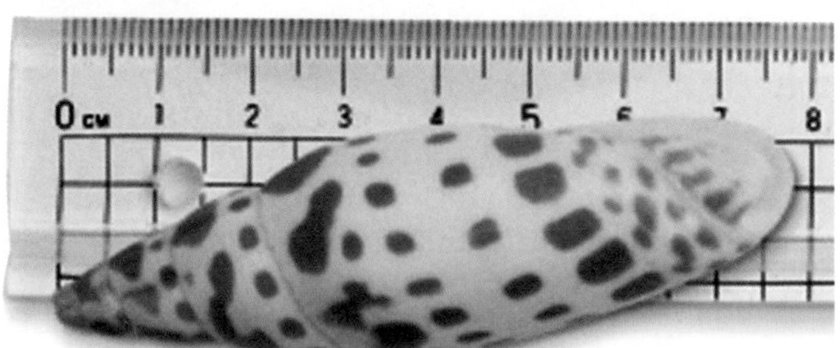

Liquid Volume To measure the volume of a liquid, or the amount of space it takes up, you will use a unit of measure known as the **liter (L).** One liter is the approximate volume of a medium-size carton of milk. Smaller volumes are measured in milliliters (mL). Scientists use graduated cylinders to measure liquid volume.

Activity

The graduated cylinder in the picture is marked in milliliter divisions. Notice that the water in the cylinder has a curved surface. This curved surface is called the *meniscus*. To measure the volume, you must read the level at the lowest point of the meniscus. What is the volume of water in this graduated cylinder?

Common Conversion		
1 L	=	1,000 mL

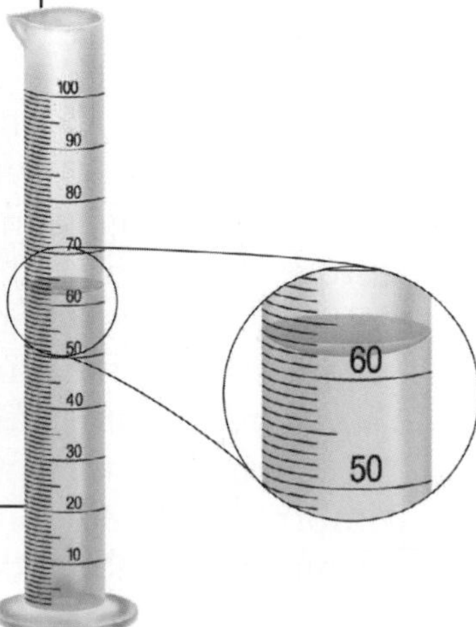

Mass To measure mass, or the amount of matter in an object, you will use a unit of measure known as the **gram (g).** One gram is approximately the mass of a paper clip. Larger masses are measured in kilograms (kg). Scientists use a balance to find the mass of an object.

Common Conversion
1 kg = 1,000 g

Activity

The mass of the potato in the picture is measured in kilograms. What is the mass of the potato? Suppose a recipe for potato salad called for one kilogram of potatoes. About how many potatoes would you need?

0.25 KG

Temperature To measure the temperature of a substance, you will use the **Celsius scale.** Temperature is measured in degrees Celsius (°C) using a Celsius thermometer. Water freezes at 0°C and boils at 100°C.

Time The unit scientists use to measure time is the **second (s).**

Activity

What is the temperature of the liquid in degrees Celsius?

Converting SI Units

To use the SI system, you must know how to convert between units. Converting from one unit to another involves the skill of **calculating,** or using mathematical operations. Converting between SI units is similar to converting between dollars and dimes because both systems are based on powers of ten.

Suppose you want to convert a length of 80 centimeters to meters. Follow these steps to convert between units.

1. Begin by writing down the measurement you want to convert—in this example, 80 centimeters.
2. Write a conversion factor that represents the relationship between the two units you are converting. In this example, the relation ship is 1 meter = 100 centimeters. Write this conversion factor as a fraction, making sure to place the units you are converting from (centimeters, in this example) in the denominator.
3. Multiply the measurement you want to convert by the fraction. When you do this, the units in the first measurement will cancel out with the units in the denominator. Your answer will be in the units you are converting to (meters, in this example).

Example

80 centimeters = ■ meters

$$80 \text{ centimeters} \times \frac{1 \text{ meter}}{100 \text{ centimeters}} = \frac{80 \text{ meters}}{100}$$

$$= 0.8 \text{ meters}$$

Activity

Convert between the following units.

1. 600 millimeters = ■ meters
2. 0.35 liters = ■ milliliters
3. 1,050 grams = ■ kilograms

Conducting a Scientific Investigation

In some ways, scientists are like detectives, piecing together clues to learn about a process or event. One way that scientists gather clues is by carrying out experiments. An experiment tests an idea in a careful, orderly manner. Although experiments do not all follow the same steps in the same order, many follow a pattern similar to the one described here.

Posing Questions

Experiments begin by asking a scientific question. A scientific question is one that can be answered by gathering evidence. For example, the question "Which freezes faster—fresh water or salt water?" is a scientific question because you can carry out an investigation and gather information to answer the question.

Developing a Hypothesis

The next step is to form a hypothesis. A **hypothesis** is a possible explanation for a set of observations or answer to a scientific question. In science, a hypothesis must be something that can be tested. A hypothesis can be worded as an *If . . . then . . .* statement. For example, a hypothesis might be *"If I add table salt to fresh water, then the water will freeze at a lower temperature."* A hypothesis worded this way serves as a rough outline of the experiment you should perform.

Designing an Experiment

Next you need to plan a way to test your hypothesis. Your plan should be written out as a step-by-step procedure and should describe the observations or measurements you will make.

Two important steps involved in designing an experiment are controlling variables and forming operational definitions.

Controlling Variables In a well-designed experiment, you need to keep all variables the same except for one. A **variable** is any factor that can change in an experiment. The factor that you change is called the **manipulated variable.** In this experiment, the manipulated variable is the amount of table salt added to the water. Other factors, such as the amount of water or the starting temperature, are kept constant.

The factor that changes as a result of the manipulated variable is called the **responding variable.** The responding variable is what you measure or observe to obtain your results. In this experiment, the responding variable is the temperature at which the water freezes.

An experiment in which all factors except one are kept constant is called a **controlled experiment.** Most controlled experiments include a test called the control. In this experiment, Container 3 is the control. Because no salt is added to Container 3, you can compare the results from the other containers to it. Any difference in results must be due to the addition of salt alone.

Forming Operational Definitions Another important aspect of a well-designed experiment is having clear operational definitions. An **operational definition** is a statement that describes how a particular variable is to be measured or how a term is to be defined. For example, in this experiment, how will you determine if the water has frozen? You might decide to insert a stick in each container at the start of the experiment. Your operational definition of "frozen" would be the time at which the stick can no longer move.

Experimental Procedure	
1.	Fill 3 containers with 300 milliliters of cold tap water.
2.	Add 10 grams of salt to Container 1; stir. Add 20 grams of salt to Container 2; stir. Add no salt to Container 3.
3.	Place the 3 containers in a freezer.
4.	Check the containers every 15 minutes. Record your observations.

Interpreting Data

The observations and measurements you make in an experiment are called **data.** At the end of an experiment, you need to analyze the data to look for any patterns or trends. Patterns often become clear if you organize your data in a data table or graph. Then think through what the data reveal. Do they support your hypothesis? Do they point out a flaw in your experiment? Do you need to collect more data?

Drawing Conclusions

A **conclusion** is a statement that sums up what you have learned from an experiment. When you draw a conclusion, you need to decide whether the data you collected support your hypothesis or not. You may need to repeat an experiment several times before you can draw any conclusions from it. Conclusions often lead you to pose new questions and plan new experiments to answer them.

Activity

Is a ball's bounce affected by the height from which it is dropped? Using the steps just described, plan a controlled experiment to investigate this problem.

Technology Design Skills

Engineers are people who use scientific and technological knowledge to solve practical problems. To design new products, engineers usually follow the process described here, even though they may not follow these steps in the exact order. As you read the steps, think about how you might apply them in technology labs.

Identify a Need

Before engineers begin designing a new product, they must first identify the need they are trying to meet. For example, suppose you are a member of a design team in a company that makes toys. Your team has identified a need: a toy boat that is inexpensive and easy to assemble.

Research the Problem

Engineers often begin by gathering information that will help them with their new design. This research may include finding articles in books, magazines, or on the Internet. It may also include talking to other engineers who have solved similar problems. Engineers often perform experiments related to the product they want to design.

For your toy boat, you could look at toys that are similar to the one you want to design. You might do research on the Internet. You could also test some materials to see whether they will work well in a toy boat.

Drawing for a boat design ▼

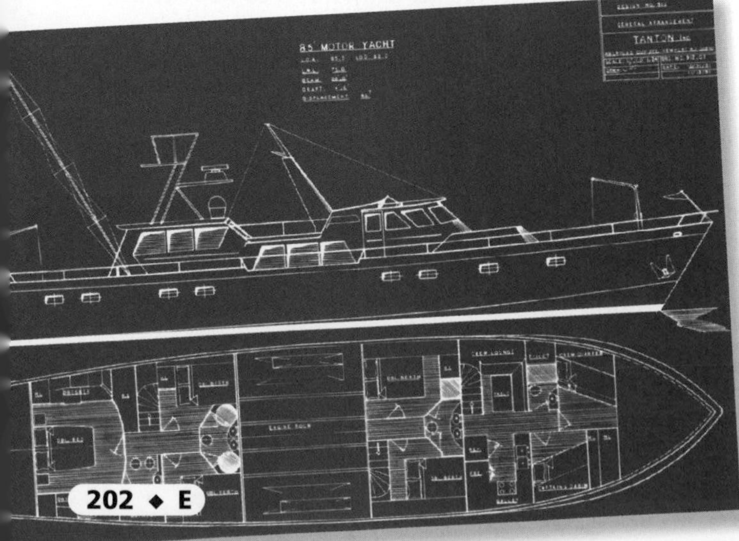

Design a Solution

Research gives engineers information that helps them design a product. When engineers design new products, they usually work in teams.

Generating Ideas Often design teams hold brainstorming meetings in which any team member can contribute ideas. **Brainstorming** is a creative process in which one team member's suggestions often spark ideas in other group members. Brainstorming can lead to new approaches to solving a design problem.

Evaluating Constraints During brainstorming, a design team will often come up with several possible designs. The team must then evaluate each one.

As part of their evaluation, engineers consider constraints. **Constraints** are factors that limit or restrict a product design. Physical characteristics, such as the properties of materials used to make your toy boat, are constraints. Money and time are also constraints. If the materials in a product cost a lot, or if the product takes a long time to make, the design may be impractical.

Making Trade-offs Design teams usually need to make trade-offs. In a **trade-off,** engineers give up one benefit of a proposed design in order to obtain another. In designing your toy boat, you will have to make trade-offs. For example, suppose one material is sturdy but not fully waterproof. Another material is more waterproof, but breakable. You may decide to give up the benefit of sturdiness in order to obtain the benefit of waterproofing.

Build and Evaluate a Prototype

Once the team has chosen a design plan, the engineers build a prototype of the product. A **prototype** is a working model used to test a design. Engineers evaluate the prototype to see whether it works well, is easy to operate, is safe to use, and holds up to repeated use.

Think of your toy boat. What would the prototype be like? Of what materials would it be made? How would you test it?

Troubleshoot and Redesign

Few prototypes work perfectly, which is why they need to be tested. Once a design team has tested a prototype, the members analyze the results and identify any problems. The team then tries to **troubleshoot,** or fix the design problems. For example, if your toy boat leaks or wobbles, the boat should be redesigned to eliminate those problems.

Communicate the Solution

A team needs to communicate the final design to the people who will manufacture and use the product. To do this, teams may use sketches, detailed drawings, computer simulations, and word descriptions.

Activity

You can use the technology design process to design and build a toy boat.

Research and Investigate

1. Visit the library or go online to research toy boats.
2. Investigate how a toy boat can be powered, including wind, rubber bands, or baking soda and vinegar.
3. Brainstorm materials, shapes, and steering for your boat.

Design and Build

4. Based on your research, design a toy boat that
   - is made of readily available materials
   - is no larger than 15 cm long and 10 cm wide
   - includes a power system, a rudder, and an area for cargo
   - travels 2 meters in a straight line carrying a load of 20 pennies
5. Sketch your design and write a step-by-step plan for building your boat. After your teacher approves your plan, build your boat.

Evaluate and Redesign

6. Test your boat, evaluate the results, and troubleshoot any problems.
7. Based on your evaluation, redesign your toy boat so it performs better.

Creating Data Tables and Graphs

How can you make sense of the data in a science experiment? The first step is to organize the data to help you understand them. Data tables and graphs are helpful tools for organizing data.

Data Tables

You have gathered your materials and set up your experiment. But before you start, you need to plan a way to record what happens during the experiment. By creating a data table, you can record your observations and measurements in an orderly way.

Suppose, for example, that a scientist conducted an experiment to find out how many Calories people of different body masses burn while doing various activities. The data table shows the results.

Notice in this data table that the manipulated variable (body mass) is the heading of one column. The responding variable (for Experiment 1, the number of Calories burned while bicycling) is the heading of the next column. Additional columns were added for related experiments.

Calories Burned in 30 Minutes

Body Mass	Experiment 1: Bicycling	Experiment 2: Playing Basketball	Experiment 3: Watching Television
30 kg	60 Calories	120 Calories	21 Calories
40 kg	77 Calories	164 Calories	27 Calories
50 kg	95 Calories	206 Calories	33 Calories
60 kg	114 Calories	248 Calories	38 Calories

Bar Graphs

To compare how many Calories a person burns doing various activities, you could create a bar graph. A bar graph is used to display data in a number of separate, or distinct, categories. In this example, bicycling, playing basketball, and watching television are the three categories.

To create a bar graph, follow these steps.

1. On graph paper, draw a horizontal, or *x*-, axis and a vertical, or *y*-, axis.
2. Write the names of the categories to be graphed along the horizontal axis. Include an overall label for the axis as well.
3. Label the vertical axis with the name of the responding variable. Include units of measurement. Then create a scale along the axis by marking off equally spaced numbers that cover the range of the data collected.
4. For each category, draw a solid bar using the scale on the vertical axis to determine the height. Make all the bars the same width.
5. Add a title that describes the graph.

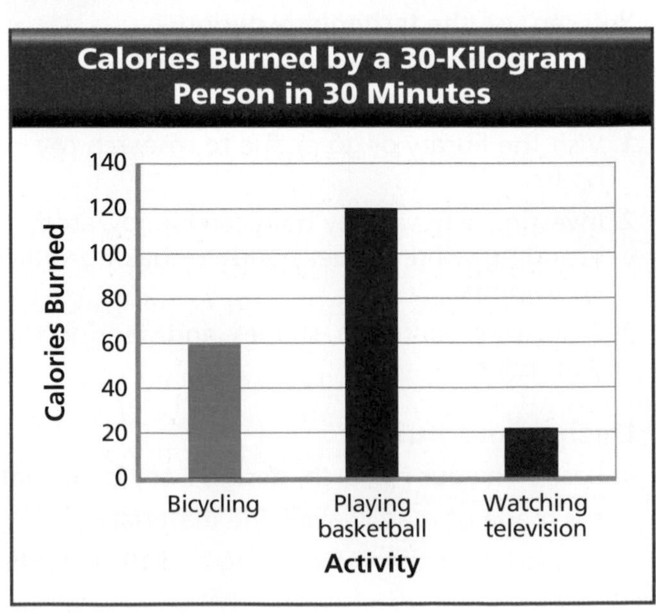

Line Graphs

To see whether a relationship exists between body mass and the number of Calories burned while bicycling, you could create a line graph. A line graph is used to display data that show how one variable (the responding variable) changes in response to another variable (the manipulated variable). You can use a line graph when your manipulated variable is **continuous,** that is, when there are other points between the ones that you tested. In this example, body mass is a continuous variable because there are other body masses between 30 and 40 kilograms (for example, 31 kilograms). Time is another example of a continuous variable.

Line graphs are powerful tools because they allow you to estimate values for conditions that you did not test in the experiment. For example, you can use the line graph to estimate that a 35-kilogram person would burn 68 Calories while bicycling.

To create a line graph, follow these steps.

1. On graph paper, draw a horizontal, or *x*-, axis and a vertical, or *y*-, axis.
2. Label the horizontal axis with the name of the manipulated variable. Label the vertical axis with the name of the responding variable. Include units of measurement.
3. Create a scale on each axis by marking off equally spaced numbers that cover the range of the data collected.
4. Plot a point on the graph for each piece of data. In the line graph above, the dotted lines show how to plot the first data point (30 kilograms and 60 Calories). Follow an imaginary vertical line extending up from the horizontal axis at the 30-kilogram mark. Then follow an imaginary horizontal line extending across from the vertical axis at the 60-Calorie mark. Plot the point where the two lines intersect.

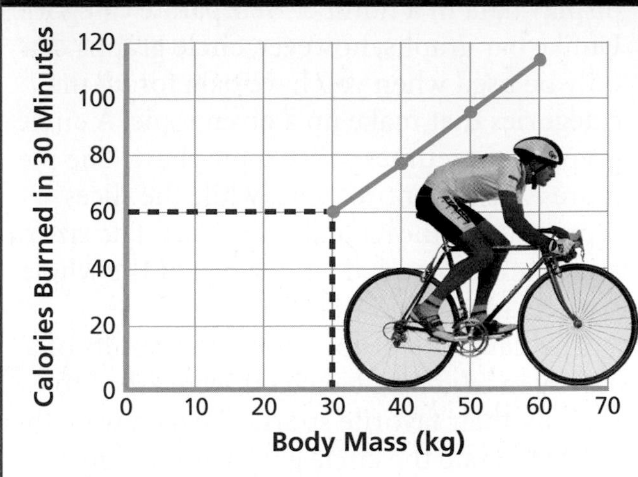

5. Connect the plotted points with a solid line. (In some cases, it may be more appropriate to draw a line that shows the general trend of the plotted points. In those cases, some of the points may fall above or below the line. Also, not all graphs are linear. It may be more appropriate to draw a curve to connect the points.)
6. Add a title that identifies the variables or relationship in the graph.

Activity

Create line graphs to display the data from Experiment 2 and Experiment 3 in the data table.

Activity

You read in the newspaper that a total of 4 centimeters of rain fell in your area in June, 2.5 centimeters fell in July, and 1.5 centimeters fell in August. What type of graph would you use to display these data? Use graph paper to create the graph.

Circle Graphs

Like bar graphs, circle graphs can be used to display data in a number of separate categories. Unlike bar graphs, however, circle graphs can only be used when you have data for *all* the categories that make up a given topic. A circle graph is sometimes called a pie chart. The pie represents the entire topic, while the slices represent the individual categories. The size of a slice indicates what percentage of the whole a particular category makes up.

The data table below shows the results of a survey in which 24 teenagers were asked to identify their favorite sport. The data were then used to create the circle graph at the right.

Favorite Sports	
Sport	Students
Soccer	8
Basketball	6
Bicycling	6
Swimming	4

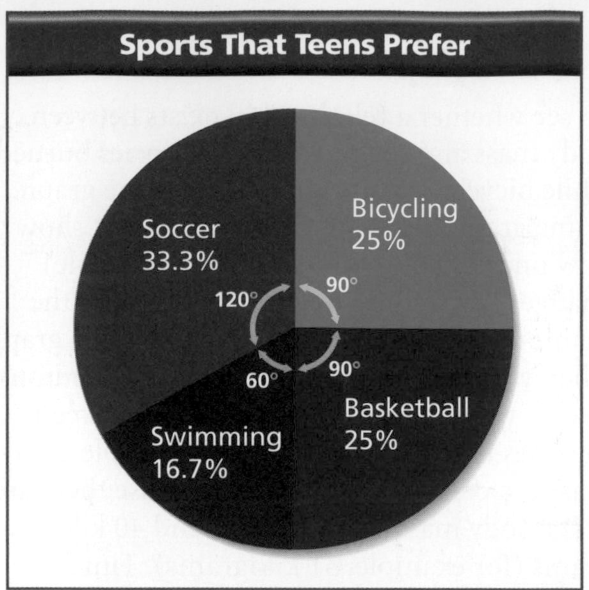

To create a circle graph, follow these steps.

1. Use a compass to draw a circle. Mark the center with a point. Then draw a line from the center point to the top of the circle.
2. Determine the size of each "slice" by setting up a proportion where x equals the number of degrees in a slice. (*Note:* A circle contains 360 degrees.) For example, to find the number of degrees in the "soccer" slice, set up the following proportion:

$$\frac{\text{Students who prefer soccer}}{\text{Total number of students}} = \frac{x}{\text{Total number of degrees in a circle}}$$

$$\frac{8}{24} = \frac{x}{360}$$

Cross-multiply and solve for x.

$$24x = 8 \times 360$$
$$x = 120$$

The "soccer" slice should contain 120 degrees.

3. Use a protractor to measure the angle of the first slice, using the line you drew to the top of the circle as the 0° line. Draw a line from the center of the circle to the edge for the angle you measured.
4. Continue around the circle by measuring the size of each slice with the protractor. Start measuring from the edge of the previous slice so the wedges do not overlap. When you are done, the entire circle should be filled in.
5. Determine the percentage of the whole circle that each slice represents. To do this, divide the number of degrees in a slice by the total number of degrees in a circle (360), and multiply by 100%. For the "soccer" slice, you can find the percentage as follows:

$$\frac{120}{360} \times 100\% = 33.3\%$$

6. Use a different color for each slice. Label each slice with the category and with the percentage of the whole it represents.
7. Add a title to the circle graph.

Activity

In a class of 28 students, 12 students take the bus to school, 10 students walk, and 6 students ride their bicycles. Create a circle graph to display these data.

Math Review

Scientists use math to organize, analyze, and present data. This appendix will help you review some basic math skills.

Mean, Median, and Mode

The **mean** is the average, or the sum of the data divided by the number of data items. The middle number in a set of ordered data is called the **median.** The **mode** is the number that appears most often in a set of data.

Example

A scientist counted the number of distinct songs sung by seven different male birds and collected the data shown below.

Male Bird Songs

Bird	A	B	C	D	E	F	G
Number of Songs	36	29	40	35	28	36	27

To determine the mean number of songs, add the total number of songs and divide by the number of data items—in this case, the number of male birds.

$$\text{Mean} = \frac{231}{7} = 33 \text{ songs}$$

To find the median number of songs, arrange the data in numerical order and find the number in the middle of the series.

27 28 29 35 36 36 40

The number in the middle is 35, so the median number of songs is 35.

The mode is the value that appears most frequently. In the data, 36 appears twice, while each other item appears only once. Therefore, 36 songs is the mode.

Practice

Find out how many minutes it takes each student in your class to get to school. Then find the mean, median, and mode for the data.

Probability

Probability is the chance that an event will occur. Probability can be expressed as a ratio, a fraction, or a percentage. For example, when you flip a coin, the probability that the coin will land heads up is 1 in 2, or $\frac{1}{2}$, or 50 percent.

The probability that an event will happen can be expressed in the following formula.

$$P(\text{event}) = \frac{\text{Number of times the event can occur}}{\text{Total number of possible events}}$$

Example

A paper bag contains 25 blue marbles, 5 green marbles, 5 orange marbles, and 15 yellow marbles. If you close your eyes and pick a marble from the bag, what is the probability that it will be yellow?

$$P(\text{yellow marbles}) = \frac{15 \text{ yellow marbles}}{50 \text{ marbles total}}$$

$$P = \frac{15}{50}, \text{ or } \frac{3}{10}, \text{ or } 30\%$$

Practice

Each side of a cube has a letter on it. Two sides have *A*, three sides have *B*, and one side has *C*. If you roll the cube, what is the probability that *A* will land on top?

Area

The **area** of a surface is the number of square units that cover it. The front cover of your textbook has an area of about 600 cm^2.

Area of a Rectangle and a Square To find the area of a rectangle, multiply its length times its width. The formula for the area of a rectangle is

$$A = \ell \times w, \text{ or } A = \ell w$$

Since all four sides of a square have the same length, the area of a square is the length of one side multiplied by itself, or squared.

$$A = s \times s, \text{ or } A = s^2$$

Example

A scientist is studying the plants in a field that measures 75 m × 45 m. What is the area of the field?

$$A = \ell \times w$$

$$A = 75 \text{ m} \times 45 \text{ m}$$

$$A = 3{,}375 \text{ m}^2$$

Area of a Circle The formula for the area of a circle is

$$A = \pi \times r \times r, \text{ or } A = \pi r^2$$

The length of the radius is represented by r, and the value of π is approximately $\frac{22}{7}$.

Example

Find the area of a circle with a radius of 14 cm.

$$A = \pi r^2$$

$$A = 14 \times 14 \times \frac{22}{7}$$

$$A = 616 \text{ cm}^2$$

Practice

Find the area of a circle that has a radius of 21 m.

Circumference

The distance around a circle is called the circumference. The formula for finding the circumference of a circle is

$$C = 2 \times \pi \times r, \text{ or } C = 2\pi r$$

Example

The radius of a circle is 35 cm. What is its circumference?

$$C = 2\pi r$$

$$C = 2 \times 35 \times \frac{22}{7}$$

$$C = 220 \text{ cm}$$

Practice

What is the circumference of a circle with a radius of 28 m?

Volume

The volume of an object is the number of cubic units it contains. The volume of a wastebasket, for example, might be about 26,000 cm^3.

Volume of a Rectangular Object To find the volume of a rectangular object, multiply the object's length times its width times its height.

$$V = \ell \times w \times h, \text{ or } V = \ell wh$$

Example

Find the volume of a box with length 24 cm, width 12 cm, and height 9 cm.

$$V = \ell wh$$

$$V = 24 \text{ cm} \times 12 \text{ cm} \times 9 \text{ cm}$$

$$V = 2{,}592 \text{ cm}^3$$

Practice

What is the volume of a rectangular object with length 17 cm, width 11 cm, and height 6 cm?

Fractions

A **fraction** is a way to express a part of a whole. In the fraction $\frac{4}{7}$, 4 is the numerator and 7 is the denominator.

Adding and Subtracting Fractions To add or subtract two or more fractions that have a common denominator, first add or subtract the numerators. Then write the sum or difference over the common denominator.

To find the sum or difference of fractions with different denominators, first find the least common multiple of the denominators. This is known as the least common denominator. Then convert each fraction to equivalent fractions with the least common denominator. Add or subtract the numerators. Then write the sum or difference over the common denominator.

Example

$$\frac{5}{6} - \frac{3}{4} = \frac{10}{12} - \frac{9}{12} = \frac{10 - 9}{12} = \frac{1}{12}$$

Multiplying Fractions To multiply two fractions, first multiply the two numerators, then multiply the two denominators.

Example

$$\frac{5}{6} \times \frac{2}{3} = \frac{5 \times 2}{6 \times 3} = \frac{10}{18} = \frac{5}{9}$$

Dividing Fractions Dividing by a fraction is the same as multiplying by its reciprocal. Reciprocals are numbers whose numerators and denominators have been switched. To divide one fraction by another, first invert the fraction you are dividing by—in other words, turn it upside down. Then multiply the two fractions.

Example

$$\frac{2}{5} \div \frac{7}{8} = \frac{2}{5} \times \frac{8}{7} = \frac{2 \times 8}{5 \times 7} = \frac{16}{35}$$

Practice

Solve the following: $\frac{3}{7} \div \frac{4}{5}$.

Decimals

Fractions whose denominators are 10, 100, or some other power of 10 are often expressed as decimals. For example, the fraction $\frac{9}{10}$ can be expressed as the decimal 0.9, and the fraction $\frac{7}{100}$ can be written as 0.07.

Adding and Subtracting With Decimals To add or subtract decimals, line up the decimal points before you carry out the operation.

Example

$$\begin{array}{r} 27.4 \\ +\ 6.19 \\ \hline 33.59 \end{array} \qquad \begin{array}{r} 278.635 \\ -\ 191.4 \\ \hline 87.235 \end{array}$$

Multiplying With Decimals When you multiply two numbers with decimals, the number of decimal places in the product is equal to the total number of decimal places in each number being multiplied.

Example

$$\begin{array}{rl} 46.2 & \text{(one decimal place)} \\ \times\ 2.37 & \text{(two decimal places)} \\ \hline 109.494 & \text{(three decimal places)} \end{array}$$

Dividing With Decimals To divide a decimal by a whole number, put the decimal point in the quotient above the decimal point in the dividend.

Example

$$15.5 \div 5$$

$$5\overline{)15.5} = 3.1$$

To divide a decimal by a decimal, you need to rewrite the divisor as a whole number. Do this by multiplying both the divisor and dividend by the same multiple of 10.

Example

$$1.68 \div 4.2 = 16.8 \div 42$$

$$42\overline{)16.8} = 0.4$$

Practice

Multiply 6.21 by 8.5.

Ratio and Proportion

A **ratio** compares two numbers by division. For example, suppose a scientist counts 800 wolves and 1,200 moose on an island. The ratio of wolves to moose can be written as a fraction, $\frac{800}{1,200}$, which can be reduced to $\frac{2}{3}$. The same ratio can also be expressed as 2 to 3 or 2 : 3.

A **proportion** is a mathematical sentence saying that two ratios are equivalent. For example, a proportion could state that $\frac{800 \text{ wolves}}{1,200 \text{ moose}} = \frac{2 \text{ wolves}}{3 \text{ moose}}$. You can sometimes set up a proportion to determine or estimate an unknown quantity. For example, suppose a scientist counts 25 beetles in an area of 10 square meters. The scientist wants to estimate the number of beetles in 100 square meters.

Example

1. Express the relationship between beetles and area as a ratio: $\frac{25}{10}$, simplified to $\frac{5}{2}$.
2. Set up a proportion, with x representing the number of beetles. The proportion can be stated as $\frac{5}{2} = \frac{x}{100}$.
3. Begin by cross-multiplying. In other words, multiply each fraction's numerator by the other fraction's denominator.

   $$5 \times 100 = 2 \times x, \text{ or } 500 = 2x$$

4. To find the value of x, divide both sides by 2. The result is 250, or 250 beetles in 100 square meters.

Practice

Find the value of x in the following proportion: $\frac{6}{7} = \frac{x}{49}$.

Percentage

A **percentage** is a ratio that compares a number to 100. For example, there are 37 granite rocks in a collection that consists of 100 rocks. The ratio $\frac{37}{100}$ can be written as 37%. Granite rocks make up 37% of the rock collection.

You can calculate percentages of numbers other than 100 by setting up a proportion.

Example

Rain falls on 9 days out of 30 in June. What percentage of the days in June were rainy?

$$\frac{9 \text{ days}}{30 \text{ days}} = \frac{d\%}{100\%}$$

To find the value of d, begin by cross-multiplying, as for any proportion:

$$9 \times 100 = 30 \times d \qquad d = \frac{900}{30} \qquad d = 30$$

Practice

There are 300 marbles in a jar, and 42 of those marbles are blue. What percentage of the marbles are blue?

Significant Figures

The **precision** of a measurement depends on the instrument you use to take the measurement. For example, if the smallest unit on the ruler is millimeters, then the most precise measurement you can make will be in millimeters.

The sum or difference of measurements can only be as precise as the least precise measurement being added or subtracted. Round your answer so that it has the same number of digits after the decimal as the least precise measurement. Round up if the last digit is 5 or more, and round down if the last digit is 4 or less.

Example

Subtract a temperature of 5.2°C from the temperature 75.46°C.

$$75.46 - 5.2 = 70.26$$

5.2 has the fewest digits after the decimal, so it is the least precise measurement. Since the last digit of the answer is 6, round up to 3. The most precise difference between the measurements is 70.3°C.

Practice

Add 26.4 m to 8.37 m. Round your answer according to the precision of the measurements.

Significant figures are the number of nonzero digits in a measurement. Zeroes between nonzero digits are also significant. For example, the measurements 12,500 L, 0.125 cm, and 2.05 kg all have three significant figures. When you multiply and divide measurements, the one with the fewest significant figures determines the number of significant figures in your answer.

Example

Multiply 110 g by 5.75 g.

$$110 \times 5.75 = 632.5$$

Because 110 has only two significant figures, round the answer to 630 g.

Scientific Notation

A **factor** is a number that divides into another number with no remainder. In the example, the number 3 is used as a factor four times.

An **exponent** tells how many times a number is used as a factor. For example, $3 \times 3 \times 3 \times 3$ can be written as 3^4. The exponent ^{4} indicates that the number 3 is used as a factor four times. Another way of expressing this is to say that 81 is equal to 3 to the fourth power.

Example

$$3^4 = 3 \times 3 \times 3 \times 3 = 81$$

Scientific notation uses exponents and powers of ten to write very large or very small numbers in shorter form. When you write a number in scientific notation, you write the number as two factors. The first factor is any number between 1 and 10. The second factor is a power of 10, such as 10^3 or 10^6.

Example

The average distance between the planet Mercury and the sun is 58,000,000 km. To write the first factor in scientific notation, insert a decimal point in the original number so that you have a number between 1 and 10. In the case of 58,000,000, the number is 5.8.

To determine the power of 10, count the number of places that the decimal point moved. In this case, it moved 7 places.

$$58{,}000{,}000 \text{ km} = 5.8 \times 10^7 \text{ km}$$

Practice

Express 6,590,000 in scientific notation.

Reading Comprehension Skills

Each section in your textbook introduces a Target Reading Skill. You will improve your reading comprehension by using the Target Reading Skills described below.

Using Prior Knowledge

Your prior knowledge is what you already know before you begin to read about a topic. Building on what you already know gives you a head start on learning new information. Before you begin a new assignment, think about what you know. You might look at the headings and the visuals to spark your memory. You can list what you know. Then, as you read, consider questions like these.

- How does what you learn relate to what you know?
- How did something you already know help you learn something new?
- Did your original ideas agree with what you have just learned?

Asking Questions

Asking yourself questions is an excellent way to focus on and remember new information in your textbook. For example, you can turn the text headings into questions. Then your questions can guide you to identify the important information as you read. Look at these examples:

Heading: Using Seismographic Data

Question: How are seismographic data used?

Heading: Kinds of Faults

Question: What are the kinds of faults?

You do not have to limit your questions to text headings. Ask questions about anything that you need to clarify or that will help you understand the content. *What* and *how* are probably the most common question words, but you may also ask *why*, *who*, *when*, or *where* questions.

Previewing Visuals

Visuals are photographs, graphs, tables, diagrams, and illustrations. Visuals contain important information. Before you read, look at visuals and their labels and captions. This preview will help you prepare for what you will be reading.

Often you will be asked what you want to learn about a visual. For example, after you look at the normal fault diagram below, you might ask: What is the movement along a normal fault? Questions about visuals give you a purpose for reading—to answer your questions.

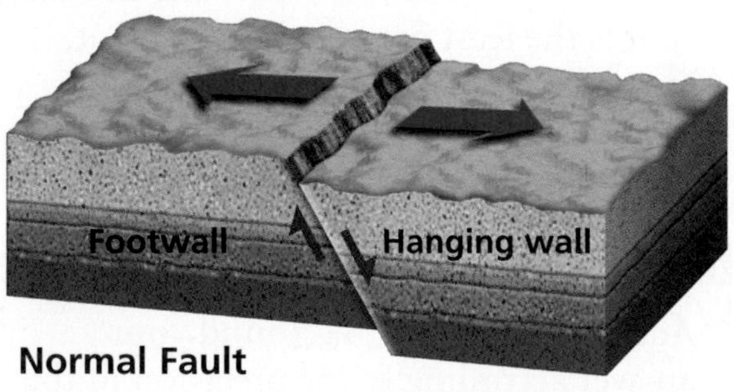

Normal Fault

Outlining

An outline shows the relationship between main ideas and supporting ideas. An outline has a formal structure. You write the main ideas, called topics, next to Roman numerals. The supporting ideas, called subtopics, are written under the main ideas and labeled A, B, C, and so on. An outline looks like this:

Technology and Society

I. Technology through history
II. The impact of technology on society
  A.
  B.

Identifying Main Ideas

When you are reading science material, it is important to try to understand the ideas and concepts that are in a passage. Each paragraph has a lot of information and detail. Good readers try to identify the most important—or biggest—idea in every paragraph or section. That's the main idea. The other information in the paragraph supports or further explains the main idea.

Sometimes main ideas are stated directly. In this book, some main ideas are identified for you as key concepts. These are printed in boldface type. However, you must identify other main ideas yourself. In order to do this, you must identify all the ideas within a paragraph or section. Then ask yourself which idea is big enough to include all the other ideas.

Comparing and Contrasting

When you compare and contrast, you examine the similarities and differences between things. You can compare and contrast in a Venn diagram or in a table.

Venn Diagram A Venn diagram consists of two overlapping circles. In the space where the circles overlap, you write the characteristics that the two items have in common. In one of the circles outside the area of overlap, you write the differing features or characteristics of one of the items. In the other circle outside the area of overlap, you write the differing characteristics of the other item.

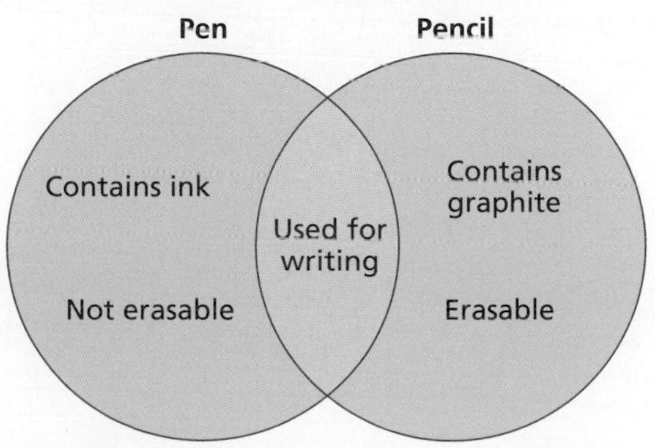

Table In a compare/contrast table, you list the characteristics or features to be compared across the top of the table. Then list the items to be compared in the left column. Complete the table by filling in information about each characteristic or feature.

Blood Vessel	Function	Structure of Wall
Artery	Carries blood away from heart	
Capillary		
Vein		

Identifying Supporting Evidence

A hypothesis is a possible explanation for observations made by scientists or an answer to a scientific question. Scientists must carry out investigations and gather evidence that either supports or disproves the hypothesis.

Identifying the supporting evidence for a hypothesis or theory can help you understand the hypothesis or theory. Evidence consists of facts—information whose accuracy can be confirmed by testing or observation.

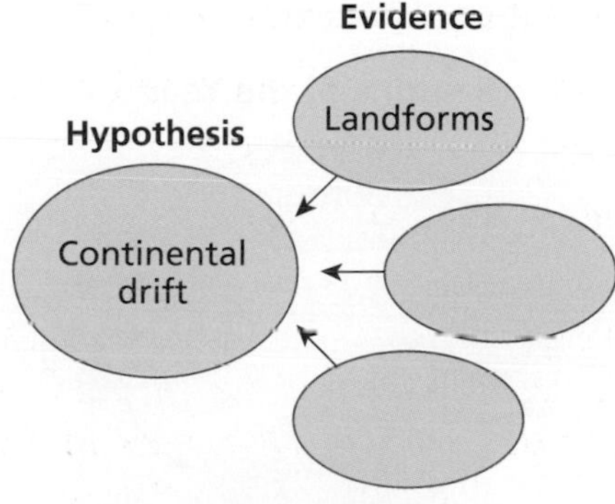

Sequencing

A sequence is the order in which a series of events occurs. A flowchart or a cycle diagram can help you visualize a sequence.

Flowchart To make a flowchart, write a brief description of each step or event in a box. Place the boxes in order, with the first event at the top of the chart. Then draw an arrow to connect each step or event to the next.

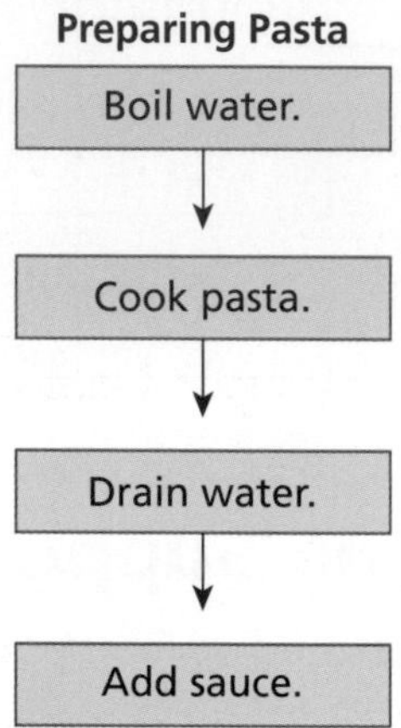

Cycle Diagram A cycle diagram shows a sequence that is continuous, or cyclical. A continuous sequence does not have an end because when the final event is over, the first event begins again. To create a cycle diagram, write the starting event in a box placed at the top of a page in the center. Then, moving in a clockwise direction, write each event in a box in its proper sequence. Draw arrows that connect each event to the one that occurs next.

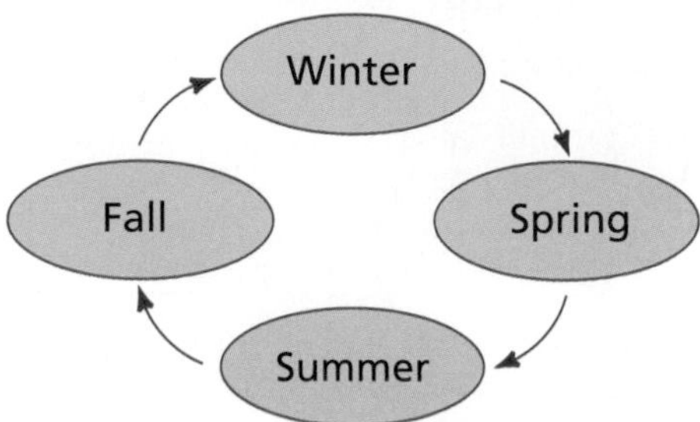

Relating Cause and Effect

Science involves many cause-and-effect relationships. A cause makes something happen. An effect is what happens. When you recognize that one event causes another, you are relating cause and effect.

Words like *cause, because, effect, affect,* and *result* often signal a cause or an effect. Sometimes an effect can have more than one cause, or a cause can produce several effects.

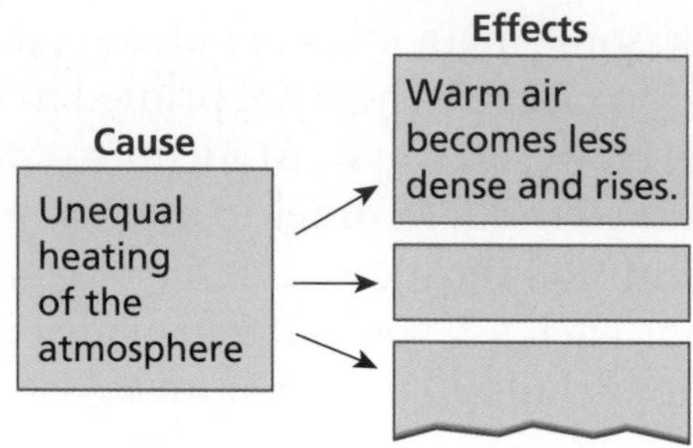

Concept Mapping

Concept maps are useful tools for organizing information on any topic. A concept map begins with a main idea or core concept and shows how the idea can be subdivided into related subconcepts or smaller ideas.

You construct a concept map by placing concepts (usually nouns) in ovals and connecting them with linking words (usually verbs). The biggest concept or idea is placed in an oval at the top of the map. Related concepts are arranged in ovals below the big idea. The linking words connect the ovals.

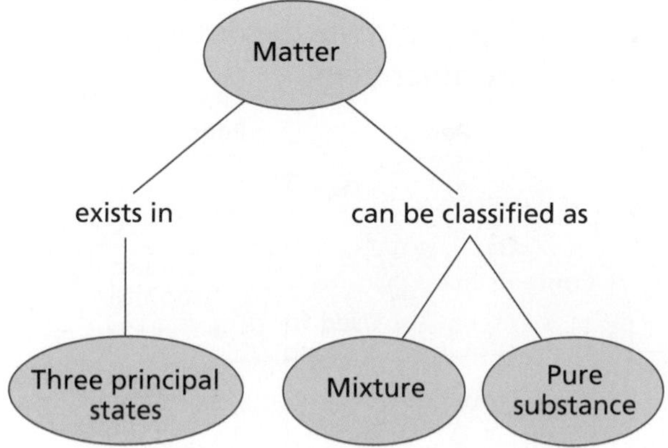

Building Vocabulary

Knowing the meaning of these prefixes, suffixes, and roots will help you understand the meaning of words you do not recognize.

Word Origins Many science words come to English from other languages, such as Greek and Latin. By learning the meaning of a few common Greek and Latin roots, you can determine the meaning of unfamiliar science words.

Prefixes A prefix is a word part that is added at the beginning of a root or base word to change its meaning.

Suffixes A suffix is a word part that is added at the end of a root word to change the meaning.

Greek and Latin Roots

Greek Roots	Meaning	Example
ast-	star	astronaut
geo-	Earth	geology
metron-	measure	kilometer
opt-	eye	optician
photo-	light	photograph
scop-	see	microscope
therm-	heat	thermostat
Latin Roots	**Meaning**	**Example**
aqua-	water	aquarium
aud-	hear	auditorium
duc-, duct-	lead	conduct
flect-	bend	reflect
fract-, frag-	break	fracture
ject-	throw	reject
luc-	light	lucid
spec-	see	inspect

Prefixes and Suffixes

Prefix	Meaning	Example
com-, con-	with	communicate, concert
de-	from; down	decay
di-	two	divide
ex-, exo-	out	exhaust
in-, im-	in, into; not	inject, impossible
re-	again; back	reflect, recall
trans-	across	transfer
Suffix	**Meaning**	**Example**
-al	relating to	natural
-er, -or	one who	teacher, doctor
-ist	one who practices	scientist
-ity	state of	equality
-ology	study of	biology
-tion, -sion	state or quality of	reaction, tension

Safety Symbols

These symbols warn of possible dangers in the laboratory and remind you to work carefully.

Safety Goggles Wear safety goggles to protect your eyes in any activity involving chemicals, flames or heating, or glassware.

Lab Apron Wear a laboratory apron to protect your skin and clothing from damage.

Breakage Handle breakable materials, such as glassware, with care. Do not touch broken glassware.

Heat-Resistant Gloves Use an oven mitt or other hand protection when handling hot materials such as hot plates or hot glassware.

Plastic Gloves Wear disposable plastic gloves when working with harmful chemicals and organisms. Keep your hands away from your face, and dispose of the gloves according to your teacher's instructions.

Heating Use a clamp or tongs to pick up hot glassware. Do not touch hot objects with your bare hands.

Flames Before you work with flames, tie back loose hair and clothing. Follow instructions from your teacher about lighting and extinguishing flames.

No Flames When using flammable materials, make sure there are no flames, sparks, or other exposed heat sources present.

Corrosive Chemical Avoid getting acid or other corrosive chemicals on your skin or clothing or in your eyes. Do not inhale the vapors. Wash your hands after the activity.

Poison Do not let any poisonous chemical come into contact with your skin, and do not inhale its vapors. Wash your hands when you are finished with the activity.

Fumes Work in a ventilated area when harmful vapors may be involved. Avoid inhaling vapors directly. Only test an odor when directed to do so by your teacher, and use a wafting motion to direct the vapor toward your nose.

Sharp Object Scissors, scalpels, knives, needles, pins, and tacks can cut your skin. Always direct a sharp edge or point away from yourself and others.

Animal Safety Treat live or preserved animals or animal parts with care to avoid harming the animals or yourself. Wash your hands when you are finished with the activity.

Plant Safety Handle plants only as directed by your teacher. If you are allergic to certain plants, tell your teacher; do not do an activity involving those plants. Avoid touching harmful plants such as poison ivy. Wash your hands when you are finished with the activity.

Electric Shock To avoid electric shock, never use electrical equipment around water, or when the equipment is wet or your hands are wet. Be sure cords are untangled and cannot trip anyone. Unplug equipment not in use.

Physical Safety When an experiment involves physical activity, avoid injuring yourself or others. Alert your teacher if there is any reason you should not participate.

Disposal Dispose of chemicals and other laboratory materials safely. Follow the instructions from your teacher.

Hand Washing Wash your hands thoroughly when finished with the activity. Use soap and warm water. Rinse well.

General Safety Awareness When this symbol appears, follow the instructions provided. When you are asked to develop your own procedure in a lab, have your teacher approve your plan before you go further.

Science Safety Rules

General Precautions

Follow all instructions. Never perform activities without the approval and supervision of your teacher. Do not engage in horseplay. Never eat or drink in the laboratory. Keep work areas clean and uncluttered.

Dress Code

Wear safety goggles whenever you work with chemicals, glassware, heat sources such as burners, or any substance that might get into your eyes. If you wear contact lenses, notify your teacher.

Wear a lab apron or coat whenever you work with corrosive chemicals or substances that can stain. Wear disposable plastic gloves when working with organisms and harmful chemicals. Tie back long hair. Remove or tie back any article of clothing or jewelry that can hang down and touch chemicals, flames, or equipment. Roll up long sleeves. Never wear open shoes or sandals.

First Aid

Report all accidents, injuries, or fires to your teacher, no matter how minor. Be aware of the location of the first-aid kit, emergency equipment such as the fire extinguisher and fire blanket, and the nearest telephone. Know whom to contact in an emergency.

Heating and Fire Safety

Keep all combustible materials away from flames. When heating a substance in a test tube, make sure that the mouth of the tube is not pointed at you or anyone else. Never heat a liquid in a closed container. Use an oven mitt to pick up a container that has been heated.

Using Chemicals Safely

Never put your face near the mouth of a container that holds chemicals. Never touch, taste, or smell a chemical unless your teacher tells you to.

Use only those chemicals needed in the activity. Keep all containers closed when chemicals are not being used. Pour all chemicals over the sink or a container, not over your work surface. Dispose of excess chemicals as instructed by your teacher.

Be extra careful when working with acids or bases. When mixing an acid and water, always pour the water into the container first and then add the acid to the water. Never pour water into an acid. Wash chemical spills and splashes immediately with plenty of water.

Using Glassware Safely

If glassware is broken or chipped, notify your teacher immediately. Never handle broken or chipped glass with your bare hands.

Never force glass tubing or thermometers into a rubber stopper or rubber tubing. Have your teacher insert the glass tubing or thermometer if required for an activity.

Using Sharp Instruments

Handle sharp instruments with extreme care. Never cut material toward you; cut away from you.

Animal and Plant Safety

Never perform experiments that cause pain, discomfort, or harm to animals. Only handle animals if absolutely necessary. If you know that you are allergic to certain plants, molds, or animals, tell your teacher before doing an activity in which these are used. Wash your hands thoroughly after any activity involving animals, animal parts, plants, plant parts, or soil.

During field work, wear long pants, long sleeves, socks, and closed shoes. Avoid poisonous plants and fungi as well as plants with thorns.

End-of-Experiment Rules

Unplug all electrical equipment. Clean up your work area. Dispose of waste materials as instructed by your teacher. Wash your hands after every experiment.

English and Spanish Glossary

abiotic factor A nonliving part of an organism's habitat. (p. 8)
factor abiótico La parte no viva del hábitat de un organismo.

acid rain Precipitation that is more acidic than normal because of air pollution. (p. 140)
lluvia ácida Precipitación que es más ácida de lo normal debido a la contaminación del aire.

adaptation A behavior or physical characteristic that allows an organism to live successfully in its environment. (p. 25)
adaptación Comportamiento o característica física que permite a un organismo vivir en su medio ambiente.

aquaculture The practice of raising fish and other water-dwelling organisms for food. (p. 93)
acuicultura Técnica del cultivo de peces y otros organismos acuáticos para consumo humano.

B

bedrock Rock that makes up Earth's crust. (p. 118)
lecho rocoso Roca que forma la corteza de la Tierra.

biodegradable Capable of being broken down by bacteria and other decomposers. (p. 125)
biodegradable Sustancia que las bacterias y otros descomponedores pueden descomponer.

biodiversity The number of different species in an area. (p. 95)
biodiversidad Número de diferentes especies en un área.

biogeography The study of where organisms live. (p. 54)
biogeografía Estudio del lugar donde viven los organismos.

biomass fuel Fuel made from living things. (p. 169)
combustible de biomasa Combustible formado a partir de seres vivos.

biome A group of land ecosystems with similar climates and organisms. (p. 58)
bioma Grupo de ecosistemas terrestres con climas y organismos similares.

biotic factor A living part of an organism's habitat. (p. 7)
factor biótico La parte viva del hábitat de un organismo.

birth rate The number of births in a population in a certain amount of time. (p. 16)
tasa de natalidad Número de nacimientos en una población en un período determinado.

canopy A leafy roof formed by tall trees in a forest. (p. 60)
bóveda arbórea Cubierta densa formada por las cimas hojeadas de los árboles altos de un bosque.

captive breeding The mating of animals in zoos or wildlife preserves. (p. 104)
reproducción en cautiverio Apareamiento de animales en zoológicos y reservas naturales.

carnivore A consumer that eats only animals. (p. 43)
carnívoro Consumidor que come sólo animales.

carrying capacity The largest population that an area can support. (p. 19)
capacidad de carga La mayor población que puede sustentar un área.

chlorofluorocarbons Human-made gases containing chlorine and fluorine (also called CFCs). (p. 148)
clorofluorocarbonos Gases producidos por el ser humano que contienen cloro y flúor (también llamados CFC).

clear-cutting The process of cutting down all the trees in an area at once. (p. 90)
tala total Proceso de cortar simultáneamente todos los árboles de un área.

climate The typical weather pattern in an area over a long period of time. (p. 57)
clima Patrón típico del tiempo en un área durante un largo período.

combustion The process of burning a fuel. (p. 159)
combustión Proceso en el que se quema un combustible.

commensalism A relationship between two species in which one species benefits and the other is neither helped nor harmed. (p. 30)
comensalismo Relación entre dos especies donde una se beneficia y la otra no obtiene ni beneficio ni perjuicio.

community All the different populations that live together in an area. (p. 9)
comunidad Todas las diferentes poblaciones que viven juntas en un área.

competition The struggle between organisms to survive as they attempt to use the same limited resource. (p. 26)
competencia Lucha entre organismos por sobrevivir a medida que usan los recursos limitados en un mismo hábitat.

composting The process of helping biodegradable wastes to decompose naturally. (p. 127)
compostaje Proceso de ayudar a que los desechos biodegradables se descompongan de manera natural.

condensation The process by which a gas changes to a liquid. (p. 49)
condensación Proceso por el cual un gas se convierte en líquido.

coniferous tree A tree that produces its seeds in cones and that has needle-shaped leaves. (p. 64)
árbol conífero Árbol que produce sus semillas en conos y sus hojas tienen forma de aguja.

consumer An organism that obtains energy by feeding on other organisms. (p. 43)
consumidor Organismo que obtiene energía alimentándose de otros organismos.

continental drift The very slow motion of the continents. (p. 55)
deriva continental Movimiento muy lento de los continentes.

control rod A cadmium rod used in a nuclear reactor to absorb neutrons from fission reactions. (p. 176)
varilla de control Varilla de cadmio que se usa en un reactor nuclear para absorber los neutrones emitidos por las reacciones de la fisión.

D

death rate The number of deaths in a population in a certain amount of time. (p. 16)
tasa de mortalidad Número de muertes en una población en un período determinado.

deciduous tree A tree that sheds its leaves and grows new ones each year. (p. 63)
árbol caducifolio Árbol cuyas hojas caen y vuelven a crecer anualmente.

decomposer An organism that breaks down wastes and dead organisms. (p. 43)
descomponedor Organismo que descompone desechos y organismos muertos.

desert An area that receives less than 25 centimeters of precipitation per year. (p. 61)
desierto Área que recibe menos de 25 centímetros de precipitación al año.

desertification The advance of desert-like conditions into areas that previously were fertile. (p. 120)
desertificación Avance de condiciones similares a las del desierto a áreas que anteriormente eran fértiles.

development The construction of buildings, roads, bridges, dams, and other structures. (p. 117)
desarrollo Construcción de edificios, carreteras, puentes, presas y otras estructuras.

dispersal The movement of organisms from one place to another. (p. 55)
dispersión Movimiento de los organismos de un lugar a otro.

drought A period of less rain than normal. (p. 120)
sequía Período de menor lluvia que lo normal.

E

ecology The study of how living things interact with each other and their environment. (p. 10)
ecología Estudio de cómo interactúan los seres vivos entre sí y con su medio ambiente.

ecosystem The community of organisms that live in a particular area, along with their nonliving surroundings. (p. 10)
ecosistema Comunidad de organismos que viven en un área determinada, junto con su medio ambiente no vivo.

efficiency The percentage of energy that is used to perform work. (p. 180)
eficiencia Porcentaje de energía usada para realizar trabajo.

emigration Leaving a population. (p. 16)
emigración Abandono de una población.

emissions Pollutants that are released into the air. (p. 138)
gases contaminantes Contaminantes liberados al aire.

endangered species A species in danger of becoming extinct in the near future. (p. 101)
especie en peligro de extinción Especie que corre el riesgo de desaparecer en el futuro próximo.

energy conservation The practice of reducing energy use. (p. 182)
conservación de la energía Práctica de reducción del uso de energía.

energy pyramid A diagram that shows the amount of energy that moves from one feeding level to another in a food web. (p. 46)
pirámide de la energía Diagrama que muestra la cantidad de energía que pasa de un nivel de alimentación a otro en una red alimentaria.

energy transformation A change from one form of energy to another; also called an energy conversion. (p. 158)
transformación de la energía Cambio de una forma de energía a otra; también se le llama conversión de energía.

environmental science The study of the natural processes that occur in the environment and how humans can affect them. (p. 86)
ciencias del medio ambiente Estudio de los procesos naturales que ocurren en el medio ambiente y cómo los seres humanos pueden afectarlos.

erosion The process by which water, wind, or ice moves particles of rock or soil. (p. 119)
erosión Proceso por el cual el agua, el viento o el hielo transportan partículas de roca o suelo.

estimate An approximation of a number, based on reasonable assumptions. (p. 14)
estimación Cálculo aproximado de un número, basándose en supuestos razonables.

estuary A habitat in which the fresh water of a river meets the salt water of the ocean. (p. 72)
estuario Hábitat en el cual el agua dulce de un río se encuentra con el agua salada del mar.

evaporation The process by which molecules of a liquid absorb energy and change to a gas. (p. 49)
evaporación Proceso por el cual las moléculas de un líquido absorben energía y pasan al estado gaseoso.

exotic species Species that are carried to a new location by people. (p. 56)
especies exóticas Especies que lleva la gente a un nuevo lugar.

extinction The disappearance of all members of a species from Earth. (p. 100)
extinción Desaparición de la Tierra de todos los miembros de una especie.

F

fertilizer A substance that provides nutrients to help crops grow better. (p. 119)
fertilizante Sustancia que proporciona nutriente para ayudar a que crezcan mejor los cultivos.

fishery An area with a large population of valuable ocean organisms. (p. 92)
pesquería Área con una gran población de organismos marinos aprovechables.

food chain A series of events in which one organism eats another and obtains energy. (p. 44)
cadena alimentaria Serie de sucesos en los que un organismo se come a otro y obtiene energía.

food web The pattern of overlapping food chains in an ecosystem. (p. 44)
red alimentaria Patrón de cadenas alimentarias sobrepuestas en un ecosistema.

fossil fuel An energy-rich substance (such as coal, oil, or natural gas) formed from the remains of organisms. (p. 160)
combustible fósil Sustancia rica en energía (como carbón mineral, petróleo o gas natural) que se forma a partir de los restos de organismos.

fuel A substance that provides energy as the result of a chemical change. (p. 158)
combustible Sustancia que libera energía como resultado de un cambio químico.

fuel rod A uranium rod that undergoes fission in a nuclear reactor. (p. 176)
varilla de combustible Varilla de uranio que se somete a la fisión en un reactor nuclear.

G

gasohol A mixture of gasoline and alcohol. (p. 169)
gasohol Mezcla de gasolina y alcohol.

gene A structure in an organism's cells that carries its hereditary information. (p. 99)
gen Estructura en las células de un organismo que contiene la información hereditaria.

geothermal energy Heat from Earth's interior. (p. 170)
energía geotérmica Calor del interior de la Tierra.

global warming The theory that increasing carbon dioxide in the atmosphere will raise Earth's average temperature. (p. 150)
calentamiento global Teoría que dice que al aumentar el dióxido de carbono en la atmósfera, aumentará la temperatura promedio de la Tierra.

grassland An area populated by grasses and other nonwoody plants. Most grasslands get 25 to 75 centimeters of rain each year. (p. 62)
pradera Área poblada de pastos y de otras plantas no leñosas. La mayoría de las praderas recibe de 25 a 75 centímetros de lluvia al año.

greenhouse effect The trapping of heat near Earth's surface by certain gases in the atmosphere. (p. 150)
efecto invernadero Calor atrapado cerca de la superficie de la Tierra por ciertos gases de la atmósfera.

groundwater Water stored in underground layers of soil and rock. (p. 132)
aguas freáticas Aguas acumuladas en capas subterráneas de suelo y roca.

H

habitat An environment that provides the things an organism needs to live, grow, and reproduce. (p. 7)
hábitat Ambiente que proporciona las cosas que un organismo necesita para vivir, crecer y reproducirse.

habitat destruction The loss of a natural habitat. (p. 102)
destrucción del hábitat Pérdida de un hábitat natural.

habitat fragmentation The breaking of a habitat into smaller, isolated pieces. (p. 102)
fragmentación del hábitat Desintegración de un hábitat en porciones aisladas más pequeñas.

hazardous waste A material that can be harmful if it is not properly disposed of. (p. 128)
desecho peligroso Material que puede ser dañino si no se elimina adecuadamente.

herbivore A consumer that eats only plants. (p. 43)
herbívoro Consumidor que come sólo plantas.

host The organism that a parasite lives in or on in a parasitism interaction. (p. 31)
huésped Organismo dentro o fuera del cual vive un parásito en una interacción de parasitismo.

hydrocarbon An energy-rich chemical compound that contains carbon and hydrogen atoms. (p. 160)
hidrocarburo Compuesto químico rico en energía que contiene átomos de carbono e hidrógeno.

hydroelectric power Electricity produced using the energy of flowing water. (p. 168)
energía hidroeléctrica Electricidad que se produce usando la energía de una corriente de agua.

I

immigration Moving into a population. (p. 16)
inmigración Ingreso a una población.

incineration The burning of solid waste. (p. 123)
incineración Quema de desechos sólidos.

insulation Material that blocks heat transfer between the air inside and outside a building. (p. 180)
aislante Material que impide la transferencia de calor entre el interior y el exterior de un edificio.

intertidal zone The area between the highest high-tide line and lowest low-tide line. (p. 72)
zona intermareal Área entre la línea más alta de la marea alta y la línea más baja de la marea baja.

K

keystone species A species that influences the survival of many others in an ecosystem. (p. 97)
especie clave Especie que influye en la supervivencia de muchas otras en un ecosistema.

L

land reclamation The process of restoring land to a more natural state. (p. 121)
recuperación de la tierra Proceso de restitución de la tierra a un estado más natural.

leachate Polluted liquid produced by water passing through buried wastes in a landfill. (p. 124)
lixiviado Líquido contaminado que se produce por el paso del agua a través de los desechos enterrados en un relleno sanitario.

limiting factor An environmental factor that causes a population to decrease. (p. 18)
factor limitante Factor ambiental que impide el crecimiento de una población.

litter The layer of dead leaves and grass on top of the soil. (p. 118)
mantillo Capa suelta de hierbas y hojas secas sobre el suelo.

M

meltdown A dangerous condition in which fuel rods inside a nuclear reactor melt. (p. 177)
fusión (del núcleo de un reactor) Condición peligrosa en la cual las varillas de combustible dentro del reactor nuclear se derriten.

municipal solid waste Waste produced in homes, businesses, and schools. (p. 123)
desechos sólidos urbanos Desechos producidos en hogares, oficinas y escuelas.

mutualism A relationship between two species in which both species benefit. (p. 30)
mutualismo Relación entre dos especies de la cual ambas se benefician.

N

natural resource Anything in the environment that is used by people. (p. 83)
recurso natural Cualquier cosa del medio ambiente que usa la gente.

natural selection A process by which characteristics that make an individual better suited to its environment become more common in a species. (p. 25)
selección natural Proceso por el cual las características que permiten a un individuo adaptarse mejor a su medio ambiente se hacen más comunes en una especie.

neritic zone The region of shallow ocean water over the continental shelf. (p. 72)
zona nerítica Región sobre la placa continental donde el agua del océano es poco profunda.

niche The role of an organism in its habitat, or how it makes its living. (p. 25)
nicho Función de un organismo en su hábitat, o cómo sobrevive.

nitrogen fixation The process of changing free nitrogen gas into a usable form. (p. 52)
fijación del nitrógeno Proceso de conversión del gas nitrógeno libre en una forma aprovechable.

nonrenewable resource A natural resource that is not replaced in a useful time frame. (p. 83)
recurso no renovable Recurso natural que no se restaura una vez usado, en un período relativamente corto.

nuclear fission The splitting of an atom's nucleus into two smaller nuclei and neutrons. (p. 175)
fisión nuclear División del núcleo de un átomo en dos núcleos más pequeños y neutrones.

nuclear fusion The combining of two atomic nuclei to produce a single larger nucleus and much energy. (p. 178)
fusión nuclear Unión de dos núcleos atómicos para producir un núcleo único más grande y liberar energía.

nucleus The central core of an atom that contains the protons and neutrons. (p. 174)
núcleo Parte central de un átomo que contiene protones y neutrones.

nutrient depletion The situation that arises when more soil nutrients are used than the decomposers can supply. (p. 119)
agotamiento de nutrientes Situación que se produce cuando se usan más nutrientes del suelo de lo que los descomponedores pueden proporcionar.

O

omnivore A consumer that eats both plants and animals. (p. 43)
omnívoro Consumidor que come tanto plantas como animales.

organism A living thing. (p. 7)
organismo Un ser viviente.

ozone A toxic form of oxygen. (p. 139)
ozono Forma tóxica del oxígeno.

ozone layer The layer of the atmosphere that contains a higher concentration of ozone than the rest of the atmosphere. (p. 147)
capa de ozono Capa atmosférica que contiene una mayor concentración de ozono que el resto de la atmósfera.

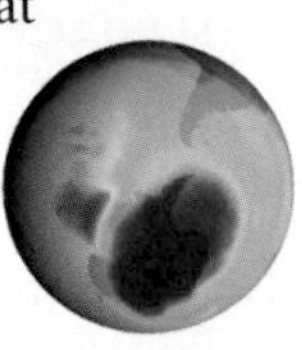

P

parasite The organism that benefits by living on or in a host in a parasitism interaction. (p. 31)
parásito Organismo que se beneficia de vivir en la superficie o en el interior de un húesped en una interacción de parasitismo.

parasitism A relationship in which one organism lives on or in a host and harms it. (p. 31)
parasitismo Relación en la cual un organismo vive en la superficie o en el interior de un huésped y lo perjudica.

permafrost Soil that is frozen all year. (p. 65)
permagélido Suelo que está congelado todo el año.

pesticide A chemical that kills crop-destroying organisms. (p. 134)
pesticida Sustancia química que mata los organismos que dañan los cultivos.

petrochemical A compound made from oil. (p. 162)
petroquímico Compuesto que se obtiene del petróleo.

petroleum Liquid fossil fuel; oil. (p. 162)
petróleo Combustible fósil líquido.

photochemical smog A thick, brownish haze formed when certain gases react with sunlight. (p. 139)
neblina tóxica fotoquímica Densa bruma parduzca que se forma cuando ciertos gases reaccionan con la luz solar.

photosynthesis The process in which organisms use water along with sunlight and carbon dioxide to make their own food. (p. 8)
fotosíntesis Proceso por el cual los organismos usan el agua junto con la luz solar y el dióxido de carbono para producir su alimento.

pioneer species The first species to populate an area. (p. 33)
especies pioneras Primeras especies en poblar una región.

poaching Illegal killing or removal of wildlife from their habitats. (p. 102)
caza ilegal Matanza o eliminación de la fauna silvestre de su hábitat.

pollutant A substance that causes pollution. (p. 133)
contaminante Sustancia que provoca contaminación.

pollution Contamination of land, water, or air. (p. 84)
contaminación Polución del suelo, agua o aire.

population All the members of one species in a particular area. (p. 9)
población Todos los miembros de una especie en un área particular.

population density The number of individuals in an area of a specific size. (p. 18)
densidad de población Número de individuos en un área de un tamaño específico.

precipitation Rain, snow, sleet, or hail. (p. 49)
precipitación Lluvia, nieve, aguanieve o granizo.

predation An interaction in which one organism kills another for food. (p. 27)
depredación Interacción en la cual un organismo mata y se come a otro.

predator The organism that does the killing in a predation interaction. (p. 27)
depredador Organismo que mata en la depredación.

prey An organism that is killed and eaten by another organism. (p. 27)
presa Organismo que otro organismo mata y come.

primary succession The series of changes that occur in an area where no soil or organisms exist. (p. 33)
sucesión primaria Serie de cambios que ocurren en un área en donde no existe suelo ni organismos.

producer An organism that can make its own food. (p. 43)
productor Organismo que puede elaborar su propio alimento.

R

radon A colorless, odorless, radioactive gas. (p. 141)
radón Gas radiactivo que no tiene color ni olor.

reactor vessel The part of a nuclear reactor where nuclear fission occurs. (p. 176)
cuba de reactor Parte de un reactor nuclear donde ocurre la fisión nuclear.

recycling The process of reclaiming and reusing raw materials. (p. 125)
reciclaje Proceso de recuperar y volver a usar materias primas.

refinery A factory in which crude oil is heated and separated into fuels and other products. (p. 162)
refinería Planta en la que el petróleo crudo se calienta y separa en combustibles y otros productos.

renewable resource A resource that is either always available or is naturally replaced in a relatively short time. (p. 83)
recurso renovable Recurso que está siempre disponible o que es restituido de manera natural en un período relativamente corto.

S

sanitary landfill A landfill that holds nonhazardous waste such as municipal solid waste and construction debris. (p. 124)
relleno sanitario Relleno que contiene desechos no peligrosos, como desechos sólidos urbanos y escombros de la construcción.

savanna A grassland close to the equator that receives as much as 120 centimeters of rain per year. (p. 62)
sabana Tierra de pastos próxima al ecuador que recibe hasta 120 centímetros de lluvia al año.

scavenger A carnivore that feeds on the bodies of dead organisms. (p. 43)
carroñero Carnívoro que se alimenta del cuerpo de animales muertos.

secondary succession The series of changes that occur in an area where the ecosystem has been disturbed, but where soil and organisms still exist. (p. 34)
sucesión secundaria Serie de cambios que ocurren en un área después de la perturbación de un ecosistema, pero donde todavía hay suelo y organismos.

sediments Particles of rock and sand. (p. 134)
sedimentos Partículas de roca y arena.

selective cutting The process of cutting down only some trees in an area. (p. 90)
tala selectiva Proceso de cortar sólo algunos árboles de un área.

sewage The water and human wastes that are washed down sinks, toilets, and showers. (p. 134)
aguas residuales Agua y desechos humanos que son desechados por lavamanos, servicios sanitarios y duchas.

solar energy Energy from the sun. (p. 166)
energía solar Energía del Sol.

species A group of organisms that are physically similar and can mate with each other and produce offspring that can also mate and reproduce. (p. 9)
especie Grupo de organismos que son físicamente semejantes, se pueden cruzar y producen crías que también se pueden cruzar y reproducir.

subsoil The layer of soil below topsoil that has less plant and animal matter than topsoil. (p. 118)
subsuelo Capa de suelo bajo el suelo superior que tiene menos material vegetal y animal que el suelo superior.

succession The series of predictable changes that occur in a community over time. (p. 32)
sucesión Serie de cambios predecibles que ocurren en una comunidad a través del tiempo.

sustainable yield An amount of a renewable resource that can be harvested regularly without reducing the future supply. (p. 91)
rendimiento sostenible Cantidad de un recurso renovable que puede ser recolectado constantemente sin reducir el abastecimiento futuro.

symbiosis A close relationship between two species that benefits at least one of the species. (p. 30)
simbiosis Relación estrecha entre dos especies de la que se beneficia al menos una de ellas.

 T

taxol A chemical in Pacific yew tree bark that has cancer-fighting properties. (p. 108)
taxol Sustancia química en la corteza del tejo del Pacífico con propiedades curativas contra el cáncer.

temperature inversion A condition in which a layer of warm air traps polluted air close to Earth's surface. (p. 139)
inversión térmica Condición en la que una capa de aire caliente atrapa aire contaminado cerca de la superficie de la Tierra.

threatened species A species that could become endangered in the near future. (p. 101)
especie amenazada Especie que puede llegar a estar en peligro de extinción en el futuro próximo.

topsoil An upper layer of soil consisting of rock fragments, nutrients, water, air, and decaying plant and animal matter. (p. 118)
suelo superior Capa superior de suelo formada por fragmentos de roca, nutrientes, agua, aire y materia animal y vegetal en descomposición.

tundra An extremely cold, dry biome. (p. 65)
tundra Bioma extremadamente frío y seco.

 U

understory A layer of shorter plants that grow in the shade of a forest canopy. (p. 60)
sotobosque Estrato de plantas de baja estatura que crecen a la sombra de la bóveda arbórea.

 W

water cycle The continuous process by which water moves from Earth's surface to the atmosphere and back. (p. 48)
ciclo del agua Proceso continuo mediante el cual el agua pasa de la superficie de la Tierra a la atmósfera y viceversa.

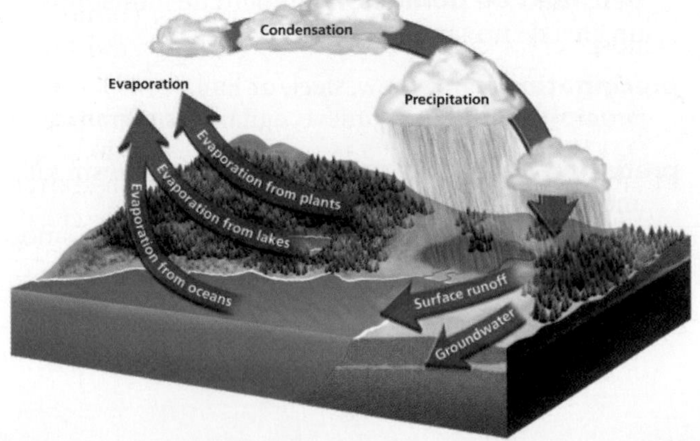

Page numbers for key terms are printed in **boldface** type.
Page numbers for illustrations, maps, and charts are printed in *italics*.

Index

B

C

Index

Page numbers for key terms are printed in **boldface** type.
Page numbers for illustrations, maps, and charts are printed in *italics*.

Index

Page numbers for key terms are printed in **boldface** type.
Page numbers for illustrations, maps, and charts are printed in *italics*.

Acknowledgments

Acknowledgment for page 194: Excerpt from "The Amateur Naturalist" by Gerald Durrell with Lee Durrell. Copyright © Gerald Durrell 1982. Reprinted by permission of Curtis Brown on behalf of The Estate of Gerald Durrell. Note: Every effort has been made to contact the copyright owner.

Staff Credits

Diane Alimena, Scott Andrews, Jennifer Angel, Michele Angelucci, Laura Baselice, Barbara A. Bertell, Suzanne Biron, Peggy Bliss, James Brady, Anne M. Bray, Sarah M. Carroll, Kerry Cashman, Jonathan Cheney, Lisa J. Clark, Bob Craton, Patricia M. Dambry, Kathy Dempsey, Emily Ellen, Leanne Esterly, Thomas Ferreira, Jonathan Fisher, Patricia Fromkin, Paul Gagnon, Kathy Gavilanes, Holly Gordon, Robert Graham, Ellen Granter, Diane Grossman, Barbara Hollingdale, Linda Johnson, Anne Jones, John Judge, Kevin Keane, Kelly Kelliher, Toby Klang, Sue Langan, Russ Lappa, Carolyn Lock, Rebecca Loveys, Constance J. McCarty, Carolyn B. McGuire, Ranida Touranont McKneally, Anne McLaughlin, Eve Melnechuk, Natania Mlawer, Janet Morris, Karyl Murray, Francine Neumann, Baljit Nijjar, Marie Opera, Jill Ort, Kim Ortell, Joan Paley, Dorothy Preston, Maureen Raymond, Laura Ross, Rashid Ross, Siri Schwartzman, Melissa Shustyk, Laurel Smith, Emily Soltanoff, Jennifer A. Teece, Elizabeth Torjussen, Amanda M. Watters, Merce Wilczek, Amy Winchester, Char Lyn Yeakley. **Additional Credits:** Tara Alamilla, Louise Gachet, Allen Gold, Andrea Golden, Terence Hegarty, Etta Jacobs, Meg Montgomery, Stephanie Rogers, Kim Schmidt, Adam Teller.

Illustration

Morgan Cain & Associates: 147, 154, 162, 175, 178, 183, 186r, 188; **Kerry Cashman:** 14–15, 55, 59–66; **John Ceballos:** 141; **John Edwards and Associates:** 124, 142, 150, 159, 161, 170, 177, 186l; **Biruta Hansen:** 24–25; **Robert Hynes:** 11; **Kevin Jones Associates:** 18t, 33, 34–35, 49, 51–52, 167; **Karen Minot:** 90, 97; **Pond and Giles:** 38, 93; **J/B Woolsey Associates:** 12, 74, 155; **XNR Productions:** 86–87, 120. **All charts and graphs by Matt Mayerchak.**

Photography

Photo Research John Judge

Cover image top, Muench Photography Inc.; **bottom,** J. David Andrews/Masterfile. **Page vi,** Tony Craddock/Getty Images, Inc.; **vii,** Richard Haynes; **viii,** Richard Haynes; **x,** Christopher G. Knight; **1,** H. Bruce Rinker; **1,** Stephen Dalton/Photo Researchers, Inc.; **2bl,** Meg Lowman; **2br,** Meg Lowman/Australian Journals of Scientific Research; **2t,** Raphael Gaillarde/Gamma Press Images; **3,** Christopher G. Knight.

Chapter 1

Pages 4–5, Getty Images, Inc.; **5 inset,** Richard Haynes; **6t,** Tom Lazar/Animals Animals/Earth Scenes; **6b,** C.K. Lorenz/Photo Researchers, Inc.; **7,** C.W. Schwartz/Animals Animals/Earth Scenes; **8t,** Konrad Wothe/Minden Pictures; **8m,** Christoph Burki/Getty Images, Inc.; **8b,** John Cancalosi/Tom Stack & Associates; **9,** Breck P. Kent/Animals Animals/Earth Scenes; **13,** Frans Lanting/Minden Pictures; **14l,** Fred Bruemmer/Peter Arnold, Inc.; **14r,** C. Allan Morgan/DRK Photo; **15l,** Thomas Mangelsen/Minden Pictures; **15r,** Wallace J. Nichols; **17t,** Alan D. Carey/Photo Researchers, Inc.; **17b,** Leonard Lee Rue III/Photo Researchers, Inc.; **18,** Kenneth W. Fink/Photo Researchers, Inc.; **19t,** Anthony Bannister/Animals Animals/Earth Scenes; **19b,** Tony Craddock/Getty Images, Inc.; **20,** Tom & Pat Leeson/Photo Researchers, Inc.; **21,** Dave King/Dorling Kindersley; **22–23t,** Gary Griffen/Animals Animals/Earth Scenes; **22b,** Raymond Gehman/Corbis; **26tl,** Ron Willocks/Animals Animals/Earth Scenes; **26ml,** Patti Murray/Animals Animals/Earth Scenes; **26bl,** Rob Simpson/Visuals Unlimited; **26r,** Wally Eberhart/Visuals Unlimited; **27,** F. Stuart Westmorland/Photo Researchers, Inc.; **28,** S. Dalton/OSF/Animals Animals/Earth Scenes; **29tl,** Leroy Simon/Visuals Unlimited; **29tr,** Dante Fenolio/Photo Researchers, Inc.; **29mr,** Nigel J. Dennis/Photo Researchers. Inc.; **29bl,** Art Wolfe; **29br,** Brian Rogers/Visuals Unlimited; **30,** Daryl Balfour/Getty Images, Inc.; **31t,** Volker Steiger/SPL/Photo Researchers, Inc.; **31b,** Richard Haynes; **32 both,** Tom & Pat Leeson/Photo Researchers, Inc.; **36t,** Leroy Simon/Visuals Unlimited; **36b,** Dave King/Dorling Kindersley.

Chapter 2

Pages 40–41, Daniel J. Cox/Getty Images, Inc.; **41 inset,** Richard Haynes; **42–43,** Kent Foster/Photo Researchers, Inc.; **43t inset,** David Northcott/DRK Photo; **43m inset,** Adam Jones/Photo Researchers, Inc.; **43b inset,** S. Nielsen/DRK Photo; **46t,** Frank Greenaway/Dorling Kindersley; **46tm,** Kim Taylor & Jane Burton/Dorling Kindersley; **46bm,** Dorling Kindersley; **46bm,** Frank Greenaway/Dorling Kindersley Media Library; **46b,** Kim Taylor & Jane Burton/Dorling Kindersley; **47,** Andy Rouse/DRK Photo; **48,** Richard Haynes; **50,** Asa C. Thoresen/Photo Researchers, Inc.; **53,** E. R. Degginger/Photo Researchers, Inc.; **54t,** Richard Haynes; **54b,** Penny Tweedie/Getty Images, Inc.; **56l,** Gregory K. Scott/Photo Researchers, Inc.; **56m,** Kenneth H. Thomas/Photo Researchers, Inc.; **56r,** Runk/Schoenberger/Grant Heilman, Inc.; **59,** Jim Zipp/Photo Researchers, Inc.; **59 inset,** S. Nielsen/DRK Photo; **60l,** Frans Lanting/Minden Pictures; **60m,** Renee Lynn/Getty Images, Inc.; **60r,** Michael & Patricia Fogden/Minden Pictures; **61,** Barbara Gerlach/DRK Photo; **61 inset,** Maslowski/Photo Researchers, Inc.; **62,** Art Wolfe/Getty Images, Inc.; **62 inset,** Gerry Ellis/Minden Pictures; **63,** Carr Clifton/Minden Pictures; **63t inset,** Nick Bergkessel/Photo Researchers, Inc.; **63b inset,** Stephen J. Krasemann/DRK Photo; **64l,** Stephen J. Krasemann/DRK Photo; **64r,** Jeff Lepore/Photo Researchers, Inc.; **65,** Michio Hoshino/Minden Pictures; **65 inset,** Yva Momotiuk/John Eastcott /Minden Pictures; **66,** Douglas E. Walker/Masterfile Corporation; **66 inset,** John Cancalosi/National Geographic Society; **69,** Richard Haynes; **70t,** Tom & Pat Leeson/Photo Researchers, Inc.; **70b,** Bill Kamin/Visuals Unlimited; **71,** David Weintraub/Photo Researchers, Inc.; **71 inset,** Steven David Miller/Animals Animals/Earth Scenes; **72,** Michele Burgess/Corbis; **75,** Russ Lappa; **76t,** Andy Rouse/DRK Photo; **76b,** Steven David Miller/Animals Animals/Earth Scenes.

Chapter 3

Pages 80–81, Robert Yin/SeaPics.com; **81 inset,** Russ Lappa; **82–83,** Key Sanders/Getty Images, Inc.; **84l,** Corbis; **84m,** Corbis; **84r,** UPI/Corbis-Bettmann; **85l,** Erich Hartmann/Magnum Photos; **85m,** Kevin Fleming/Corbis; **85r,** William Campbell/Peter Arnold, Inc.; **86t,** Corbis; **86b,** Warren Morgan/Corbis; **87t,** Ariel Skelley/Corbis; **87b,** Marc Epstein/DRK Photo; **88–89,** Richard Haynes; **91,** Inga Spence/Visuals Unlimited; **92,** G.R. Robinson/Visuals Unlimited; **93,** Greg Vaughn/Tom Stack & Associates; **94,** Russ Lappa; **95,** Richard Haynes; **96t,** C Squared Studios /Getty Images, Inc.; **96b,** Frans Lanting/Minden Pictures; **97t,** David Wrobel/Visuals Unlimited; **97b,** Stephen J. Krasemann/DRK Photo; **98t,** Wayne Lynch/DRK Photo; **98b,** Fred Bavendam/Minden Pictures; **99,** D. Cavagnaro/DRK Photo; **100tl,** David Sieren/Visuals Unlimited; **100tr,** David Dennis/Animals Animals/Earth Scenes; **100b,** Jeff Lepore/Photo Researchers, Inc.; **101tl,** David Liebman; **101ml,** Stephen J. Krasemann/DRK Photo; **101bl,** Marilyn Kazmers/Peter Arnold, Inc.; **101r,** Ken Lucas/Visuals Unlimited; **102,** Kent Gilbert/AP/Wide World Photos; **103,** James H. Robinson/Animals Animals/Earth Scenes; **104t,** Roy Toft/Tom Stack & Associates; **104b,** Tom Uhlman/AP/Wide World Photos; **105,** James H. Robinson/Animals Animals/Earth Scenes; **106,** Doug Perrine/DRK Photo; **107l,** Walter H. Hodge/Peter Arnold, Inc.; **107m,** Doug Perrine/DRK Photo; **107r,** Ed Reschke/Peter Arnold, Inc.; **108t,** Greg Vaughn/Tom Stack & Associates; **108b,** Bill Greenblatt/Getty Images, Inc.; **109,** G. Payne/Liaison/Getty Images, Inc.; **110t,** David Dennis/Animals Animals/Earth Scenes; **110bl,** Greg Vaughn/Tom Stack & Associates; **110br,** Walter H. Hodge/Peter Arnold, Inc.

Chapter 4

Pages 114–115, Jim Wark/Airphoto; **115 inset,** Richard Haynes, **116t,** Richard Haynes; **116b,** Corbis; **117,** David Zalubowski/AP/Wide World Photos; **118l,** Peter Griffiths/Dorling Kindersley Media Library; **118t inset,** Michael Habicht/Animals Animals; **118m inset,** S.L. Rose/Visuals Unlimited; **118b inset,** Gilbert S. Grant/Photo Researchers, Inc.; **119l,** Martin Benjamin/The Image Works; **119r,** Tom Bean 1994/DRK Photo; **120l,** Peter Johnson/Corbis; **120r,** Walt Anderson/Visuals Unlimited; **121 both,** Department of Environmental Protection, Commonwealth of Pennsylvania/Mineral Information Institute; **122–123,** Nick Vedros, Vedros & Assoc./Getty Images, Inc.; **125,** David Joel/Getty Images, Inc.; **126l,** Richard Haynes; **126r,** Randy Faris/Corbis; **127t,** Larry Lefever/Grant Heilman Photography, Inc.; **127b,** Rosemary Mayer/Holt Studios/Photo Researchers, Inc.; **128 all,** Russ Lappa; **129 all,** Russ Lappa; **130,** Russ Lappa; **131,** Russ Lappa; **133l,** Richard Hutchings/Photo Researchers, Inc.; **133r,** Michael S. Yamashita/Corbis; **135,** Dorling Kindersley; **136,** Norman McGrath; **137,** Armando Franca/ AP/Wide World Photos; **138t,** Russ Lappa; **138b,** Derek Trask/Corbis; **139,** P. Baeza/ Publiphoto/Photo Researchers, Inc.; **140,** Richard Megna/Fundamental Photographs; **142,** Eric Pearle/Getty Images, Inc.; **143,** Ed Pritchard/Getty Images, Inc.; **145,** Richard Haynes; **146 both,** Richard Haynes; **148 all,** NASA/Goddard Space Flight Center Scientific Visualization Studio; **151,** NASA Goddard Space Flight Center; **152,** Russ Lappa.

Chapter 5

Pages 156–157, Didier Dorval/Masterfile Corporation; **157 inset,** Visuals Unlimited; **158t,** E.R. Degginger; **158b,** Toby Talbot/AP/Wide World Photos; **161t,** Colin Keates/Dorling Kindersley; **161m,** Andreas Einsiedel/Dorling Kindersley; **161b,** Andreas Einsiedel /Dorling Kindersley; **162,** Bill Ross/Corbis; **163,** Roger Ball/Corbis; **164,** Owen Franken/Corbis; **165,** Lawrence Migdale/Photo Researchers, Inc.; **166,** Nadia MacKenzie/Getty Images, Inc.; **168t,** Tom Bean/DRK Photo; **168b,** Doug Sokell/Tom Stack & Associates; **169t,** Daniel Putterman/Stock Boston, Inc./PictureQuest; **169b,** Brian Branch-Price/AP/Wide World Photos; **171,** NASA; **172,** Richard Haynes; **173,** Richard Haynes; **174t,** Russ Lappa; **174b,** Bettmann-Corbis; **176t,** Joseph Sohm/ChromoSohm, Inc./Corbis; **176b,** E.R. Degginger; **179,** Richard Haynes; **180l,** Mitch Kezar/Getty Images, Inc.; **180m,** Tony Freeman/PhotoEdit; **180r,** Scott Olson/Getty Images, Inc.; **181l,** Anthony Meshkinyar/Getty Images, Inc.; **181m,** Yves Marcoux/Getty Images, Inc.; **181r,** Mike Fiala/Getty Images, Inc.; **182l,** Michael Newman/Photo Edit; **186,** Scott Olson/Getty Images, Inc.

190, Devez/CNRS/Photo Researchers, Inc.; **191b,**Tom Brakefield/DRK Photo; **191ml,** Mc Donald Wildlife Photography/Animals Animals/Earth Scenes; **191mr,** Peter Steyn/Ardea London, Ltd.; **191t,** M.C. Chamberlain/DRK Photo; **192–193,** Chinch Gryniewicz/Ecoscene/Corbis; **193b,** Jose Anzel/Aurora Photos; **193t,** Christie's Images; **194t,** Corbis-Bettmann; **194–195,** M. Harvey/DRK Photo; **195bl,** Wolfgang Kaehler/Corbis; **195bm,** Frans Lanting/Minden Pictures; **195br,** Tim Davis/Photo Researchers, Inc.; **195t,** Neil Lucas/Nature Picture Library; **196,** Tony Freeman/PhotoEdit; **197b,** Russ Lappa; **197m,** Richard Haynes; **197t,** Russ Lappa; **198,** Richard Haynes; **200,** Richard Haynes; **202,** Morton Beebe/Corbis; **203,** Catherine Karnow/Corbis; **205b,** Richard Haynes; **205t,** Dorling Kindersley; **207,** Image Stop/Phototake; **210,** Richard Haynes; **217,** Richard Haynes; **222,** NASA/Goddard Space Flight Center Scientific Visualization Studio.